The Mafia's Greatest Hits

The Mafia's Greatest Hits

David H. Jacobs

CITADEL PRESS
Kensington Publishing Corp.
www.kensingtonbooks.com

CITADEL PRESS BOOKS are published by

Kensington Publishing Corp.
850 Third Avenue
New York, NY 10022

All Kensington titles, imprints, and distributed lines are available at special quantity discounts for bulk purchases for sales promotions, premiums, fund-raising, educational, or institutional use. Special book excerpts or customized printings can also be created to fit specific needs. For details, write or phone the office of the Kensington special sales manager: Kensington Publishing Corp., 850 Third Avenue, New York, NY 10022, attn: Special Sales Department; phone 1-800-221-2647.

CITADEL PRESS and the Citadel logo are Reg. U.S. Pat. & TM Off.

First printing: July 2006

10 9 8 7 6 5 4 3 2 1

Printed in the United States of America

Library of Congress Control Number: 2005938606

ISBN 0-8065-2757-9

Contents

Acknowledgments

Special thanks to Pat O'Donnell and the gang at Devil Bat Media and Idea Men Productions.

Introduction

"It's an old Sicilian message. It means Luca Brasi
sleeps with the fishes."
—*The Godfather* by Mario Puzo

When you're in the mob, trying not to get killed is almost a way of life.

Billy Batts was a made guy with John Gotti's crew out of the Ozone Park–Howard Beach section of Queens, New York, and a stone's throw from John F. Kennedy International Airport. He'd just gotten sprung from jail after an eight-year stretch and was having himself a party at The Suite, a joint I owned. He was knocking them back and was pretty boozed up when he started busting balls— but not just any balls. This particular pair belonged to Tommy "Tommy D" DeSimone, an associate with the Lucchese family run by Paulie "Big Paul" Vario out of Brooklyn. It was 1970.

Tommy D suffered from what mental health experts today would describe as a personality disorder, "characterized by a pervasive pattern of instability of interpersonal relationships, self-image, and affects, and marked impulsivity that begins by early adulthood and is present in a variety of contexts" or some shrink-speak like that.

Bullshit. Tommy D was a psycho, a remorseless killer who'd shoot you in the face and then order a pizza—something Billy Batts was about to find out the hard way.

To make a long story shorter, Billy pissed Tommy off. Tommy, with the help of Jimmy Burke (who later masterminded the 1976 Lufthansa heist, at the time the largest cash robbery in American history, and no pillar of sanity himself), beat Billy Batts to death. Or so we thought. We stuffed him into the trunk of Tommy D's car and drove him upstate to bury him—stopping at Tommy D's mother's house for a late snack first. The problem was that Billy Batts wasn't quite dead (we heard him banging around in the trunk), a situation Tommy D and Jimmy rectified by stabbing and shooting him as Billy lay helpless, trying not to choke on his own blood as he begged for mercy. He got none. Not surprisingly, Tommy D got himself whacked a few years later for killing Billy Batts. Payback really was a bitch.

If this story sounds familiar, it's because you may have seen it portrayed in the movie that was made about me, *Goodfellas*, in 1990, that Marty Scorsese adapted from Nick Pileggi's bestselling book *Wiseguy*. I mention it here to show how easy it is, when you're mobbed up, to wind up in the trunk of a Caddy, buried in a Staten Island landfill, or dismembered in the back of a social club and having your body parts disposed of in dumpsters all over New York. (In the mob, the expression "being a man about town" takes on a whole new meaning.) Whether you're a low-level street hood or the head of an entire Mafia family, mob hits are the great equalizer. No one is ever immune from two shots behind the ear or a close—and permanent—encounter with a gun, a knife, or even a chainsaw.

Strike or otherwise disrespect a "made" guy? Two in the head.

The envelope's a little light this week? Tomorrow they'll find you in the weeds.

Rat out a fellow wiseguy by talking to the feds or the cops? They'll find you at the bottom of Sheepshead Bay with a jukebox tied around your neck.

And these are the ones you *don't* read about. Other hits have become the stuff of Mafia legend:

Joey Gallo—killed in Umberto's Clam House in Little Italy in 1975. Abe "Kid Twist" Reles, the Murder, Inc. stoolpigeon who was tossed out of a hotel window in Coney Island in 1941. Albert Anastasia, cut down in a barber's chair in 1957. Carmine Galante,

Preface: Handicapping the Hits

A kill stirs things up. It's like having a winning ball club. The
fans gather to talk about it, to speculate and chew it to pieces.
— *Killer Mine* by Mickey Spillane

It's been said that every game is a kind of combat. If so, the reverse
is true, that every combat is a kind of game. For centuries, games
such as chess and Go have been used to sharpen the wits of strate-
gists. In World War II, game theory first began to be applied to battle-
field conditions, and later to the spheres of business and even human
social interactions.

Murder may be considered as a game in which the challenger
contends with the opposition with the life of the intended victim as
prize. One area where professional killers abound is in organized
crime. Other such spheres are law enforcement and the military.

The field of study discussed in this book is big-time gangland executions: "hits." Think of the underworld as a major league, the top
crime bosses as the team owners and managers, and their enforcers
and hitmen as the players. A gang killing is an event; a gang war is
like a World Series.

In the belief that almost everything can be quantified, this system
proposes to rate the highest-profile hits on a point system. Each
murder event can win a possible 20 points. Five points are awarded
for strategy, 5 for tactics, and 10 for results.

Strategy is, simply, the plan. The murder plan. The assassination killed in a hail of bullets as he finished lunch in a Brooklyn restaurant in 1977. Joe "Joe the Boss" Massiera, one of the earliest Mafia chieftains, whacked in a Coney Island restaurant in 1933. And the list goes on.

In *The Mafia's Greatest Hits*, David H. Jacobs provides an energetic survey of over 100 years of mob mayhem. He details the Mafia's splashiest and most infamous murders, from the perspective of a fan at a sporting event—celebrated episodes of big-time gangland executions are told in the breezy, yet vividly direct tone of a sportswriter covering a ball game or heavyweight championship bout.

So read and enjoy—this book is killer entertainment.

—Henry Hill
January 2006

HENRY HILL is the author (with Gus Russo) of *Gangsters and Goodfellas: Wiseguys, Witness Protection, and Life on the Run* and *A Goodfella's Guide to New York: Your Personal Tour through the Mob's Notorious Haunts, Hair-Raising Crime Scenes, and Infamous Hot Spots* (with Bryon Schreckengost). He can't tell you where he lives.

of a top mobster encompasses many variables that the plan must address: whether the human target—the "mark"—is unwary or alert for trouble; how hard or soft the security is surrounding the mark; the mark's routines, behavioral patterns, and personal quirks; and so on. What was the plan? How well did it work? Was the right approach made, the correct personnel chosen?

Tactics is how the plan was carried out. It combines mechanics, tradecraft, the ability to improvise, and the determination to see the job through.

Results are what happen in the hit's aftermath, in the short, medium, and long term. Hitting the target and eliminating the mark are a big part of the results, but not all. What, apart from liquidating the mark, was the hit designed to do? How well did it achieve its goal? These are the key factors in tallying up the results.

Sometimes a killing that's flawless in execution may bring about the exact opposite of the original desired objective. It may bring about the capture or death not only of the hitter but also of the planners who put him on the game board and set him into action. That's why the results carry a possible 10-point maximum score instead of the possible 5 each allotted for strategy and tactics.

The theory and rules for handicapping the hits are reviewed and expanded on in chapter 1, to give the reader further grounding.

But enough of theory. The fact is that while the rankings of each of the classic, epoch-making hits that follow are based on speculation and analysis, real flesh-and-blood players staked all on the outcome of these grim games of life and death. You've got the best seat in the house, one that's safely out of the line of fire.

Let the games begin!

1

A Bullet for Big Jim

Jim Colosimo was a big man who lived big. That's why they called him "Big Jim." He was also a big crook, pimp, whoremonger, political fixer, extortionist, and killer. For the first two decades of the twentieth century, he was Chicago's top vice lord and lived the part. A show-off with a mania for grandeur and a penchant for flashy clothes and high living, he toted a pearl-handled revolver. An avaricious diamond collector, he habitually went about town with a pocket or two filled with loose gems.

His vice ring forced scores of innocent young girls into prostitution and routinely trafficked in the bodies of hundreds—thousands—more.

If there was anyone who should have been unsentimental about romance, it was him. Yet in the finest storybook tradition, when at the height of his power, he put himself on the spot for a kill—all for the love of a good (and good-looking) woman.

His death was the first major organized crime killing of the twentieth century, ultimately paving the way for the American Mafia's historic expansion into nationwide big business.

* * *

Between 1900 and 1920—a period roughly paralleling Colosimo's tenure in Chicago vice—America saw a quickening in industrialization. Factories adopted the assembly-line method. The automobile, telephone, and electric light became vital parts of the national life. Motion pictures (silent movies) seized the crown of popular entertainment. Radio piped invisible voices and music into the home. The federal government grew, extending its reach into spheres of activity previously immune to its influence.

It was an era of mass production, mass communication, mass culture, and, in the case of World War I, mass slaughter.

In America, Chicago's wealth and power was second only to that of New York City's, giving rise to its nickname, the Second City. The advent of Prohibition would see Chicago claim first place as the capital of organized crime and gang violence, pioneering a particularly new, fast-paced, and industrialized model of U.S. racketeering that laid the groundwork for today's national crime syndicate.

Big Jim Colosimo's fate was to find himself in the unenviable position of being a roadblock on that path to progress.

Giacomo Colosimo was born in 1877 in the province of Calabria, Italy. Southern Italy is a harsh environment and Calabria was one of its most impoverished areas. The 1880s saw a massive exodus from the region, with hundreds of thousands of immigrants settling in the United States. Among them in 1895 were the Colosimos, who settled in Chicago's First Ward.

The First Ward was possibly the most corrupt district in the city. Its seething heart was the Levee, a neighborhood bounded from Clark Street to Wabash Avenue and from Eighteenth Street to Twenty-second Street.

This was the era of so-called segregated vice, the practice of centralizing prostitution in a specific locale, what used to be called the "red-light district." The Levee was made up of scores of such operations, ranging from opulent, high-line whorehouses to the meanest, lowest dives and cribs—and all stops in-between.

The houses catering to the carriage trade were at the top of the social pyramid, with a leavening of midlevel houses and a vast base of lower-end sites. Patrons at the middle and bottom rungs of the ladder ran the risk of being stabbed or knocked on the head and robbed by any of the countless toughs who thronged the milieu. Some had their throats cut and were dumped in the river or a vacant lot.

Others were drugged: the "Mickey Finn," an alcoholic beverage doped with a knockout drug, took its name from one of its most assiduous dispensers, a notorious Levee bartender named (what else?) Mickey Finn.

Victims were lucky if they found themselves waking up in an alley, plucked clean of their possessions right down to their underwear. More than a few received overdoses and never woke up.

Apart from the ever lucrative business of whoremongering, the Levee was awash in booze, from bonded to bootlegged. The area was a magnet for a collection of underworld characters: gamblers, grifters, thieves, dealers in stolen goods, thugs, and killers, as well as a plethora of pimps, panders, and procurers. Thrill-seekers high and low provided a steady stream of customers and cash.

One element conspicuous by its absence in the area was the law. Chicago, in that era, was notoriously underpoliced. When they did show themselves, uniformed cops were most likely to be seen ducking into a Levee saloon for a drink or five.

Protecting and profiting from Levee vice was the political powerhouse team of committeeman Michael "Hinky-Dink" Kenna and his sidekick, alderman John "Bathhouse John" Coughlin. The duo could and did regularly deliver large blocks of votes to both party candidates on election day. That was the source of their power. With it came all the benefits: the ability to get people jobs and to sell offices and privileges.

They and their associates made fortunes in "honest graft" by the letting of city building contracts and similar projects. A vital source of revenue was the selling of permission to operate in the vice business as long as the appropriate political officeholders and law enforcers were properly greased with payoff money. That's how business was done.

Such was the environment in which young Colosimo, who'd now

Americanized his name to "James," came of age. He ripened into a fine physical specimen of manhood, causing him to be tagged with the nickname "Big Jim," which would follow him for the rest of his life. By his late teens, he was already a fledgling thief and pimp and a dabbler in Black Hand–type extortion.

The Black Hand was not so much an organized criminal conspiracy as a technique. It came from Italy, where the intended victim would receive one or several notes, often drafted with flowery politeness, threatening him and his family with violence and death if he did not make a sizable cash payment to his extortioners. The notes, usually anonymous or signed with false names, were often sealed with a black imprint of a hand; thus, the Black Hand. Since violent reprisal almost inevitably followed a refusal, most victims usually paid. Having paid once, they could be made to pay again and again.

A racket so successful in the Old World could hardly fail to be transplanted to the New. Black Hand notes were sent by individual thugs or small gangs. The targets were members of Italian American communities who had achieved some degree of prosperity, or at least had enough money to make it worth a crook's time to pry it out of them.

Back in the old country, the police were in such ill repute that it was regarded as not only futile but also dangerous to appeal to them for help from Blackhanders, with whom they were often in league. The immigrants carried this same distrust of the police with them when they came to America, a trait that the New World extortionists traded on.

Young Big Jim's early ventures into blackhanding must not have been too successful, since he was temporarily scared out of a life of crime and even into holding a regular job for a while.

Colosimo wangled himself a post as a "wing," that is, a streetsweeper who cleaned up horse droppings left in the road, a vital function in the days before the horseless carriage. His talent for organization showed itself when he organized his fellow streetsweepers into a club whose votes he could deliver for the Party. This brought him to the attention of the ward powerbrokers, who marked him as a young man on the way up.

He learned early on the important lesson that in Chicago, power came out of the ballot box. He who could deliver live bodies to vote early and often was a useful tool and might go far. (For that matter, in a pinch the dead could also be pressed into service to vote the ticket.)

The Kenna-Coughlin combine tabbed Big Jim for the plum post of bagman, collecting payoff money from Levee brothel owners and saloon keepers. The up-and-coming Colosimo decided it was time to take a wife and embraced his destiny in the ample form of Victoria Moresco, twenty years his senior and one of the premier whorehouse madams in the district. They were soon wed and Big Jim took on the congenial task of supervising and managing her properties and human chattels.

Prostitution was a leading industry in the First Ward, where it was coddled and milked. It generated fabulous profits for those on the top, with returns diminishing to insignificance (if not downright nullity) by the time they reached the whores who were actually doing the work.

A handful of houses were distinguished by beautiful women, luxurious surroundings, and elegant champagne suppers. A modest-sized middle sector supplied more or less clean young women in workmanlike surroundings with few niceties but relatively safe conditions. Below that lay a huge mass of dives and cribs seething with omnipresent criminality, a last way station for used-up prostitutes before dropping into the social pit.

Health and hygiene were dubious prospects at best, with the ever present danger of sexually transmitted diseases (STDs)—at a time when the lack of penicillin and similar antibiotics made contracting an STD a serious and potentially lethal threat not only for the infected but also for their sexual partners and offspring.

Beer and liquor were readily available throughout the Levee. Many saloons and ginmills featured rooms in the back or upstairs with some mattresses on the floor where barmaids and house whores could turn quick tricks.

High and low, all such establishments had one thing in common: they had to pay to stay in business. That meant kicking in the weekly payoff tab for ward bosses who had the say-so as to whether they could keep operating. In the First Ward, this meant the Kenna-Coughlin combine.

The bosses took care of incidental expenses along the line, mostly bribes to crooked cops for looking the other way. Even precinct captains came more or less cheap for ignoring something they generally had no inclination to interfere with in any case. Graft percolated downward at the station house, making its way in sharply decreasing amounts to the lower ranks and street cops.

Vice was big business, a "service industry" with a high turnover in the whores who made up its personnel. In an average midlevel house, records show that each inmate turned over from ten to twenty tricks per night, totaling several hundred customers a week. The physical demands on the prostitutes were strenuous and debilitating. This was a grind that used up women fast.

Most of them were young, in their teens, but the work took its toll. Generally, even the youngest and prettiest would be worn out after a year or two. As their looks and freshness faded, they were shipped down the line to the high-volume houses and, ultimately, to the dives, cribs, and finally the streets, a descent that took on average about five years. Drug addiction, drink, and the lack of fresh air and sunlight also accelerated the toll.

The trade required a continual stream of fresh flesh. To meet this demand, the so-called white slave trade existed.

The economics of the racket were simple. The city was a magnet for girls and young women, most of them from rural areas. A prime target were girls who worked in service as housemaids. Young and handsome suitors from the procurement rings would court the girls and invite them out on "dates." The victims were lured to an out-of-the-way place. They were then gang-raped for several days and nights as a way of being broken into the business and hooked on drugs before being sold to the houses.

Their new owners (panders, pimps, and madams) kept the new-comers in virtual slavery, often penning them behind locked doors and barred windows and keeping all their hard-earned gains (hence the term "inmate").

White slave rings occupied a kind of transitional stage in the evo-lution of the vice trade, existing in profusion in every big city in the country. There is evidence that rings from different cities occasion-ally worked together, as for example the pipeline in two-way human trafficking between Chicago and New York.

The Colosimo name appeared in several investigations of white slavery but no arrests were made.

Such investigations were cyclical phenomena, like outbreaks of sunspots. They fell into a drearily familiar pattern, where some out-rage against the common weal would get into the press, the reform-ers and church groups would set up a howl, and city hall politicoes would posture and bluster. A few token raids and arrests would be carried out by the police, nothing would really be achieved, and within a short time, the fickle public would lose its sense of outrage and things would go back to "normal."

Big Jim was at the heart of the Levee's vice trade, where he thrived and prospered, looking after his and his wife's interests, an extensive network of hundreds of brothels and saloons, including a highline whorehouse that bore her name, "Victoria's." He fielded a squad of some of the Midwest's toughest gunmen to protect those interests. He was one of the biggest men in the Levee, a leading purveyor of vice and graft.

Naturally, he became a citywide celebrity. He was not one to shun the limelight—in fact, he courted it. He lived in the high, wide, and handsome style associated with the Gilded Age of the 1890s and rode it well into the next century.

A leading light of what used to be called the "sporting fraternity," a raffish half-world of gamblers, touts, swells, and men-about-town, he dressed the part in flashy checked suits and other overstated ap-parel. He was mad for diamonds and made a practice of constantly acquiring precious stones from fences and thieves. He habitually carried a handful of the pricey rocks inside a vest pocket, passing them out by way of tips or calling cards. He was, in short, a character, of a type that is a magnet for newspaper ink.

His showpiece nightspot was Colosimo's Café, located at 2128 South Wabash Avenue. A popular venue where society swells rubbed elbows with crooks and mugs in opulent settings that featured a mahagony bar and ornate dining room, the café was one of Chicago's major draws and tourist attractions.

Big Jim reveled in what would later come to be known as "gangster chic," attracting the interest and attention of the city's movers and shakers. He was taken up by the ritzy set, with his club becoming a prime watering hole for the high and mighty of Chicago.

Changing times and social climes failed to dislodge him from the top of the vice pyramid.

The first decade of the twentieth century saw the passing of the last holdouts of legal or at least officially tolerated red-light districts, as the concept of segregated vice came into disrepute. An alliance of reformers, good government types, church groups, and ladies clubs exerted significant political pressure. In city after city, the red-light districts were closed and shuttered.

Chicago was no exception. The Levee's finish was not unlike that of any other business that goes under. One day it was a going concern; the next, a ghost town, abandoned by its rogue denizens to forestall a full-scale cleansing by the police. Pimps and whores quit their haunts, packed their grips, and moved elsewhere. The houses went dark.

It was the end of the Levee as a thriving red-light district, but hardly the end of Chicago vice. The decline of the houses saw the rise of the call flats—that is, apartments near the saloons where the whores turned their tricks. Big Jim continued his rise, weathering the transition with aplomb, his fortunes not only undiminished but growing.

Success brought its own perils, however. He was subject to Black Hand extortion attempts on a regular basis. Even though Colosimo bossed an elite squad of killer gunmen, they couldn't protect him all the time and the Blackhanders knew it.

Some Blackhanders he ignored, others he had killed. Sometimes he paid because it was cheaper and less aggravating than not doing so.

Business was good, so good that in 1910 he hired a newcomer to help manage his operations. By so doing, he brought to Chicago a man regarded by some experts as one of the few genuine criminal masterminds of the twentieth century: John Torrio.

Torrio was a cousin of Victoria Moresco Colosimo. He hailed from New York City, where he'd been a thief, a brothel keeper, and a power in the infamous Five Points gang, a longtime presence and one of the old-time Gangs of New York whose roots went well back into the nineteenth century. He co-owned a bar in Brooklyn, a bucket-of-blood dive that was the sight of a number of slayings. His partner in the venture was Frankie Yale (Uale), the stellar Mafia assassin and national president of Unione Siciliane, a Sicilian American workers and self-help organization that had been taken over by the Mafia and used as a vehicle for extortion, labor racketeering, theft, and the like.

Torrio was a deep player, a strategist who preferred cunning and stealth to out and out violence, though he was not hesitant to order killings when necessary. A dealer in women's flesh, he shunned sleeping with whores and was faithful to his wife, with whom he enjoyed spending quiet nights at home. He never carried a gun, an affectation that would someday later come to haunt him.

Torrio picked up stakes and headed west to Chicago to work for Big Jim. His first task was to deal with a Black Hand gang that was pressing Colosimo hard by trying to shake him down. Torrio dealt with it by luring its members to an ambush where his gunmen shot them dead.

With this latest batch of extortionists eliminated and with Torrio handling much of the management chores, life was better than ever for Big Jim. The period from 1910 to 1920 was his golden decade.

Torrio's effective management style left Big Jim with perhaps too much time on his hands. He met Dale Winter in 1919, an attractive nineteen-year-old showgirl who went to work singing in one of his clubs. Colosimo fell hard. It must have been love: he even wanted to marry the girl, who apparently reciprocated his affection.

First, though, he would have to be shed of his current matrimonial encumbrance, Victoria Moresco Colosimo, the original wellspring of his good fortune and Torrio's cousin. Her brother was even one of Big Jim's elite, handpicked gunmen. A settlement was made, Victoria was divorced, and Colosimo was quick to wed Dale.

Torrio viewed the developments with equanimity. His business interests as Colosimo's manager far outweighed any family feeling he might have had for Cousin Victoria.

No, that was not what irked Torrio about Big Jim. What rankled him was Colosimo's blind indifference to the dazzling prospects of the newly enacted Eighteenth Amendment to the U.S. Constitution prohibiting the sale, distribution, and private consumption of alcoholic beverages.

The temperance movement to ban booze had flourished during the latter half of the nineteenth century, its ranks swelled by cranks, crackpots, reformers, idealists, religious personalities, and church and ladies groups. The Drys were the Prohibition Party; the anti-Prohibitionists were the Wets.

Scoffers mocked the idea that the United States could ever become a land where liquor, wine, and even beer were banished. Some of the same folks had also disbelieved that the red-light districts would go dark.

The 1918 election sent a pro-Dry majority to Congress, which quickly enacted the Eighteenth Amendment, making it the law of the land. The accompanying Volstead Act gave the law some teeth by providing for enforcement, prosecution, and punishment of violators.

Visionary John Torrio saw Prohibition as the road to riches, a gold rush for organized crime. He reasoned that Americans were going to drink, the law be damned. Someone would have to supply that need. Crookdom was uniquely positioned to do so, and the profits would be fabulous, gargantuan.

The Chicago mobs were nicely positioned to ride the gravy train. Not far to the north lay Canada, where Prohibition was naught. Canadian spirits could be trucked down across the border or shipped across Lake Michigan.

Torrio's cunning brain grasped all the fabulous, wealth-generating possibilities. Alas, like other visionaries, he was soon to discover the difficulty of persuading others of what he regarded as a self-evident truth. One other, specifically: Big Jim. Colosimo just couldn't or wouldn't get the message. Torrio gave him the pitch, laying out the bright promise of golden riches awaiting all who got into bootleg booze in a big way.

The boss failed to see the light. He told Torrio to stick to the tried and true vice racket. The whores were good enough for them, they always had been and always would be.

His obtuseness frustrated Torrio. Was Big Jim a hidebound traditionalist and reactionary too set in his ways to adapt to changing times? Or was it simply that his heart just wasn't in the business anymore?

That Big Jim's main interests lay in another direction seemed likely. He was more in love than ever with his new bride, doting on Dale, his time with her increasingly monopolizing his attentions. He wanted to enjoy the good life with her. His vice rackets were making money and, thanks to Torrio's skillful management, required little of his time. He had a good thing going.

A gang boss may commit many sins, but the most unforgiveable of all is to be too stupid to make money.

To Torrio, the equation was simple. There was a fortune to be made from Prohibition. If Colosimo's gang didn't make it, other, rival gangs would. And the vast sums they would realize from it would increase their power and influence at the Colosimo crowd's expense. Therefore, going all-out into illegal booze became not only a matter of profitability but also of survival itself.

Big Jim had no use for Torrio's bootleg schemes but he had no intention of retiring, either. He liked things fine the way they were. His appetite for vice trade profits remained insatiable. He would stay right where he was, a roadblock on the highway to progress. Like an unwanted building in the path of a projected highway, he was ripe for condemnation and demolition.

Sometime in early 1920, Torrio sent east for a fellow Brooklynite of his acquaintaince, a strapping young hoodlum named Alphonse Capone. As Torrio had done ten years earlier, Capone followed the siren call to Chicago. He found gainful employment as Torrio's man—not Big Jim's, significantly.

It was quite a trifecta: Colosimo, the Second City's number-one vice lord; Johnny Torrio, the crafty fox of the underworld; and Scarface Al Capone, whose power and notoriety would someday eclipse that of the others.

Another Brooklyn-based Torrio associate, one far more notorious at that time than Capone, was Frankie Yale, the national president of the Unione Siciliane. Yale's nickname, the "Undertaker," was not solely predicated on the fact that he indeed was the owner of a funeral parlor. Before too long, the Undertaker would be heeding that siren call and taking a trip out west to Chicago, too.

The Hit

On the afternoon, of May 11, 1920, Big Jim went to his show-place, Colosimo's Café on South Wabash Avenue. The club faced east on the west side of the thoroughfare, which ran north–south. The building was divided lengthwise into two sections, north and south. Both sections shared a common entrance on the structure's east side, an entryway that included a coatroom and a telephone booth.

Colosimo spent some time going over that evening's planned dinner menu with the maître d'. A handful of kitchen staff were also on the premises. Colosimo mentioned that he had an appointment with someone who was scheduled to meet him at the club at four o'clock. He did not say who that person was. At one point, he looked at his watch and noted that that the person he was to meet was not on time.

He went into the entryway. Shots sounded.

Club staffers went into the entryway and found Big Jim lying on the floor, bleeding from a head wound, dead. The assassin was nowhere to be seen.

The killer must have entered the building and hid in the coatroom. When Colosimo entered the hallway, the killer fired twice. One shot scored, the other missing the target. The killer had then exited by the front door, losing himself on Wabash Avenue. Whether he fled by car or on foot is unknown, but his getaway was clean.

A sweet job—simple, straightforward, and brutally effective.

A NOTE ON RATING THE HITS

Each hit can earn a possible twenty points maximum. Five points maximum may be awarded for strategy and 5 for tactics. Simply put, strategy is the plan and tactics is how it is carried out. A maximum of 10 points may be earned for results. Results may be described as: What was the kill intended to do and how well did it do it? A successful assassination, however, is no guarantee of a high-level score. Results take the big picture into account. A man's death, while successfully achieved, may bring about consequences that are quite different from those that are intended. For example, the assassination of Julius Caesar resulted in putting his nephew on the throne, hardly the goal that Brutus, Cassius, and Casca had in mind.

Handicapping the Colosimo Kill

STRATEGY

Big Jim seemed to his associates to have lost some of the fire in the belly necessary to be a bigtime crook. His obstinate refusal to go into bootlegging was costing them plenty of money, and that's a capital offense. He wouldn't retire, but he had to go. Nobody wanted him to suffer unduly, but they wanted him dead more.

There was a way such things were done. The killer or killers, professionals in such things, would be brought in from out of town (if possible) to prevent the likelihood of their being recognized. The intended victim, the mark, must be lured to the ambush sight, where death would come swiftly, inexorably, and without warning. This was no sport. It was cold-blooded murder with the killer optimizing every exploitable angle.

Often, it is necessary to make a victim's body disappear, keeping his fate a mystery, but that would not be needed where Colosimo was concerned. That was a plus, because it circumvented the need for any complicated body disposal maneuvers.

The main thrust of the plan was to get Colosimo to the ambush site and lower the boom. He would be lured to the killing ground at a time and place of the opposition's choice. The killing ground was his own club, his headquarters and place of power whose familiar surroundings would lull him into a false sense of safety and incline him to lower his guard.

A Judas was needed, someone trusted by Colosimo who could put him on the spot. Who that person was is unknown. We know that someone filled the Judas role, someone who had an appointment to meet Big Jim at the club at four in the afternoon, because Colosimo said so and there was no reason for him to lie. It had to be someone important enough for him to meet personally, rather than delegating the task to Torrio or another underling. Someone who Colosimo had no reason to suspect of treachery.

Torrio was well known at the club; had the appointment been with him, there would have been no reason for Colosimo not to say so, especially when he failed to arrive on time. The betrayer's identity remains a mystery.

A weakness in the plan lay in setting it in the club when some of the staff were on the scene. That was a potential complication. Witnesses might see the killer clearly enough to make an identification to police, were they lacking in wit enough to realize that such public-mindedness would put them on the chopping block. Someone might even try to play hero and do something stupid and get shot for his troubles or even worse, somehow gum up the works and muff the kill.

Deduct 1 point for locating the hit in Colosimo's club.

STRATEGY: 4

Tactics

The approach was stealthy, with smooth clandestinity. Colosimo never dreamed he was slated for demolition. Which is another sign of why he had to go. A smart gang boss knows that he's always slated for demolition by somebody, either a rival or an upstart in his own organization, and acts accordingly. Colosimo had gotten too cocky. His heart was no longer in the game that had brought him fame and fortune, it was with his lovely young bride. He was slipping.

Had he sensed trouble, he would have taken precautions and supplied himself with bodyguards. That he did not proves he'd been lulled into a false sense of security. He suspected no trouble, nothing out of the ordinary, when he arrived at the club to keep that fatal appointment.

The plotters were well acquainted with Colosimo's schedule, daily habit and routine. This intelligence was obtained without tipping him off that he was being stalked. He was set up by someone who knew him very well.

The four o'clock appointment was also well planned, taking place as it did in broad daylight, a circumstance likely to cause Colosimo to lower his guard. That added an element of risk, maximizing as it did the chance of the killer being seen by witnesses and detracting from his ability to lose any possible pursuit in darkness and so endangering or at least encumbering his getaway.

The ambush site was good, with the club entryway being screened from view of those in the north and south rooms. Additional cover was provided by the coatroom, which served as the shooter's lair, allowing him to conceal himself to avoid being seen by the mark, staffers, or passersby.

The killer had to have some way of knowing if Colosimo was in the building. Did he have the place staked out and saw Big Jim entering? Or was there an inside man, a spotter, who gave the signal that Big Jim was in the house? The answer is unknowable.

The evidence showed that Colosimo was shot from behind. There was no chance for him to draw the pearl-handled gun with which he armed himself. Presumably, he never knew what hit him. Two shots were fired, one striking him fatally in the head, the other missing.

The killshot did its job, leaving no mortally wounded man behind to make any verge-of-death identifications of his slayer or any other statements that might be potentially incriminating to his associates.

The killer made the fatal strike and followed it up with a quick getaway. So quick, that it is not known if he fled on foot or by car. A quick getaway and a clean one.

Deduct 1 point for a risky daylight shoot.

TACTICS: 4

RESULTS

Colosimo's death had no real downside—except to him, of course, and to a lesser degree, his new wife and any other claimants to his estate. Big Jim was reputed to go about with a big bankroll worth a small fortune stuffed into one of his pockets as he went about his business around town. No such bankroll was officially reported to have been found on him. Had it existed, it could have been pocketed by his killer, by one of the café staffers, or by sticky-fingered police who arrived early at the crime scene.

It was also widely held that he must have squirreled away hundreds of thousands of dollars in loot from his vice trade profits over the years, but an exhaustive search of his belongings failed to turn up anything more than a few thousand dollars. Neither the first nor second Mrs. Colosimo laid claim to the money, which went to Big Jim's father.

So much for the downside.

The upside was that now Johnny Torrio was in the driver's seat, master of the Colosimo organization and the financial and political clout that came with it. He was in position to inaugurate his grand scheme of empire building based on bootleg booze.

His lieutenant, Al Capone, likewise benefitted, moving up in the organization to the number-two spot under Torrio.

The organization they forged would dominate Chicago, expand underworld crime to unprecedented levels, and lay the groundwork for a national crime syndicate. Not a bad return for the blotting out of Big Jim!

RESULTS: 10

Murder Meter Box Score
   STRATEGY: 4
   TACTICS: 4
   RESULTS: 10

TOTAL: 18

Who done it? Who slew Colosimo?

A likely candidate for the shooter was Frankie Yale, who wore many hats: Unione Siciliane president, mafioso, cigar vendor, and funeral parlor owner, to name a few. The mainstay of his various businesses, and the secret of his success, was that he was an icy and relentless professional killer, a top notch hitman. He and Torrio were more than old acquaintances back in Brooklyn, they were partners in a low dive bar and other, more sinister ventures.

Hot on the heels of the Colosimo hit, Chicago police arrested Yale at the railroad depot, where he was waiting to catch a train out of town. He was a prime suspect but there was nothing to hold him on and the law soon released him.

But Yale fit the pattern. He was a hired killer, way off his home turf of Brooklyn, just the kind of out-of-town top gun that plotters like to bring in to whack one of their own. He and Torrio had a long history of working together.

Another, less likely candidate for the hit was Al Capone. A story surfaced out of Chicago newsroom gossip to the effect that it was Capone who'd lurked in the coatroom and potted Big Jim.

Several factors work against Capone being the shooter. Torrio had brought in Capone to be his right-hand man. Capone was a power-house with a zest for the kind of violence and brutality needed for the coming struggle for control of Chicago, action that was less congenial to the more rational and flexible Torrio. Torrio would not want to risk losing this valuable tool in the event that something went wrong with the Colosimo kill to put the spotlight on Al. Capone was his protégé, his creature, and if he was suspected in Big Jim's murder, suspicion would likely fall on Torrio, too.

Capone was a brash killer with plenty of guts and nerve, but Yale was a specialist. Colosimo's was the kind of delicate case that called for Yale's lethal expertise.

All this is theory, though Yale's presence in Chicago during the window of opportunity for the Colosimo kill adds substance to the speculation. However, the killer need not have been Yale or Capone, but an unknown third party who did the deed and left behind not a trace. It's less likely but not impossible.

Those who knew for sure have long since passed on without breaking silence.

So much for the shooter. Who ordered the hit?

In the old Roman Senate, whenever a new bill or piece of legislation was proposed, the key question was: *Cui bono*? (Who benefits?) Who benefitted from the Colosimo kill?

Johnny Torrio, first and foremost. With the boss dead, he became the new boss, inheriting the title to go with the power he already wielded. No more would Big Jim, all puffed up with himself, complacently wave aside Torrio's ambitious master plan for reaping a bootleg bonanza. Now, Torrio was calling the shots, with Capone backing and enforcing the play.

There remained one final ceremony to be performed, one last rite of passage: the burial of Big Jim. He went to the hereafter with all the grandiose pomp and circumstance befitting a gangland kingpin and vice lord: an avalanche of floral bouquets and memorial tributes, a lengthy cortege of limousines, and a roster of distinguished mourners.

They were burying not only a man but also an era, the last of the old-time, old-school vice barons. His death opened the way for the Mafia to establish its powerful and profitable retooling into a sleek, twentieth-century corporate business model.

The funeral was of a scope and scale befitting the late Mr. Colosimo: big.

2

"Only Capone Kills Like That": The St. Valentine's Day Massacre

The art of the gangland funeral would reach its highest development in the 1920s. And why not? There was no shortage of gang killings, especially not in Chicago, where the John Torrio–Al Capone combine spent the better part of the decade battling rival gangs for total supremacy.

Dion "Deanie" O'Bannion knew plenty about gangland funerals, both as owner of a floral shop and as trigger-tempered boss of the Irish North Side gang. As a florist, he'd supplied spectacular memorial wreaths, arrangements, and tributes to any number of the Chicago underworld's most high-profile funerals. As a gang chief and killer, he'd supplied any number of corpses for some of those same funerals. O'Bannion's North Siders had been butting heads with the Torrio-Capone West Side outfit since the Colosimo kill in 1920.

On November 10, 1924, three men entered O'Bannion's floral shop. It was a busy time for the owner and his assistants. Mike Merlo, the head of the Chicago branch of the Unione Siciliane, had only recently passed away. He and O'Bannion had been friends. In fact, it was his moderating influence that had kept the West Side enemies of O'Bannion from making a move on him.

O'Bannion and his assistants in the backroom were hard at work preparing memorial wreaths and tributes for the Merlo funeral. When the three men entered, O'Bannion went to greet them. He knew them.

Two of them were John Scalise and Albert Anselmi, two professional gunmen and killers associated with the West Side Genna crime family. The third man has been variously identified as Frankie Yale or, less likely, one of the Genna brothers.

O'Bannion was expecting them. James Genna had earlier ordered a floral tribute for the Merlo rites. O'Bannion had received a phone call telling him that some men were coming over to pick up the piece. He knew Anselmi and Scalise, and he knew they worked for the Gennas.

Also, he was not entirely defenseless. O'Bannion habitually carried three guns in different pockets, placed so he could get to one fast when he needed it.

"Hello, boys," he said. "You must be here for Merlo's funeral."

He advanced with one hand outstretched, reaching to shake hands. The third man took O'Bannion's hand as if to shake and gripped it tightly, immobilizing it and preventing him from drawing any of the three guns he was carrying.

Anselmi and Scalise drew their guns, blasting O'Bannion at point-blank range. One of them delivered the coup de grâce, a bullet in the head. O'Bannion hit the floor. The killers exited, escaping via getaway car.

The quarrelsome O'Bannion had been feuding with the Gennas, but when he had recently crossed the Torrio-Capone combine on a bootlegging deal that not only cost them money but also socked Torrio on a federal rap for which he would do nine months in jail, he set in motion the forces that would destroy him. The death of his friend, Mike Merlo, removed the last obstacle in the way of obliterating O'Bannion. The O'Bannion hit was a combined Genna-Torrio-Capone operation.

O'Bannion was given a grand sendoff, the most opulent and ostentatious gangland funeral ever seen in Chicago or anywhere else in the United States, then or now. For pageantry and spectacle, it was the highwater mark of the genre.

His death opened a five-year-long war between the North Siders and the Capone mob, one that culminated in the notorious St. Valentine's Day Massacre—itself a peak experience, in the annals of gangland slayings.

It must have seemed a whole lot simpler and less bloody in concept several years earlier, when Torrio had ascended to the throne of the Colosimo operation.

The way he saw it, the coming bootlegging bonanza would generate so much cash beyond the wild dreams of avarice of even the greediest gangster, that it only made sense for Chicago's rival mobs to cease their incessant sniping and feuding and agree to a truce where they could all get rich. Torrio made a fundamental error in judgment here. Sane and level-headed, he underestimated the career criminal's need for violence and insatiable appetite for more than a fair share.

Chicago was a city divided into various ethnic neighborhoods, with Irish, Italians, blacks, and Poles being among the most prominent groups. Each group had its own gangs and bosses. Italian and Sicilian gangs were located largely on the city's West Side, while the Irish gangs claimed the North Side as their territory.

The first major achievement of Johnny Torrio's tenure as West Side boss was to negotiate a kind of truce or treaty between the major gangs, with the goal of suppressing costly and bloody territorial disputes and maximizing profits.

It's always difficult to persuade crooks to put a check on their endless greed and acquisitiveness. The only way to do so is show them that they'll make more money by cooperation than conflict. Even then, it's usually a sure bet that the participants are only biding their time, waiting for the right moment to eliminate their opponents and take it all.

Agreeing to the treaty was the North Side triumvirate of Dion O'Bannion, Hymie Weiss, and George "Bugs" Moran. O'Bannion was of Irish descent, Weiss was Polish, and Moran was Irish and

Polish. The West Side Torrio-Capone combine was sided by the Gennas, six brothers of Sicilian ancestry whose greed and violence had caused gangland to label them the "Terrible Gennas."

Torrio's vision was quickly proved right, as bootlegging became the gangsters' royal road to riches. Illegal alcohol was what made the Roaring Twenties roar. Now that it was prohibited, it became more popular than ever, a textbook case of the lure of the forbidden.

The era of raccoon coats, short skirts, bobbed hair, Flaming Youth, flappers, and petting parties floated on a sea of booze. No party was a party without it. Collegiate romeos went equipped with hip flasks in their back pockets when courting Betty Coed. No aspiring man about town could afford to be without his own personal bootlegger. Speakeasies, restricted or private clubs where booze was sold, seemed to pop up on every corner.

Prohibition had only fired America's thirst to a raging need. Satisfying that thirst was a gargantuan task, but crookdom met the challenge.

It was illegal to make or sell beer, wine, or spirits. That was the law of the land, amended to the Constitution. There were some loopholes. For example, pharmacists were allowed to possess stocks of alcohol for medicinal purposes. But these stores (much of which were diverted to gangsters and bootleggers) were only a drop in the bucket.

Some booze was smuggled in by boat on the coasts or overland from Canada and Mexico. Truck convoys guarded by machine gun–wielding guards smuggled stocks of whiskey by night. A little, a very little of this prime bonded stock wound up intact and undiluted in the hands of a wealthy few. Much of it was watered down and sold in its adulterated state to maximize profits.

The real fountainhead of the trade was homemade hooch. Moonshine. Home brew. When they called it "bathtub gin," they weren't kidding. Much of it was actually whipped up in bathtubs or "alky cookers" by legions of small producers who sold their stock directly to gangsters.

Violence was endemic to the bootlegger's trade. Every load of booze was subject to hijacking by anybody else tough enough to take it. Rivals sought to eliminate the competition by gunning them out.

Prohibition didn't exactly spawn a readymade army of hoodlums. They were already in place, in every big city and town. Civilizations come and go, but crooks are forever. Bootlegging gave them a calling. Opportunities were many. Firepower was fierce: automatic pistols and submachine guns, shotguns, and dynamite. Lawlessness was motorized: fast and mobile.

The situation was the same in Chicago, only more so. Nature seemed to have a special sauce for the Second City.

The truce that Torrio had brokered held good only for the big fish. It was a mutual nonaggression pact allowing them to gobble up the small fish and consolidate their holdings before once more starting in on each other. The period from 1920 to 1924 was the era of the Chicago beer wars as the big gangs sought to monopolize bootlegging in their respective territories.

The Italian West Siders and Irish North Siders came out on top. The rivals tested each other, probing for weaknesses, looking to open and exploit any toehold or wedge into the other guy's turf. Incidents that exploded into violence and killing tested the fabric of the truce, straining but not breaking it.

Gangsters being gangsters, with their greedy, grasping, and disputacious natures, it was only a matter of time before the guns started barking between the North and West Side mobs. The time came when all the small fish had been eaten and the big ones started eyeing each other, sizing up their foes for the inevitable showdown.

North Side boss Dion O'Bannion tried to move some of the beer across the line in Genna territory. Expressing contempt in reaction to reports of the brothers' displeasure, he added insult to injury by saying, "To hell with them Sicilians."

The Gennas came from the Sicilian village of Marsala, as did Albert Anselmi and John Scalise. Anselmi and Scalise were hired killers who worked in tandem. Things got too hot for them in Sicily, so they moved to Chicago, where they sold their guns to the Gennas. The two were among the most feared killers in the city.

Not by O'Bannion, though. He kept on jousting with the Gennas. His friend, Mike Merlo, used his considerable influence as head of the Unione Siciliane's Chicago branch to convince the Gennas to hold their fire.

O'Bannion was something of a prankster, and he came up with a scheme to stick it to the Torrio-Capone combine but good. He was tipped off that one of his distilleries was slated to be raided by federal investigators. Announcing that he was planning to retire, he sold the distillery at a bargain price to Torrio.

Torrio was present when the site was hit by the feds. He was arrested and faced charges on a federal rap, rather than on more easily quashed city or state charges. Around this time, Merlo died of natural causes, removing the bar to action that had stymied the Gennas until then. Torrio and Capone were equally agreed that Deanie was long overdue for a reckoning.

The day came on November 10, 1924, when O'Bannion was shot dead in his flower shop. The guns that blew the life out of him fired the opening volley of a five-year-long gang war that would see scores of casualties on both sides and reach its peak on St. Valentine's Day 1929.

The murder of their chief quite naturally outraged the North Siders, of whom none was more inconsolable than O'Bannion's lieutenant, Hymie Weiss. The gang wasted no time in striking back hard. Their target? Johnny Torrio, who prided himself on not carrying a gun.

He could have used one on the night of January 24, 1925, when a trio of would-be killers caught him out in the open with no bodyguards, his arms laden with packages bought on a shopping trip from which he and his wife had just returned.

The gunmen were Hymie Weiss, George "Bugs" Moran, and Vincent "Schemer" Drucci. The opening blast from their shotguns cut down Torrio, felling but not killing him. Moran moved in to deliver the coup de grâce, a bullet in the head. The gun was jammed. The late Deanie O'Bannion hadn't once tagged Moran the "Shooting Fool" for nothing.

Believing him dead, the shooters fled. Torrio *was*—but not mortally. He held on, lingering in a hospital bed for months, in agony (one of the slugs had hit him in the groin), but he finally pulled through to a full recovery.

He'd had enough. His diplomatic skills were irrelevant in the dawning era of Chicago gang warfare, (fire)powered by the Thompson submachine gun and the grenade—the Typewriter and the Pineapple, respectively, in underworld argot.

He turned his entire operation over to Al Capone, who was well poised to receive it. Scarface would not shrink from doing whatever had to be done to be the Big Boss. Torrio did his nine-month federal rap on the distillery beef, was released from jail, and with his wife left first Chicago and then the United States to avoid North Sider guns, spending a few years in Europe before returning to the States.

He would continue to play a leading role in organized crime, but his role as a player and power in Chicago was done.

Now began in earnest the irresistible rise of Al Capone to the top of the Chicago heap. And by extension, occupancy of the apex of the pyramid of U.S. organized crime. Under his leadership, the Second City became number one in crookdom's roster of sin cities.

For the next five years, Capone waged a relentless struggle to consolidate his West Side gang's hold over the city. His primary antagonists were the North Siders, but there were plenty of other pitched battles with lesser but still murderous foes. His meteoric career is well-covered elsewhere, so a quick summary will serve our purpose here.

A prime source of Capone's strength was his alliance with Frankie Yale's organization in Brooklyn, New York. Yale set up a pipeline between New York and Chicago. Rum-running ships brought in quantities of high-grade booze to the New York coast, from which it was then shipped in truck convoys to Chicago.

A major asset was Capone's first-rate execution squad (he called them "bodyguards"). He had a legion of strongarm men and shooters at his call, but these were the killer elite. Among them were Anselmi and Scalise, Fred "Killer" Burke, and "Machine Gun" Jack

McGurn, who was fated to be the architect of the St. Valentine's Day Massacre.

Meanwhile, the war with the North Side continued to play out its stark game of natural selection.

In 1925, the Gennas moved to fill the power vacuum that the death of Mike Merlo had left at the top of the Chicago branch of the Unione Siciliane. It was a plum prize, rich with cash and clout, and one that Capone himself coveted but could not fill, due to his being of Neapolitan descent. His parents had come from Naples, while he had been born in the United States. But his lack of Sicilian ancestry barred him from claiming the Unione crown.

In possession of the Unione, the Gennas now fell out with Capone, whose name was firmly placed on their better-dead list. But they held high priority on the North Siders' own kill list, and a ferocious campaign by Weiss and his troops resulted in most of the brothers being killed and the rest being driven into exile in Sicily.

Capone retaliated for the botched hit on Torrio with a successful one on Hymie Weiss. Assassins rented an apartment with a firing line on Weiss's headquarters in O'Bannion's old flower shop and turned it into a machine gun nest, catching Weiss on the sidewalk in the open and chopping him down.

Capone's association with Frankie Yale turned into a liability when Capone became suspicious that Yale was hijacking his own westbound bootleg booze shipments that were being convoyed to Chicago. In 1927, Capone dissolved his partnership with Yale, courtesy of a quartet of Chicago torpedoes who went to New York and caught Yale out driving his car on a Sunday in Brooklyn. Yale's machine was plated with bulletproof armor, but in an odd fit of omission, he'd neglected to outfit it with bulletproof glass.

The quartet's car was stocked with machine guns that they turned on Yale. His was the first murder to be committed by submachine gun in New York City, a famous first.

Back in Chicago, the North Side continued to target Capone, making over a dozen attempts on his life. They also took out any number of lesser lights of his organization. Capone longed to deliver one bold stroke that would eliminate his foes.

The Hit

By 1929, Capone was at the top of his game and was the most powerful gang leader in the nation. He was known nationwide, even internationally. In Chicago he was the Big Boy and the Big Fellow, and when either of those names came up, it was understood that they referred to Capone. Much of city hall was on his payroll, not least of which was Mayor William "Big Bill" Thompson, with whom Capone enjoyed the friendliest of relations. He had little to fear from the police, many of whom were also on his payroll.

He was a celebrity, a role to which he was not averse. He loved the publicity, the cheers of the crowd when he went to a baseball stadium or boxing match. He gave interviews portraying himself as a "simple businessman" who flaunted a Prohibition that nobody wanted by supplying the myriad thirsty with bootleg booze. Periodically, he said that he was retired from the game, fooling no one.

Yet, there was discord in the Capone barony. His killers had eliminated most of his major enemies, but not Bugs Moran.

Moran was now boss of the North Siders, a tough, scrappy bunch of unregenerate hoodlums who refused to lay down and die. They kept up the pressure, searching for vulnerabilities.

Two of them, brothers Pete and Frank Gusenberg, caught Capone top-gun Jack McGurn in an unguarded moment while he was making a call from a pay phone booth. They sprayed him with machine gun bullets until they were sure he was dead. But he wasn't, and lived to recover.

He was an aggressive, athletic guy who'd been born James De Mora. In his late teens he did a stint as a boxer, billed as an Irishman and fighting under the name "Jack McGurn." He was nineteen when his grocer father was killed by gangsters. McGurn plunged into the criminal life, becoming a gunman and enforcer.

Along the way, he killed four of the men who'd killed his father. Each was found with a nickel pressed into his hand—McGurn had learned that the killers had slightingly referred to his father as a small-time "nickel and dimer."

He was a smart, tough, and ruthless prankster and punisher. As

"Machine Gun" Jack McGurn (so named for his weapon of choice), he was one of Capone's ace executioners. His clean-cut good looks, athleticism, and smooth front gave him a kind of Gatsbyesque aura in the Chicago underworld. But his smooth front was just that—a front; his well-tailored suits and well-spoken demeanor masked an icy ruthlessness.

Just how ruthless McGurn could be was demonstrated in the matter of singer-performer Joe E. Lewis, one of the most notorious and grotesque acts of violence in an era replete with same.

Lewis grew eager to quit McGurn's club and go work for another nightspot. McGurn replied that if he left, Lewis would never live to open his act. Lewis went to the other club, where on opening night he rubbed salt in the wound by making some ill-timed cracks about the gangster.

McGurn's response was not long in coming. A couple of his enforcers invaded Lewis's hotel room and overpowered the performer. One of them stuck a knife in Lewis's throat, cutting his vocal chords in a deliberate attempt to end his career as a singer.

Lewis survived, suffering through a long and painful convalescence from which he never fully recovered, although by heroic efforts he managed to overcome his affliction to the point of reinventing his performing career as a successful nightclub comic.

He was the victim of a terrorist act whose purpose was to terrorize. Instead of killing him, he was left alive as a reminder to others that not even a popular entertainer could defy Jack McGurn with impunity.

That's what McGurn did to a nightclub singer who'd crossed him. What he would do to the Gusenberg brothers, who'd had the effrontery to shoot him, and to their boss Bugs Moran was soon to be demonstrated.

The botched attempt on McGurn's life was a warning to Al Capone that the war that had begun with the execution of Dion O'Bannion in 1924 would end only with the death of Capone or Moran.

Capone was under no illusions. It was kill or be killed. Either he eliminated the North Side gang or they would eliminate him.

* * *

The recuperating McGurn was put in charge of the Get Moran operation. McGurn moved with the bold ruthlessness for which he was known. Like any good planner, his first need was for intelligence about the enemy.

Capone was headquartered in a fancy Chicago hotel, the Hawthorne. Moran's command post was a North Side garage housing the S.M.C. Cartage Company at 2122 North Clark Street.

McGurn sent two brothers, Harry and Phil Keywell, to keep watch on the garage. They rented a room across the street from it, in a building at 2119 North Clark Street, using it as an observation post.

McGurn staffed the operation, tabbing for the hit squad the indispensable Anselmi and Scalise; Elmer "Killer" Burke, of St. Louis's Egan's Rats gang, a bank robber and shooter; James Ray, a Burke cohort; and Joseph Lolordo, brother of Capone ally Pasquale Lolordo, who was recently slain by a mutual foe.

McGurn set a trap for Moran with some tempting bait. One of his men not on the execution squad posed as a hijacker who had a load of freshly plundered Canadian whiskey, "the real stuff," that he was looking to unload fast and cheap. He approached the Moran gang, who were receptive to the deal. The exchange (whiskey for cash) was made at the Clark Street garage.

Moran, well pleased, was highly receptive when he was subsequently contacted by the front man who proposed doing a second deal along the lines of the first.

The date for the next exchange was set for February 14, 1929— St. Valentine's Day. Moran would be present for it, as he'd been for the first. In their apartment across the street, the Keywell brothers kept the garage under surveillance, watching for Bugs. On February 14 at about 10:30 A.M., they saw Moran enter the garage and quickly reported the sighting to the executioners.

Unknowingly, they'd made a serious error. The man they'd seen going into the garage was not Moran but Albert Weinshank, a gang member who looked like him. Weinshank was a saloon keeper whose resemblence to Moran was widely noted, but not by the Keywells.

Inside the garage were seven men and a dog. Besides Weinshank, those present were Pete and Frank Gusenberg; safecracker John May; James Clark, a bankrobber and Moran's brother-in-law; Adam Heyer, Moran's business manager; and optometrist Dr. Reinhardt H. Schwimmer. The dog, a German shepherd named Highball, belonged to May.

A police car unexpectedly arrived on the scene, manned by three uniformed and two plainclothes cops. Armed with shotguns and machine guns, they quickly entered the garage.

Again, fate took a hand. The real Bugs Moran and two of his sidemen were nearby, walking toward the garage when they saw the police car drive up. Thinking it was a raid, they kept on walking, putting some distance between themselves and the site.

Inside the garage, the police had gotten the drop on the gangsters, covering them with drawn guns. The North Siders might well have solaced themselves with the thought that these had to be the dumbest cops in town. Moran paid good money and lots of it to the top brass at the police station house to immunize himself from such nuisances as raids.

The gangsters made no attempt to resist what must have seemed to them a ridiculous mix up. If they must be arrested and taken to the station house, so be it. They'd all been arrested plenty of times before, it was no big deal. It would all be straightened out later, either by crooked cops on the payroll or by Moran's lawyers. That's when these straight-arrow cops who were dumb or crazy enough to roust the gang would find out the facts of life, before being transferred to patrolling a beat out in the middle of nowhere at the far reaches of the city limits.

The intruders lined the seven men up facing the rear garage wall, and frisked and relieved them of their weapons (disarming and defanging them). That's when the Moran gang found out the real facts of life, that what they'd thought was a police raid was actually a mass execution.

The cops weren't cops at all, but killers disguised as cops. They cut loose, opening up on the unarmed men with machine guns and shotguns, spraying them with high-velocity streams of lead and filling the garage with noise, gunsmoke, blood, and corpses.

When the shooting stopped, seven bodies lay bleeding and twitching on the floor. The executioners exited the garage, got into their car, and drove away.

Inside, all that remained alive was a fear-crazed dog and the mortally wounded Frank Gusenberg. Gusenberg lingered on for a few hours, remaining true to the underworld code by keeping silent to the last despite repeated entreaties by lawmen pleading with him to tell who'd shot him.

In the initial chaos and confusion surrounding the slaughter, there was a very real suspicion that perhaps the killing had been done by members of the Chicago police. A not unwarranted assumption, considering the pervasive corruption enveloping the force.

The Clark Street massacre created a mass sensation, not only in Chicago but also nationwide and even around the world. Its impact was electrifying, becoming headline news everywhere, even on the front page of the staid, sober *New York Times*.

The Prohibition era in general and Chicago gangland in particular were steeped in sensational murders, but the massacre was a new high (or low) in ultra-violence, retaining the capacity to shock even the most jaded jazz age denizens. Its seven-man body count equalled wholesale murder. For those concerned about gangland violence, here was proof positive that organized crime was raging out of control. The macabre association of St. Valentine's Day with mobdom's most brutal massacre to date helped to amplify the impact.

Suspicion soon turned to Al Capone, the obvious beneficiary of the liquidation of a large part of the Moran gang. Capone himself was wintering in Florida's Miami Beach, his home away from home, far away from the violence of Chicago.

Bugs Moran had no doubt as to the massacre's author, noting bitterly, "Only Capone kills like that."

Capone fired back, "The only person who kills like that is Moran."

Like his boss Capone, McGurn had been careful to establish an ironclad alibi for the time frame of the massacre, claiming to have been holed up in a hotel room with his girlfriend, Louise Rolfe, soon to gain fame as his "blonde alibi."

No one was ever arrested and charged with participating in the slaughter.

Handicapping the St. Valentine's Day Massacre

STRATEGY

McGurn's strategy was a first-rate blueprint for a masterpiece of murder, but the X factor crept in. The heart of it was the false flag ploy: sneak the executioners in place to deliver the killing stroke by disguising them as something else—that is, cops. The vehicle in which the killers arrived and departed was a real police car, one that had been stolen for the occasion. The police uniforms worn by some of the imposters were no less authentic and convincing.

A second imperative was ensuring that Bugs Moran was present when the axe fell. This was done by appealing to good, old-fashioned greed, offering Moran a great deal on some quality whiskey. The nature of the transaction was such that Moran would have to be present to make the payment and also to guard against any of the shipment falling into the sticky fingers of his underlings.

The Moran gang had no idea that the intruders were anything but what they seemed. Otherwise, they would hardly have gone to the wall like sheep to the slaughter but gone down fighting. Their suspicions were disarmed; then they themselves were disarmed. In the last few seconds when the machine gunners unlimbered their weapons and made them ready, some or all of the victims might have known what their fate was to be—but it was too late for them to do anything about it but die.

STRATEGY: 5

TACTICS

Here's where a master plan meets the unexpected, unpredictable variable: the X factor. An integral part of the scheme was the elimination of Bugs Moran along with the rest of his gang. Moran was a dangerous man; for him to slip the net meant that a planned final solution was only a work in progress. Alive, he would always be a threat, able to recruit more guns and mount a retaliatory attack on Capone.

The plan stumbled badly when the Keywell brothers mistook Moran lookalike Albert Weinshank for Moran himself. By wrongfully identifying him as Moran and giving the signal that the North Side gang leader was actually in the garage, the spotters set the plan into irreversible motion.

Moran narrowly escaped death by arriving at the garage slightly after the "police" were already on the scene and in place. Had he arrived a few minutes earlier, he would have been inside the garage when the killers struck and would have died along with the others. But he didn't, and so he escaped.

Deduct 2 points for Moran's escape.

TACTICS: 3

RESULTS

The main objective was simple: kill Bugs Moran. Capone and the North Siders were locked in a five-year duel to the death that had begun in 1924 with the O'Bannion kill. The Gusenbergs' recent botched hit on McGurn sent Capone a message that the struggle was still very much alive, that it was a hot war, a shooting war, and that it must play out until one side or the other was nullified.

Chicago could have only one boss and his rule must be absolute. If it was possible to liquidate the North Side gang in toto, why not? The criminal code—which is the law of the jungle—demands that the winner takes all and losers go to the wall. The hardest lesson for a predator is knowing when to stop eating.

There were good reasons for not exercising the master stroke of massacring a mess of North Side gangsters along with their boss.

The death of Bugs Moran, if doable, would have been part of the natural order of things in jazz age Chicago. Gang chiefs were constantly being eliminated and replaced, here and in every big city in the United States. Killing Moran would have made a splash in the press, perhaps even gone nationally due to its linkage with the high-profile Capone, but its impact would have been minor and its duration short lived. Ultimately, it would have translated into a local phenomenon, one more bigshot gangster being put on the spot.

But the St. Valentine's Day Massacre was horrific stuff that was tailor-made to become a national sensation. It generated the kind of heat that made even a confirmed publicity hound like Capone sweat. It hardened the federal government's determination to take him down. The feds had what local and state governments didn't: money, manpower, resources, and the will to battle to the finish.

So began the weaving of the net whose strands most famously included Internal Revenue Service (IRS) investigators and the U.S. Treasury's Eliot Ness and his Untouchables, a net that would ultimately ensnare Capone in a tax evasion case that earned him an eleven-year federal prison term and broke the Big Fellow's power forever.

Not only did the St. Valentine's Day Massacre fail in its primary objective of killing Moran but it also set into motion the federal forces that would destroy Capone (though not his kingdom).

Moran survives as possible threat: deduct 3 points;
provoking ultimately successful anti-Capone reaction: deduct 5 points.

RESULTS: 2

Murder Meter Box Score
   STRATEGY: 5
   TACTICS: 3
   RESULTS: 2

TOTAL: 10

McGurn's fate was inextricably linked with that of his boss. As Capone faded, so too did McGurn, with the one-time ace enforcer falling away into what he must eventually have hoped would be a peaceful and quiet obscurity.

It was not to be. On February 13, 1936, the eve of St. Valentine's

Day, McGurn's past caught up with him at a bowling alley where gang guns cut him down. One of the killers placed in his dead hand an insulting Valentine's Day card—a memento from Bugs Moran, whose lucky escape from the Clark Street slaughter had resulted in the demise of Machine Gun Jack McGurn.

3

Two Bosses Too Many

Two men, a boss and his trusted lieutenant, are eating a midday meal in an out-of-the-way restaurant. Apart from a few staffers, they have the place to themselves. After eating, they play cards to kill some time. The junior man, the lieutenant, excuses himself and goes into the men's room.

In the dining room, shots—lots of them—ring out. The senior man, riddled with bullet holes, slumps dead over the tabletop. He is—was—Mafia chief Joe "the Boss" Masseria. The lieutenant (and new boss) is Charles "Lucky" Luciano.

There was something remote, distant, and elusive in Luciano's make up that makes him difficult to categorize. Most crime bosses may be summarized by a single outstanding trait. Al Capone: Napoleonic. Albert Anastasia: hot tempered. Vito Genovese: cunning. Frank Costello: statesmanlike. Meyer Lansky: brainy. Joe Bonnano: prideful.

Luciano is tougher to pin down. Ambitious? He became the de facto boss of the national crime syndicate. Cunning? He knocked off his boss, Masseria, to become the new boss. Statesmanlike? He welded together the five leading Mafia families of New York into the nucleus, the central organizing principle of American organized crime that exists to this today. Brainy? From a prison cell, he manipulated events on the outside so as to put a military intelligence division in his debt and win his release.

Perhaps the best way to characterize Luciano, if labels are needed, is to look to the nickname that his contemporaries and colleagues who knew him best tagged him with: "Lucky." Charlie Lucky Luciano.

But luck is often the residue of planning and desire. More than luck was needed to take Luciano to the top spot in U.S. crime. It took smarts, ruthlessness, vision, and more than a few well-timed murders.

In 1931, two men stood between Luciano and the crown: Joe Masseria and Salvatore Maranzano, two Mafia bosses who hated each other; two bosses too many for Luciano's ambitious career plans.

By 1900, every big city in the United States had a Mafia component to its underworld, but the ancient society was then still one of many competing factions and not yet the "first among equals" it was soon to become.

The first really major mafioso to make a name for himself in New York City starting in the pre–World War I era was Ignazio Saietta, the feared and fearsome "Lupo the Wolf," a sadistic psychopath of the first water.

He maintained a headquarters in an East Harlem stable, the notorious Murder Stable, which was equipped with meathooks and a furnace for disposing of bodies alive or dead. He burned at least six victims and probably more alive in the furnace, incinerating them on the hot coals.

Saietta was the national president of the Unione Siciliane, an organization that as previously noted occupies an important if shadowy place in the annals of the Mafia's rise.

By the time of his "presidency," the once legitimate self-help organization for Sicilian immigrants had morphed into a Mafia-dominated crime machine. Saietta milked it as a cash cow and vehicle for extortion, labor racketeering, loansharking, and suchlike illegal activities. He was arrested for extortion in 1919, imprisoned, and heard from no more.

His successor was the redoutable Frankie Yale, the "Undertaker," who took Saietta's place as head of the Unione Siciliane. A feared professional killer, Yale plied his trade on Big Jim Colosimo, clearing the way for Johnny Torrio to take over the Chicago vice operation.

The Unione Siciliane was a vital ally during Capone's battle with the North Siders and other gangs for dominance as city crime boss. Torrio, originally from Orsara, Italy, and Capone, American-born of Neapolitan descent, lacked the proper Sicilian bloodline to establish themselves at the head of the Unione. By the 1930s though, the American Mafia had loosened its strictures to allow candidates of Italian heritage to join the previously Sicilians-only society.

Torrio and Capone had come from New York to boost Chicago's status from Second City to the nation's Capital of Crime.

Now, in 1931, three Mafia bosses, Masseria, Maranzano, and Luciano, would wrest the title of crime capital away from Chicago and back to New York.

A key Mafia power in New York in the 1920s was Guiseppe "Joe the Boss" Masseria, an accomplished killer, bootlegger, and racketeer. He was short, stocky, but surprisingly light on his feet, as several would-be assassins learned to their frustration as the agile Masseria dodged their bullets. Those on the business end of his gun were less nimble, falling victim to his traps, stratagems, and ambushes. Masseria was the first mafioso to christen himself with the Americanized title of "the Boss."

His New York associates included Brooklyn's Yale (and later, Augusto "Little Augie" Pisano and Joe Adonis); the Bronx's Ciro Terranova (the Artichoke King); and the boss's own junior boss and lieutenant, Charles "Lucky" Luciano. Sicilian-born as Salvatore Lucania, at age nine he arrived with his immigrant parents in the United States, changing his name along the way to Charles Luciano. He grew up on the edges of Manhattan's Lower East Side, a teeming Jewish and Italian immigrant neighborhood, where he made the acquaintance of Jewish gangsters Meyer Lansky and Benjamin

"Bugsy" Siegel, two future luminaries of crookdom. The acquaintance would hold him in good stead, as the duo would later feature heavily in Luciano's eventual dominance of the American Mafia and by extension the national crime syndicate.

A marked aversion to honest employment saw Luciano graduate in his teens to becoming a thief and narcotics dealer. He took a fall on a dope-peddling charge and did six months in jail. On release, he was inducted into the Five Points gang, where he made the acquaintance of such worthies as Torrio, Frankie Yale, and Al Capone.

A later arrest for selling heroin had more serious repercussions. Luciano turned informer, fingering an even bigger dope stash of a competitor. The rival was busted and the cops let Luciano go. This was not his finest hour, but he managed to keep it a secret. It came out only much later, in 1936, when he was being tried by Special Prosecutor Thomas E. Dewey. Crookdom tried to brush away its embarrassment and disillusion at Charlie Lucky's dealings with the law by arguing as a mitigating factor that he hadn't fingered a fellow Mafia member but an unconnected guy.

But that incident was unknown to the underworld back when Luciano was a young hoodlum on the way up. He was smart, slick, and tough, attributes that resulted in his becoming Masseria's right-hand man. Joe the Boss was quite fond of the polite, well-spoken Luciano, claiming to regard him almost as a son.

Events in Sicily in the mid-1920s created repercussions that were to be felt in the ranks of the American Mafia. Benito Mussolini, Italy's fascist dictator, would tolerate no competing power centers in his new Imperium. He launched a campaign against the Mafia, unleashing ruthless crime-crusher Cesare Mori ("the Iron Prefect") and granting him extraordinary police powers.

A strength of the police state is its ability to suppress crime, organized and otherwise. Unhampered by any constitutional safeguards, defendants' rights, or adversary press, Mussolini and Mori had a free hand in hammering the Mafia. Mori jailed hundreds of mafiosi, who were sentenced to long prison terms. Many others still at large stayed that way by staging a hasty departure from Sicily, ultimately landing in the United States. Their arrival had a destabilizing effect on the American Mafia.

One such notable newcomer was Salvatore Maranzano. A product of the Mafia stronghold of Sicily's Castellammare del Golfo (Castle by the sea), Maranzano was an odd combination of visionary and thug. He was a student of antiquity and a fervent admirer of Julius Caesar. He was already an established Mafia chieftain who had earned the honorific title of "Don Salvatore" before arriving in the United States.

He soon established a gang of his fellow Castellammarese expatriates. Among these newcomers were several who would become powers in their own right: Joseph "Joe Bananas" Bonnano and Joe Profaci, both Brooklyn based; Stefano Magaddino in Buffalo, New York; and Chicago's Joseph Aiello. Aiello tried to take on Capone and was squashed on the spot in 1930, but Bonnano and Magaddino thrived and enjoyed decades-long terms as Mafia bosses.

The self-important Maranzano felt (not without reason) that his Castellammarese faction was looked down on by other American Mafia members, whose antecedents lay in different parts of Sicily. A bitter rivalry developed between Maranzano and Masseria, fueled in some measure by regional rivalries but mostly from basic greed and envy. Their gangs kept bumping into each other and crowding each other's territories all over New York City.

Masseria greedily eyed Maranzano's territories and in 1930 tried to move in on them. This set off the Castellammarese War of 1930–31, which racked up an impressive body count: twenty-four soldati (soldiers) from both sides.

An early casualty was Gaetano Reina, a top Maranzano man and by virtue of a daughter's recent marriage, the father-in-law of Joe Valachi. Valachi was far down in the organizational table, a street soldier and sometime bodyguard for Maranzano. Then relatively insignificant, Valachi would be heard from much later, at great length in the 1960s, as a government informant whose sensational testimony would lift the lid on the secretive inner workings of the Mafia.

In a fit of murderous megalomania, Joe the Boss escalated the conflict by declaring "war" on all Castellammarese gangsters, not only in New York but also nationwide, giving permission to his men to kill their rivals wherever they found them. The gang war raged for eighteen months, piling up corpses on both sides. The balance shifted against Masseria, who lost men and ground to Maranzano, who was hitting Joe the Boss hard. Masseria was the first to cry uncle by swallowing his pride and offering to negotiate a peace treaty. Maranzano would have none of it. He rejected the offer and continued the war.

The party was also getting rough for Luciano, who entered into secret negotiations with Maranzano, archenemy of Joe the Boss— Lucky's boss.

Luciano now occupied a place not unlike that of Johnny Torrio when the latter's tenure as Colosimo's lieutenant was nearing its end. Like Big Jim, Joe the Boss was an impediment to progress, namely the progress of the ambitious Luciano, who wanted his post.

Sicilian-born Luciano had grown up on the streets of New York and was acculturated with an American sensibility—the criminal kind. He and others of his generation were disdainful of the likes of Joe the Boss, with his Old World airs and and pretensions and his obliviousness to the illegal money-making potentialities in America. Such two-legged relics were uncomplimentarily referred to by the young hoodlums as "Mustache Petes" and "greasers."

Luciano had valuable associations and alliances with powerful Irish and Jewish gangsters. But Masseria forbade him from entering into any joint ventures with the outsiders, no matter how potentially profitable they might be. Luciano didn't see the sense in "guys killing guys because they came from a different part of Sicily," either. Masseria's ill-considered war with Maranzano now imperiled all the members of his crime family, Luciano especially.

Joe had to go.

Luciano made a deal with Maranzano: he would deliver Masseria to the headman's axe and in return Maranzano would recognize him as the new boss of the Masseria gang. They would make peace and end their mutually destructive war.

The Hit

So it was that on April 15, 1931, at around midday, Masseria, Luciano, and three of his bodyguards found themselves in Coney Island at Scarpato's Restaurant. Joe the Boss and Charlie dined on seafood and pasta and drank plenty of wine. They enjoyed a slow, leisurely meal. Joe the Boss, Luciano recounted, loved to eat.

The lunchtime crowd ebbed and the dining room emptied, leaving the gangsters alone in the place. What few staffers were on the premises maintained a respectful distance. Masseria and his lieutenant were in no hurry to leave. Luciano suggested that they play some cards, a suggestion to which Masseria happily acceded.

Later, Luciano said that at around 3:30 P.M. he excused himself and went to the men's room. While he was washing his hands at the sink, shots sounded from the dining room. He emerged to find Masseria dead.

That was his story. "I was takin' a leak," Lucky said. "I take a long leak." The police couldn't break it, not that there's any indication to show that they tried.

The physical evidence, ballistics, and so forth showed that Joe the Boss had been massacred by several gunmen, who fired twenty shots in all. Six of them scored in his head and torso, killing him instantly.

Handicapping the Masseria hit

STRATEGY

The execution of Joe the Boss was a classic textbook hit. Mafia etiquette decreed that when a chief of Masseria's stature had to go, certain formalities had to be observed.

The process applied to those who were being removed not for any disloyalty, infamy, or breaking the sacred law of *omerta* (silence and no cooperation with the police), but to those who, like Masseria, had served honorably and well but were just in the way and had to be forcibly retired. The intended victim should be treated with as much respect as circumstances allowed. Ideally, he should enjoy a last meal and be shot unawares from behind, so that he would be dead before he knew it.

That was the ideal, though it wasn't exactly cast in concrete. A man marked for death must die and his assassin or assassins must do what was necessary for him to die. That was the elastic clause, the standard disclaimer. But all things being equal, if the niceties could be observed without risk to the life-takers, it was well that it be so.

So it was for Joe the Boss. The condemned man ate a hearty meal, unaware that he was condemned. And who better to deliver him to the chopping block than a man he trusted? Luciano was that man.

There were several weak spots in Luciano's plan. One was his presence at the hit. As the chief beneficiary (along with Maranzano) of Masseria's demise, Luciano had the potential to be fingered as a prime suspect. Torrio had been absent from the Colosimo hit and Al Capone was in Florida when the St. Valentine's Day Massacre went down. Luciano was on the scene when Joe the Boss was bumped.

It may be argued that Luciano's presence was the factor that convinced Masseria that he was secure and had nothing to worry about. That makes it a trade-off, with Luciano's assumption of the element of risk that came from being present at the hit being offset by the fact that his presence made the hit possible.

A second soft spot in the plan was its public venue. Witnesses are always a complicating factor. After the act, they sometimes require firm, not to say harsh, measures that present a further risk of exposure to both plotters and enforcers.

Scarpato's staffers, while few and off scene, were present at the restaurant. Possibly, they knew that something was up and that they should make themselves scarce. But such knowledge is dangerous to giver and recipient alike. The teller must fear that the one he told may tell the tale to the authorities. Dead men tell no tales.

On September 10, 1935—a date to remember—the body of Gerardo Scarpato, the proprietor of the restaurant where Masseria was gunned down, was found dead in the trunk of a parked car. He'd been hog-tied and rigged with a sliding noose around his neck, one fixed in such a way that the more he struggled against his bonds, the more he strangled himself.

Deduct 1 point for Luciano being present at the murder scene.
Deduct 1 point for staging the hit in a public venue.

STRATEGY: 3

TACTICS

The game was well played. The plan required Masseria's trust. Masseria knew that Maranzano was gunning for him. But he didn't know that Luciano had him, or events would have taken a radically different turn.

A hallmark of how well the game was played is the issue of the bodyguards. There weren't any—not officially. The official version of Masseria's death, the way it went into the files, is that Joe the Boss and Luciano were dining alone.

Yet, this is patently absurd. Masseria was locked deep in a bloody gang war with Maranzano that showed no sign of stopping. Joe the Boss was a good gunman who could take care of himself in a pinch and had in the past, but he wouldn't have put himself in a public place where only he and Luciano stood against however many guns Maranzano might send against him. Masseria had bodyguards who screened him when he showed his face in the open. They would have been at Scarpato's with him. The logic of survival demands it and Masseria was nothing if not a survivor.

But the police seem to have accepted at face value the story that Masseria and Luciano were dining alone. That shows real mastery of tactics—on Luciano's side. The cops had been squared away. Maybe they plain just didn't give a damn if a troublemaker like Joe the Boss was iced, or maybe some key police personnel had been paid off to not give a damn. Whatever the reason, they didn't kick.

What's most likely is that the bodyguards were there, only they had been fixed, too, and at the appointed hour made themselves scarce so the shooters could do in Masseria.

Were the bodyguards the assassins? It's unlikely but not impossible. They certainly were in position to do the deed. The option can't be ruled out.

What is impossible is that the hit was carried out by Maranzano's men. Luciano was too smart to put himself in the line of fire of Don Salvatore's shooters. Not when they could take the opportunity to kill two birds in the same bush, knocking off both Joe the Boss and his top lieutenant, making it that much easier for Maranzano to absorb or eliminate the rest of Masseria's gang.

A feasible scenario has the bodyguards withdrawing, while others stepped in and did the shooting. They might have been Luciano loyalists from the Masseria gang or an outside bunch provided by Luciano's associates such as Louis "Lepke" Buchalter or the Bug and Meyer (Siegel-Lansky) mob.

Joe Valachi believed that Masseria had been killed by Luciano, Ciro Terranova, and Vito Genovese. But he hadn't been there and had the information secondhand. Valachi spent most of his career in crime as a second-tier operator at best and was a long way from the inside where the big decisions were made.

Luciano could have done it if he had to, but he didn't have to. He'd already assumed a significant risk by being present at the hit— offstage, according to him. Being a trigger puller would have risked contaminating him with gunpowder residue on his gun hand and clothes that a paraffin test might have detected.

TACTICS: 5

RESULTS

The death of Joe the Boss may be fairly compared in its impact to the death of Big Jim Colosimo. In each case, an old-fashioned, out-of-date crime boss was supplanted by a younger, savvier challenger with modern ideas.

Masseria's death put Luciano at the head of the gang and halfway to supreme mastery over the New York Mafia.

RESULTS: 10

Murder Meter Box Score
   STRATEGY: 3
   TACTICS: 5
   RESULTS: 10

   TOTAL: 18

The aftermath of Joe the Boss's death was the occasion for one of the most singular mob meetings ever held in New York City—or anywhere else. Salvatore Maranzano called a mass meeting of the citywide Mafia factions to lay out his plans for the new era.

The gathering was held at a rental hall in the Bronx with about 500 mafiosi in attendance. The stage was hung with religious trappings as potential camouflage to mislead any outsiders (i.e., cops) who might stick their heads in to see what the meeting was all about.

Maranzano took the stage and held it doggedly as he maintained his claim to leadership of the society. During the speech, he repeatedly referred to the Mafia in a roundabout way by the phrase "la Cosa Nostra," meaning "this thing of ours" or "our thing." Mafia members of that and later generations would adopt the phraseology and in conversation frequently substitute "Cosa Nostra" for "Mafia."

He put forward a plan that was an odd, unique hybrid of Mafia tradition and modern-day styling, one shaped by his idolatry of Julius Caesar and his reading of the history of antiquity. He decreed nothing less than the reorganization of the American Mafia.

Henceforth, the ancient society would be organized along the lines of the Old Roman legions. At the head of all would be the *capo de tutti capi*, the boss of all bosses, the superboss. Maranzano let no false modesty keep him from publicly claiming that title for himself.

Below him were the bosses or representates, the heads of the various crime families. Each boss was served by an underboss (*sotto-capo*) and lieutenant (*caporegime*, "commander of the troops"). The family's main organizational grouping would be the *decine*, ten-man crews (of street soldiers), each headed by a *capodecine* or *capo*.

Maranzano then laid out the nuts and bolts of who got what.

New York City would be apportioned out to four (ultimately five) families. One was Maranzano's group, with his powerful underlings and Castellammarese sidemen Joe Profaci and Joe Bonnano. (Post-Maranzano, the organization split into a Profaci family and a Bonnano family.)

Joe the Boss Masseria's group went to Luciano and his lieutenant, the crafty, treacherous Vito Genovese.

The Reina group (Gaetano Reina was the Maranzano man whose death sparked the Castellammarese War) went to Tom Gagliano and Thomas "Three-Finger Brown" Lucchese.

Brooklyn would be headed by Joe "Mr. A." Adonis and brothers Phillip and Vincent Mangano, bolstered by the mob's future Lord High Executioner, Albert Anastasia.

Thus the New Order as decreed by Don Salvatore. The boss of bosses celebrated his self-coronation by staging a series of fund-raising (i.e., shakedown) parties by which he extracted about a $100,000 in cash from lesser chieftains and vassals of his kingdom. The Big Fellow himself, Al Capone, sent along a fat cash gift.

Flush with success, Maranzano set up headquarters in a suite of offices at Manhattan's New York Central Building at 230 Park Avenue above Grand Central Terminal.

When they first conspired against Joe the Boss, Maranzano and Luciano both knew that the day would come when one or the other of them must die. That day came soon enough for both.

Joe Valachi later testified that Maranzano had shown him a kill list of those who must die to secure the reign of the new boss of bosses. Names on the list included Luciano, Vito Genovese, and Al Capone. Maranzano moved to liquidate Luciano. But Luciano was just a shade faster.

The Hit

Maranzano was having tax troubles. Now that the jazz age had given way to the Great Depression, Uncle Sam was mightily interested in all those unpaid taxes on the loot raked up by Prohibition-era gangsters. IRS agents in Chicago pored over entries in Al Capone's ledgers. Closer to home, New York's Dutch Schultz, the beer baron of the Bronx, was being pressed by those pesky boys in the green eyeshades from the Treasury Department.

Maranzano, too, was being targeted by the IRS, whose investigators were apt to pop in anytime unannounced at his office. Not wanting to stir up any more heat, he told his torpedoes that he didn't want them hanging around the Park Avenue office with their hardware to avoid having them hit with an illegal gun possession rap. There were still some guns ready at hand at his headquarters, but the level of firepower had been damped down.

On September 10, 1931, Maranzano had scheduled a "peace conference" for later in the afternoon at his Park Avenue suite, a sit-down to iron out his troubles with Luciano and Genovese.

Before the appointed hour, four men entered the outer office and claimed to be IRS investigators. They were gunmen. They got the drop on the group in the outer office and lined them up facing along the wall.

Maranzano came out to greet them and walked into the trap. One gunman covered the group in the outer office while the others backed Maranzano into his inner office.

They planned to do the job quietly—with a knife—but Maranzano fought back and reached for a gun he kept in his desk drawer. The assassins were quicker. Maranzano went down dead with four gunshot wounds, a slashed throat, and six stab wounds. The killers fled. As they rushed out, they crossed paths with Vincent Coll, who was coming in. Talk about a small world!

Coll was one of the most notorious killers of the era. A daylight attempt to gun down Joey Rao, a rival, in East Harlem went sour, resulting in the prey escaping and five children who were playing in the street being mowed down by machine gun fire, one fatally. This led to the tabloids hanging the label "Mad Dog" on Coll, who managed to beat the rap thanks to the premier legal talent of defense lawyer Samuel S. Leibowitz, later to become a celebrated judge.

Coll was entering Maranzano's office in the line of duty, having been hired by Don Salvatore to lay a fatal ambush for Luciano and Genovese, due later at the office for the peace conference.

In what perhaps was an act of professional courtesy, one of the killers who'd slain Maranzano waved off Coll, telling him to "beat it." Coll got the message and made himself scarce.

It had been a close-run thing. Maranzano meant to get Luciano but was gotten to first. They didn't call him Lucky for nothing.

Handicapping the Maranzano Hit

STRATEGY

Luciano had good intelligence on Maranzano. The tax woes that had caused the boss of bosses to downsize his bodyguards' firepower was the opening wedge for a Luciano strike.

Luciano contracted the hit to killers outside the Mafia. Luciano biographer and veteran crime reporter Sid Feder offers that the hit squad comprised Bo Weinberg, Dutch Schultz's top hatchet man; two hoodlums from Newark, New Jersey; and two members of the Bug and Meyer mob.

Luciano used the false-flag gambit, with the killers posing as IRS agents. Their front was smooth enough for them to gain entrance, get the drop on those in the outer office, and lure Maranzano out of his inner office. It was something of a cowboy job, but as Maranzano's dealings with Vince Coll indicated, there was a need for speed.

It was risky to try to take Maranzano in his headquarters. The inside information that his men had shed most of their firearms to avoid a beef with federal investigators was promising but in no way ironclad. One or more gang members in the outer office might have been armed as a safeguard or even in defiance of the mandate. If one of them had reached a weapon when the killers made their play, gunfire could have erupted. Forewarned, Maranzano could have armed and defended himself, possibly even shooting his way clear.

Those in the outer office were gangsters or hangers-on; therefore, they were more likely to know the facts of life and not talk to the cops, unlike civilians unschooled in the underworld code of silence. That was a plus for the killers going in and coming out.

Deduct 2 points for calculated risk of confronting Maranzano gang members.

STRATEGY: 3

TACTICS

It is said that Thomas "Three-Finger Brown" Lucchese was in the outer office when the hit went down, that he was a spotter who signalled the killers, pointing them to Maranzano. Perhaps Lucchese was the source for the information about the firearms being downsized at Maranzano's headquarters, or perhaps Luciano had several informants in place.

Many things could have gone wrong during the hit. But they didn't. That speaks to the skill of the assassins, who executed all the right moves in gaining entrance to and securing the outer office and then executing Maranzano. They did what they had to do, and made the hit and then their getaway. Even the handling of Coll was nice, avoiding provoking the trigger-tempered gunman into violence and adroitly sending him on his way.

Good tactics can make an iffy plan work. Good tactics—and of course luck.

TACTICS: 5

RESULTS

The immediate result of the Maranzano hit was that Lucky Luciano did not die.

The two were in a breakneck race to see who would kill the other first. Had events gone differently that day, Luciano still might not have walked into a Coll ambush in Maranzano's lair and presented himself for slaughter. But one of the two of them had to die. Maranzano was a relentless foe, as the course of the Castellammarese War had proven, and he would have kept after Luciano until one or the other of them was no more.

They even thought alike in their homicidal schemings. Like Luciano, Maranzano had gone outside Mafia channels to pick an assassin. He'd picked one of the best. Coll was known as a fearless professional who could and would see the job through.

But Luciano's hired guns got there first. Because of that quickness, he lived while the other fell.

Underworld history might be vastly different indeed had Luciano not lived to set his hand on the tiller of the Mafia's course. Maranzano was a man of grandiose ambitions who had a first-rate organizational mind. The proof of this is seen in the fact that Luciano and the Mafia ultimately did adopt almost all of Don Salvatore's reorganization plans. They liked his plan, they just didn't like him.

New York City was divided into territories controlled by the five families that he had designated, while all the other U.S. cities had one Mafia family.

Luciano improved on Maranzano's blueprint by establishing a Commission consisting of the heads of the five families and the heads of families in such strongholds as Chicago and Buffalo. In effect, the Commission became the board of directors of the American Mafia and the extended national crime syndicate that it controlled.

Unlike Maranzano, Luciano declined to claim the title of capo de tutti capi, a title that by rights belonged to him. He was content to exercise a single vote in the Commission's majority-rules system, instead of demanding that his be the deciding vote. His thinking was that the coveted power and glory of being the boss of bosses was an open invitation to intrigue, treachery, and bloodshed. So he declined the post, and by doing so, he abolished it.

The wisdom of the decision is proved by the fact that despite periodic flareups of violence, the Mafia structure that was assembled in the post-Maranzano era lasted virtually intact for decades, and continues to do so to this day. That's not luck—it's skill.

RESULTS: 10

Murder Meter Box Score
STRATEGY: 3
TACTICS: 5
RESULTS: 10

TOTAL: 18

4

The Dying Dutchman: Dutch Schultz

What's in a name? Shakespeare famously observed that a rose by any other name would smell as sweet. In a somewhat different context, top New York mobster Dutch Schultz was known to lament having changed his handle from the name he was born with— Arthur Flegenheimer—to the Schultz handle. He felt that the shorter, snappier Schultz label lent itself to the tabloid newspaper headlines that repeatedly bannered his criminal exploits on the front page. Whereas "Flegenheimer," by virtue of its length and lack of punch, was less likely to find itself bannered across the top of the front page in the tabs' sensationalistic quest to sell more papers.

If only he'd kept his original name, he reasoned, he'd have been featured a lot less in the headlines and out of the now-unwanted public spotlight, and some other high-profile hoodlum would have the dubious honor of being Public Enemy Number One.

In this, he was probably wrong, not reckoning on the ingenuity of headline writers to punch their point across. Had he kept his original name, the tabloid press would have found some way to jazz it up for their purposes. They would have christened him with some snappy appellation such as, say, "Flegie." As in, "Police Seek Fugitive Flegie," or "Mad Dog Coll Vows Flegie Finish," and so on.

With apologies to Shakespeare, a Schultz by any other name, including Flegenheimer, would still have inevitably followed his irascible criminal nature to the finish.

That finish neared on the night of October 23, 1935, as Schultz lay mortally wounded and near death in a Newark, New Jersey, hospital. For some hours he drifted in and out of consciousness, half-delirious, keeping up a running monologue. A police stenographer sat by the dying man's bedside, taking down his every word. Police investigators hovered over Schulz, impatiently waiting for the times when he would come to a kind of wakefulness so that they could ask their questions: "Who did it, Dutch? Who shot you?"

That was the constant refrain. But the Dutchman wasn't talking. That is, not about who shot him. He rattled on for over two hours in a sprawling, free-form stream of consciousness monologue. Mixed into it like raisins in a pudding were curious fragments, tantalizing and allusive, but nothing the law could use, nothing specific that would serve as a deathbed denouncement that would hold up in court. It was doubtful whether or not Schultz even understood where he was or what they were asking, but they kept on, ever hopeful.

"Who shot you, Dutch?"

They leaned in, intent, waiting for the answer, for a lead in one of the biggest, bloodiest gangland shootings since the St. Valentine's Day Massacre. What they got was a bit of verbal nonsense that would have been right at home in the Alice-in-Wonderland world of Lewis Carroll.

"—a boy has never wept, nor dashed a thousand kim," Schultz said.

A boy has never wept, nor dashed a thousand kim. No one in the room could make sense of that one. Nor has anyone else since, then or now. It might be shrugged off as the ravings of a man delirious and near death. But even earlier, when he was conscious and aware, the Dutchman wasn't giving out any information, either.

Dutch Schultz, the last of the big independent New York mobsters, was closing in fast on oblivion. His removal would consolidate the five families' grip on the city. He'd been put on the spot by the

Mafia to protect the life of a man they hated, racketbusting Special Prosecutor Thomas E. Dewey.

Not that the family heads had any love lost for the Dutchman. But they moved against him to save an anticrime crusader whose fondest stated wish was to eliminate them. Their ultimate reward was to have one of their chiefs sentenced to a long prison term and another to die in the electric chair.

In so doing, though, they preserved the future for the American Mafia.

Arthur Flegenheimer was born to Jewish parents, a saloonkeeping father and a hardworking, downtrodden, doting mother. He grew up in the Bronx, where he attended a public school whose principal was Dr. J. F. Condon, who years later would become known as "Jafsie," playing a cryptic and ambiguous role as go-between in the sensational Lindbergh baby kidnapping—a crime that had no tie-in with Dutch Schultz.

Father Flegenheimer deserted the family when young Arthur was at a tender age, after which Arthur decided to spend his time on the shady side of the street. His public schooling was minimal, though he remained an eager reader for the rest of his life. He joined a boys' street gang with its countless fights with rival gangs and its endless petty thefts and vandalism.

He soon went from stealing packages off delivery trucks to burglary and assault. He spent fifteen months in prison on a burglary rap. On release, he changed his name to "Dutch Schultz," adopting the name of a legendary local tough who'd once been one of the Frog Hollow gang.

Schultz opened a saloon and got into bootlegging. He became a member of the Five Points gang, meeting such luminaries as Johnny Torrio, Al Capone, and Frankie Yale. He was hard driving, ambitious, and ruthless. He got into bootlegging in a big way. His gang hijacked others' booze shipments. They muscled in on the speakeasies and dives, pressuring the owners to carry Schultz's beer and none other, or else.

Recalcitrants and slow learners were beaten and brutalized into submission while the real hardheads were simply shot dead.

Gang competitors he handled with wholesale violence and murder, eliminating them to establish himself in the 1920s as the beer baron of the Bronx. Schultz's needle beer was universally acknowledged as the worst swill in New York, no mean feat in those Prohibition days. In this, Schultz echoed Frankie Yale, the Unione Siciliane boss and master assassin, whose line of cigars (the box bearing his portrait) were such foul, unsmokable pieces of rope that the local term "a Frankie Yale" came to stand as shorthand for any product that was rotten and no good.

Schultz's mob of mostly Jewish gangsters featured the fearsome Bo Weinberg, his chief enforcer and hatchet man, a hulking hoodlum capable of handling with aplomb and dispatch both strong-arm muscle jobs and swift, sure assassinations. His brain trust included slick lawyer J. Richard "Dixie" Davis and mathematical wizard Otto "Abbadabba" Berman (immortalized as the horseplaying character Regret by Broadway columnist and bard Damon Runyon, author of *Guys and Dolls*, *Lady for a Day*, and other picaresque tales of lovable wiseguy rogues).

Vital to Schultz's success were his Tammany Hall connections. Tammany Hall was a Democratic political club that had virtually ruled New York City since the 1860s and earlier. Schultz's alliance with Jimmy Hines, the district leader and supreme political power, provided the clout with police captains and judges that largely immunized the Dutchman and his mob from prosecution and provided a speedy get-out-of-jail card to those of his troops who were arrested by street cops unaware that the fix was in.

As the saying goes, "Big fleas have lesser fleas on their backs to bite them." So it was with Schultz, who at various times was locked in gang wars with the likes of Jack "Legs" Diamond and Vincent "Mad Dog" Coll.

The Dutchman moved in on some speakeasies in territory claimed by the mercurial, fast-shooting Diamond. A few bodies fell on both sides, causing the gang chiefs to have a sitdown to iron out their differences. The peace conference seemed to go well. Afterward, on the street Diamond gunmen ambushed Schultz and sideman Joey Noe. Noe was killed but Schultz used his gun to drive off the attackers.

From that moment on, Diamond's days were numbered. Known as the "Clay Pigeon" of the underworld in recognition of all the times he'd been shot and survived, Diamond met his Waterloo in a rooming house in upstate New York, where he was surprised and shot dead by the Dutchman's ace gunner Bo Weinberg.

Vince Coll suffered from delusions of grandeur. He worked briefly for a few months as one of Schultz's shooters before deciding to go into business for himself. He wanted Schultz's wealth and power overnight and decided to shoot him out of the box and take over. He and his brother, Peter, and some other hard hoods moved hard to liquidate Schultz and take over his operation.

It came naturally for Coll and company to go from hijacking Schultz's rivals' beer to hijacking Schultz's beer shipments. Of course, that put them on the Dutchman's kill list, but Vince Coll was not one to worry about that.

Schultz had Coll's brother, Peter, abducted and executed on an East Harlem street. Never too tightly wrapped under the best of circumstances, Coll went ballistic and declared total war on Schultz, furiously knocking over Schultz's shipments and drops and killing his gunmen and drivers. He was gunning for the Dutchman personally, but Schultz exercised his considerable talent for elusiveness and managed to avoid finding himself in Coll's gunsights.

Coll also earned the enmity not only of Schultz but also of other top mobsters by his habit of kidnapping them and their associates when he was in need of some easy cash, as he did when he snatched bootlegger and club boss Owney "the Killer" Madden's lieutenant and pal Lefty DeMange in broad daylight and ransoming him back for big bucks.

The Coll challenge came to an end in February 1932, when the gunman emerged from his hideout to use the phone in a Manhattan drugstore on West Twenty-third Street. He called Madden (himself a plenty tough egg) to harangue and threaten him, trying to shake him down for some dough. Madden kept Coll talking on the line while Schultz's men traced the call.

Coll had unknowingly reached the end of the line (the telephone line). He was still yapping over the phone to Madden when two killers entered the pharmacy. One covered the staff and customers with a gun, motioning them to silence. The other—believed to be Bo Weinberg—stepped in front of the telephone booth in which Coll was making his call and pulled out a machine gun that he'd been hiding under a flap of his long overcoat. Coll looked up to find himself looking down the business end of a Thompson. He was too confined in the booth to draw his gun—not that it would have done him any good if he'd tried, since the machine gunner already had the drop on him. The shooter cut loose, chopping Coll with the chatter gun and turning the glass-and-wooden walled phone booth into a vertical coffin. The Mad Dog had been put down, dead at the age of twenty-three. This incident was recreated in the classic 1937 James Cagney movie *Angels With Dirty Faces*.

The elimination of Coll meant one less headache for Schultz to worry about. More were on the way, chief among them the repeal of Prohibition.

The so-called Noble Experiment had come to an ignoble end, trailing off not with a bang but a whimper, fated to go down in history as one of the greatest flops in social engineering ever devised by the misguided brain of man.

The object of near universal detestation, honored mainly in the breach rather than the observance, it had made the populace booze-crazy and made the jazz age of the 1920s synonymous with bootleggers, hip flasks, and speakeasies.

It not only confirmed the drinkers in their habit and pleasure but it also, by the lure of the forbidden, enticed many others who might otherwise have remained teetotalers. It engendered contempt not only for a law that could be so stupid and unpopular but also for the authorities charged with making and enforcing that law.

Most important, it was an unparalleled gold rush for organized crime, the biggest bonanza crookdom would see until the drug culture of the 1960s ignited a narcotics trafficking explosion that has continued to thrive and grow for the last fifty years—but that's another story.

Bootlegging was the vehicle by which the underworld became so flush with mountains of money that it was able to establish itself on a businesslike basis throughout the nation, fueling the unprecedented rise of the Mafia-controlled and -directed national crime syndicate.

During the critical 1932 presidential campaign, Democratic candidate Franklin D. Roosevelt's platform included the repeal of Prohibition. While not crucial to his success (incumbent opponent Herbert Hoover's mismanagement of the economic depression precipitated by the stock market crash of 1929 ensured Roosevelt's landslide win), Roosevelt's stance on repeal certainly didn't hurt him any at the polls.

In December 1933, Congress passed the Twenty-first Amendment to the Constitution, which repealed Prohibition. "Happy days are here again," as Roosevelt's campaign slogan had put it—happy days for the drinking public, certainly, but not for the legion of gangsters who'd gotten rich on bootleg booze.

And certainly not for Dutch Schultz. With booze being legal, he wouldn't be able to give away his dishwater beer. Gone was the easy bootlegging money, giving way to such traditional standbys as gambling, prostitution, narcotics, and extortion.

Ever adaptable, Schultz looked for new worlds to conquer. The field of labor-industrial racketeering was inviting. Louis "Lepke" Buchalter and his partner, Jacob "Gurrah" Shapiro, had already sewed up the lucrative garment center labor racketeering franchise.

Schultz moved in on the restaurant industry with his "merchants protective association" in midtown New York, a protection racket where restaurant and store owners paid off regularly to keep from having paving blocks pitched through their storefront windows or stinkbombs set off in their places during the lunchtime rush or dinner hour. The Dutchman also muscled his way to control key restaurant-related unions, giving him a stranglehold over owners with the threat of strikes or walkouts.

His roving eye alighted uptown, on the Harlem numbers game. Schultz's brainstorm was to move in on the numbers racket.

The numbers game (also known as policy) was centered in Harlem, many of whose residents spent their hard-earned pennies and nickels wagering on a daily number. The three-digit winning number was based on a formula derived from the amounts wagered on parimutuel horse betting at race tracks. The number paid off at odds of 600-1. The game was operated by a handful of policy bankers, whose squads of runners circulated among the public, taking their bets and writing them down on slips of paper that were collected at the central banks.

Previously, the numbers game had been left alone by New York's white crime overlords, who disdained it as a penny-ante racket unworthy of their attention. Schultz was the first to realize that those pennies and nickels added up to big money, with the leading policy bankers reaping hundreds of thousands of dollars in cash every month.

Schultz muscled in, sending his strong-arm men into Harlem to beat, rob, and kill collectors at the street level, as a prelude to his taking the top policy bankers in hand and "persuading" them of the wisdom of coming in with him. Which meant, effectively, the bankers would continue running their banks but would be turning over all their revenues to Schultz and being paid a minimal weekly salary, sometimes, when Schultz felt like it. The Dutchman struck gold, as the nickel-and-dime numbers game generated an astonishing $20 million a year.

Reform raised its ugly head in New York in 1934 with the election of Republican-Fusion candidate Fiorello LaGuardia to the office of mayor. LaGuardia had run on a reform ticket, with his ascendancy neutralizing some of Schultz's Tammany political cover.

A grand jury was charged to look into the numbers game, an investigation that was conducted halfheartedly at best by elected District Attorney William Dodge, who had received $30,000 in campaign contributions from Schultz. Taking the lead, the grand jury began actively pursuing the investigation and raising a ruckus when Dodge tried to rein them in. They grabbed headlines as the "runaway jury," prompting Governor Herbert Lehman to appoint a special prosecutor to probe organized crime in New York.

The post was filled by Republican Thomas E. Dewey, already seasoned by several years spent in the U.S. Attorney's office. Dewey was a formidable legal opponent, incorruptible, with a mind for details and a mastery of relentless cross-examination.

One area of Schultz's vulnerability was federal income taxes: he didn't pay any. Failure to pay taxes was a federal rap and one not to be discounted, as Al Capone was already learning to his sorrow. Schultz had amassed several fortunes in bootleg money and had paid no taxes on it. He set lawyer Dixie Davis to work on a solution, ideally one that would involve Schultz making a cash settlement and serving no jail time.

A warrant was issued for Schultz's arrest on tax charges but was not served, because Schultz had taken it on the lam and dropped from sight. His fugitive status caused him to be listed by the Federal Bureau of Investigation (FBI) as Public Enemy Number One. This was no laughing matter. Previous holders of the title included Midwest desperadoes John Dillinger and Lester Gillis ("Babyface Nelson"), both of whom had fallen to blazing G-men guns.

Schultz surrendered to the authorities and was put on ice in jail. Counselor Davis believed he could win the tax case. His main thrust was to get the trial moved out of New York and away from the baleful influence of Tom Dewey. He argued that Schultz could not get a fair trial in the city due to his high profile and unfavorable publicity. The court agreed and the trial was set in upstate New York.

The conventional wisdom in mobdom was that Schultz would never beat the tax rap. The Dutchman was finished, washed up. This came as not unwelcome news to the gangsters who'd enviously eyed Schultz's hefty take in his stellar rackets.

Nature abhors a vacuum and crime abhors a power vacuum. Lucky Luciano took over Schultz's numbers games lock, stock, and policy bank, and Lepke took over his labor-industrial operations.

Luciano called in Schultz's top gun, Bo Weinberg, and told him Schultz was through and he, Weinberg, should get with the program. Weinberg was already pretty chummy with Lepke and Albert Anastasia and needed little urging to accede to Luciano's directive.

Schultz's trial for tax evasion was held in Syracuse, New York, where it ended in a hung jury. The second trial was held in the tiny border town of Malone, where Schultz ingratiated himself with the locals with a largesse of expansive, free-spending generosity. The jury found him not guilty, earning them an angry scolding from the judge. But the acquittal stood and the Dutchman walked.

Not one to be caught napping, Schultz moved to shore up his position. Paramount among his concerns was the loyalty or lack of it of his top enforcer, Bo Weinberg, who'd been altogether too cozy with Luciano and company while Dutch was out of town.

Bo disappeared sometime in September 1935 and was never seen again. One version (the most colorful and therefore the most unlikely) holds that Schultz was present when Weinberg's feet were encased in cement and he was thrown living into a river. Another (more likely) version is that Schultz farmed out the Weinberg disposal to some Murder, Inc. killers. Yet another posits that Schultz arranged to have Weinberg slain by his erstwhile chum, Benjamin "Bugsy" Siegel, who is said to have stabbed Bo to death. Most agree that Bo was given cement shoes and dumped in the East River. Regardless, Bo Weinberg was thereafter seen no more by the eyes of men.

Schultz had little time to enjoy his tax case acquittal, as the government filed new tax charges against him. Pressure mounted as Special Prosecutor Dewey began probing Schultz's restaurant shakedown racket.

Never the most even-tempered individual, Schultz flew into a rage and stayed there. To him, it was personal: Dutch versus Dewey. Dewey was his "nemesis." He would have no peace as long as Dewey was around. The solution was simple: Dewey would have to go.

Schultz's indiscreet remarks in this vein soon reached the ears of other mob chiefs and alarmed them.

In that fall of 1935, bad press was hardly the worst of Schultz's woes. The mobster was laying low across the river in Newark, New

Jersey, dodging Dewey's subpoenas. He was self-exiled from his home base and power base of New York, for fear of Dewey's investigators and process servers. In New Jersey, the judges were friendlier and more likely than those in New York to set bail at low figures that Schultz could make.

He was holed up in the Robert Treat Hotel in downtown Newark, while holding court at the nearby Palace Chop House restaurant across from the public service bus terminal. He was present on sufferance of Abner "Longy" Zwillman, the mob boss of New Jersey.

On top of everything else, Schultz was having money woes. He had big tax fines and expensive legal talent looming. All in all, for the one-time beer baron of the Bronx, Harlem numbers king, and merchants protective association head, a combative alpha dog type who'd come out on top in some of the toughest gang wars ever against individuals such as Coll and Diamond, it was a hell of a comedown.

Schultz had any number of ongoing legal entanglements in different jurisdictions, but it was the Dewey heat that was really burning him. "Dewey is my nemesis," he complained. "He's gotta go!"

While no reckless cowboy shooter in the Coll model, Schultz was an aggressive and easily irritated type unwilling to shrink from a fight. He was confident that his other myriad legal problems could and would be settled, but Dewey was a harder nut to crack. Schultz personalized it: Dewey was his principal tormentor. With Dewey gone, the heat would be off. The solution was simple: Dewey must go. Dutch Schultz was determined to have Tom Dewey done in.

Lepke Buchalter and Gurrah Shapiro were the most feared of all Jewish gangsters. Shapiro was the muscle, and Lepke was the brains. They first made a real impact during the garment labor strike of 1926, where they were hired out as muscle to both sides, management and labor. When they saw the riches that could be plucked from the industry, they moved in in a big way, pioneering the labor-industrial racket.

Lepke organized a murder squad to police his operations. The members were professional killers. They were Italian and Jewish and mostly recruited from Manhattan's Lower East Side and Brooklyn's Brownsville district. A potent lineup of heavyweight hitters, they would be tagged by *World-Telegram* newsman Harry Feeney with the label "Murder, Inc."

These Triple-A assassination experts were so good at what they did that they branched out into handling key hits of all five families and of families outside of New York, expanding their murder-for-hire operation nationwide.

Lepke answered to Albert Anastasia, the underboss of Brooklyn's Adonis-Mangano family. Squat, brutal, and ruthless, Anastasia had a volatile temperament that may be imagined from his underworld nickname, the Mad Hatter. As wielder of Murder, Inc., he would presently come to be known as the Lord High Executioner.

He was the man to see about a murder. He was contacted by Dutch Schultz, who offered a contract to kill Special Prosecutor Dewey.

This was hot stuff. So big a hit that it had to be sanctioned by the Commission, which met in conclave to consider Dewey's assassination. The meeting was important enough for Schultz to risk arrest by crossing from New Jersey into New York, where a new warrant had been issued for his arrest.

Present were Luciano and the other family heads, as well as Johnny Torrio, whose long years of service and sage counsel had won him a seat on the Commission. The death of Dewey was debated. Some were for it, some against it, and some were as yet undecided.

It was agreed to consider the matter for a week before rendering a final decision. Schultz, impatiently chomping at the bit, pointed out that they could save time by using the intervening seven days to scout Dewey and work up a plan for a hit. Then, if they voted to do in Dewey, they'd be set to go right ahead with it. This was agreed to.

Dewey was watched, his routine monitored. A promising avenue of opportunity soon revealed itself. Each weekday morning, Dewey left his Manhattan Fifth Avenue apartment accompanied by two bodyguards.

He would routinely duck into a nearby drugstore while the body-guards waited outside the front door. Dewey used a pay phone to contact key aides to learn what if any new developments had occurred during the night. That the pay phone was less likely to be wiretapped than his home phone was a bonus.

The mob's homicide experts saw opportunity here, the germ of a plan. A shooter with a silenced gun could follow Dewey into the drugstore and kill Dewey and the druggist. The drugstore was usually empty of customers at this time, but if it came to that, the killer could and would kill any other potential witnesses on the premises. A nearby elevated train line was noisy and would cover and muffle the silenced gunshots. The killer would then exit the building, out the back door and away before an alarm was raised. In a pinch, he could even exit by the front door, past the unsuspecting bodyguards.

In sum: Dewey was doable. The job could be done—but should it?

The Commission met in conclave at the end of seven days' time to render their final decision. They ruled against assassinating Dewey.

The main reason was that killing a man of his prominence would bring down a firestorm of reaction from city, state, and federal law enforcement agencies. The National Guard might well be called out and there was a possibility that martial law would be declared.

Under such conditions, the national crime syndicate in general and the five families in particular would be hammered. It could be the end of the American Mafia, or at least a catastrophe that would set them back for a generation.

A second consideration was that Dewey was local. His authority encompassed only Manhattan, everything else was outside his jurisdiction. This constraint would severely limit his ability to damage the organized crime infrastructure beyond the city limits.

The third unvoiced reason was that it was Schultz who was Dewey's immediate target and not the members of the Commission. Not yet, anyway. It was Schultz's problem. Besides, his Harlem numbers racket and midtown labor-industrial operations would be better off in Mafia hands.

This was a delicate time in gangland. The five families, with Luciano as their overlord in all but title, were consolidating their grip on the New York underworld, but the Mafia did not quite yet exercise supreme power in its sphere. The last holdout, the last major independent mobster, was Dutch Schultz.

The no vote didn't sit well with Schultz. A direct actionist, he vowed to take care of Dewey himself. Someone in his orbit took the tale to the Commission, reporting that the Dutchman had bragged that Dewey would be dead within forty-eight hours.

Luciano and the others knew where they stood. In forty-eight hours, either Dewey or the Dutchman must die.

The Hit

On the night of October 23, 1935, at the Palace Chop House, Schultz was holding court (as he'd been in the habit of doing since leaving New York City for Newark). It was a quiet and slow night at the Palace. There'd been a lot of slow nights since Prohibition ended.

The chophouse featured a long room with a bar and at the end of that, a backroom that was used by Schultz and company. With him were two bodyguards and a brain. The bodyguards were two of Schultz's top guns, Abe "Misfit" Landau and Lulu Rosenkrantz. The brain was Abbadabba Berman.

Destiny appeared in the form of three men who closed in on the eatery. Two of them were Murder, Inc. stalwarts, Charlie "the Bug" Workman and Emanuel "Mendy" Weiss. The third was a man of whom only two things are known: he was a member of Willie Moretti's gang and his name was "Piggy."

Workman had won his nickname when none other than his boss, Lepke Buchalter, had said admiringly of him that "Charlie had to be bugs [i.e., crazy fearless] to do the things that he did." Workman was one of Lepke's murder squad's high-level hitmen, whose status may be determined by the name that city detectives hung on him: "The Powerhouse."

Workman was designated for the wet work; Weiss's job was to

cover the door and serve as backup; and Piggy was the wheelman, the driver of the getaway car. Workman entered the chophouse, acting like he belonged there and looking like he fit right in. He sauntered down the bar to the rear of the building.

There was a lavatory door on one side of him and the backroom door on the other. He went into the lavatory. A man stood at the sink, washing his hands. Workman thought he looked familiar and decided he was one of Schultz's bodyguards. So he shot him, putting a single bullet in him. The guy folded, hitting the floor. Workman exited the washroom and went into the backroom. Seated around a table were the two gunmen, Rosenkrantz and Landau, and Berman.

The bodyguards, alerted by the sound of gunfire, unlimbered their artillery. Workman opened up, blasting back. Fireworks erupted.

A barman manned the bar up front. A veteran of the Great War not unacquainted with the sound of shooting, he dove to the floor behind the bar, laying flat and staying there.

Workman emerged from the backroom, unwounded and intact. He was almost at the front door, where Weiss waited. Suddenly, he reversed and went back the way he came, going into the lavatory.

He later told associates that he'd realized that the familiar-looking guy he'd potted in the bathroom was Schultz himself. Schultz was known to carry a big bankroll worth thousands of dollars and Workman went back to lift it. He never told anyone whether he found anything worth taking on the wounded man, and if so, if he took it.

He returned to the front and found Weiss and the getaway car gone. He'd been abandoned. Curious spectators were arrowing toward the Palace from all directions, coming to see what the shooting was all about. No doubt police were already speeding to the scene.

Worse, bodyguard Abe Landau was not dead but only wounded and still full of fight. He came outside and exchanged shots with Workman, grazing him before collapsing. Workman fled on foot, dodging down alleys and jumping over back fences, evading pursuit and making a lone getaway.

Police arriving at the scene encountered a bloodbath. Abe Landau lay sprawled in the street outside, where he'd collapsed. In the backroom, Abbadabba Berman lay shot dead. Lulu Rosenkrantz was near death, life leaking out of the bulletholes sieving him. Dutch Schultz had somehow dragged himself from the washroom to a table in the back, where he sat slumped over it in a chair. He'd been hit once, shot under the arm with a .45 slug that bored deep into his chest and innards.

Schultz and his two bodyguards were rushed to a nearby Newark hospital, where surgeons and medicoes fought a losing battle to save their lives. Landau and Rosencrantz were both soon to succumb.

Schultz was conscious at first but only semicoherent. He said that he'd been in the men's room when someone had come in and shot him. Investigators asked who had shot him but Schultz repeatedly said that he didn't know.

He lingered for a while but began to fade, life slipping away from him. In his final hours, drifting in and out of delirium, he delivered a monologue that has intrigued and baffled crime and mystery buffs to this day.

Near the end, he muttered a sentiment so apt it could have come from a Warner Brothers gangster picture of the Cagney-Bogart-Robinson genre: "Mother is the best bet and don't let Satan draw you too fast."

This was his epitaph.

That same night of October 23, an attempt was made on the life of Schultz associate Marty Krompier, a shady figure in the boxing halfworld. Krompier was in a subway arcade barber shop when a shooter popped up and pumped several slugs into him. He was severely wounded but later recovered.

The Dutchman wasn't so lucky; he died the next day on October 24.

Years later in 1940, it was Murder, Inc.'s turn on the griddle, as Burton Turkus, a Brooklyn assistant district attorney, decimated the organization, ultimately sending seven men to the electric chair. During the course of the investigation, two hoodlum associates of Charlie Workman testified as to what Workman had told them about the Schultz hit. They filled in some of the outlines of what had happened that night.

In their version, Workman, Weiss, and Piggy were waiting in a flat not far from the Palace Chop House. A spotter called, reporting that Schultz was inside. The trio went to the restaurant. Workman went in, Weiss covered the door, and Piggy remained behind the wheel of the car, its engine running.

Workman put the blast on the foursome in the back of the building, went to the front door, then turned and went back to go through Schultz's pockets and lift his roll. When he went outside, his confederates and the getaway car were gone. He fled. The flat was nearby but he didn't know where it was.

He raced into a park, where he shed his bloodstained jacket. A nightmare odyssey followed, as he blundered through the night in strange surroundings, ultimately following a set of railroad tracks to a station, where he caught a train to New York City and got away clear.

He was mightily steamed at Weiss and Piggy. The iron law of the organization mandated death for anyone who deserted his post on a job and left a comrade behind.

Mendy Weiss made his case to the masters of Murder, Inc., arguing that he had stayed at his post during the Schultz hit. Once Workman turned around to rob Schultz, Weiss reasoned that Workman was off the clock, working on his own time and for his own benefit. Weiss was duty bound to stay in place during the shooting, but not while Workman was off working his own agenda. That was Workman's problem. The judges agreed with Weiss and let him off the hook.

Workman remained plenty sore, though. At a party, he sounded off about how the hit had gone down and the raw deal he'd gotten from Weiss. His ventings returned to haunt him in the form of testimony given by the two to whom he'd unburdened himself.

Charles Workman was convicted in 1941 of the murder of Dutch Schultz and sentenced to life in prison at hard labor. He was paroled twenty-three years later, in 1964.

Handicapping the Dutch Schultz Hit

STRATEGY

The element of urgency dominated the Schultz contract. Schultz planned to assassinate Dewey within the next forty-eight hours. The clock was ticking. Schultz had to be stopped before he brought ruin on them all.

The need for speed necessitated that this would be a cowboy job. The optimum method for removing someone was to take him for a ride and dispose of the body where it couldn't be found, leaving friends and foes equally in the dark as to the missing one's fate.

There would be no such finesse when it came to taking out Schultz. This would be messy, wet work. It was a case of putting him on the spot and blasting him. Real O.K. Corral stuff, entailing a high level of risk and demanding a cool-nerved killer.

It was something of a crapshoot. After all, if Schultz's bodyguards were on the ball or even a shade faster on the draw, the would-be assassins might fall instead of the mark.

Here's where the choice of personnel becomes a strategic decision.

Lepke nominated Workman and Weiss for the job. Hadn't Lepke himself said that Workman was "bugs," that is, fearless and implacable when it came to getting the job done? The Powerhouse was top rated as a killer by both cops and crooks. Weiss had a respectable enough rep in the lethal line, but he was nowhere in Workman's heavy-hitter league. As for Piggy, he was selected because he was a local who knew the Newark area.

Putting Workman in as chief killer worked—he got the job done.

But Workman's greed in deviating from the plan to loot Schultz's bankroll could have resulted in disaster. The delay might have caused him to be killed or worse (from his bosses' standpoint) be taken alive. The same might have resulted to his accomplices, Weiss and Piggy. They were right to depart when Workman went off on his own—proving the rightness of their being selected for the job.

The planners were helped by the fact that the Dutchman was not exactly laying low. He was maintaining a more or less visible profile as opposed to having gone underground. That no bodies needed to be disposed of was a plus, cutting out the risk of exposure time.

Deduct 1 point for not having Workman squared away to ensure his sticking to the plan with no plundering.

STRATEGY: 4

TACTICS

The assassination was flawed in its execution. The plan relied on a minimum of finesse and a maximum of balls and bullets. The idea was to get Workman inside where he could blast.

The backroom battle had odds of 4-1. Workman was going up against four men. Abbadabba Berman was no gunman and can be discounted, bringing the odds down to 3-1. Schultz might or might not have a gun, depending. If he did, he knew how to use it. That left bodyguards Landau and Rosenkrantz, both armed and danger-ous. It took a wild man like Workman to walk in and start burning them down, but that's what he did.

From the time he walked in to the time he first reached the front door, he'd done everything right. But when he reversed field and went back to lift Schultz's roll, he did everything wrong.

He was out of line. Hell, out of the ballpark. Why should Weiss and Piggy risk their necks while Workman went off on his own? They were right to leave. He made a dangerous misjudgment in ex-pecting them to be there when he finally came out.

More sloppy technique showed when he went to scavenge Schultz's pockets. Schultz was still alive. Workman should have shot him in the head, finishing him. As it was, Schultz lived a long time—long enough to tell police some pretty incriminating things, had he been of a mind to. Or even if not in his right mind, he might have in-advertently betrayed in his delirium some uncomfortable truths about his gangland associates.

Workman dropped the ball on Abe Landau, too. Landau had

enough left to drag himself into the street and exchange gunfire with Workman.

Lastly, Workman's pique over the situation was such that he eventually blabbed about it to the wrong guys, whose testimony about the event sent him to prison for twenty-three years.

Deduct 1 point for Workman going back to rob Schultz.
Deduct 1 point for Workman not finishing off Schultz.
Deduct 1 point for Workman not neutralizing Landau.

TACTICS: 2

RESULTS

Dutch Schultz was dead and Dewey was saved. That was the important thing. The assassination of Tom Dewey would have meant disaster for the mob, in New York and nationally.

It might well have brought about the one thing that could've throttled the national crime syndicate while it was still in its formative stage: martial law backed by an outraged public. The governor of the state had the power to call out the National Guard, while the federal branch could have called out the active-duty military: army, navy, marines, and coast guard. In Italy, Cesare Mori had shown how effective unchecked police power could be in suppressing the ancient society of Mafia. Dewey did not die, and so that eventuality never came to pass.

For that alone, the Schultz kill must be labeled a success.

Other factors came into play. Schultz's erratic behavior had provoked fears that he would crack if Dewey managed to get a conviction against him, causing the Dutchman to turn informer and trade what he knew about Luciano and the Commission in return for a lesser sentence.

His removal had a happy economic consequence in that it allowed Luciano and Lepke to take over Dutch's lucrative policy, labor, and protection rackets, which provided an immediate big-money payoff plus lucrative long-term profits.

Schultz had been the last major gang leader independent of the Mafia in New York. Now the big five would consolidate their control of the underworld, absorbing the lesser Irish and Jewish gangs and subordinating them to the power of Cosa Nostra.

Yet, as will be seen in the next chapter, Schultz's death would ultimately prove to have dire consequences for two of the authors of his demise, Luciano and Lepke.

Mafia law demands the sacrifice of the individual for the greater good of the organization. The trick is in finding some other individual to sacrifice while avoiding the axe oneself.

Deduct 2 points for future negative consequences for Luciano and Lepke.

RESULTS: 8

Murder Meter Box Score
    STRATEGY: 4
    TACTICS: 2
    RESULTS: 8

    TOTAL: 14

5

The Man in the Half-Moon Hotel:
Abe Reles

In 1941, the law of unintended consequences found itself embodied in the thuggish form of a tenant on the sixth floor of the Half-Moon Hotel in Coney Island, New York. He was Abe "Kid Twist" Reles, a Murder, Inc. stalwart and expert with the gun, knife, ice pick, and strangler's cord. He could do the job with his bare hands, too, if it came to that.

Reles was squat and unlovely, five feet, two inches, with powerful upper body development and too-long arms: a gorilloid physique. But looks can be deceiving. Kid Twist had a brain full of facts about the mob's top execution squad—of which until recently he'd been a star performer—and a near photographic memory for details.

Coney Island is at land's end by the sea and the area was lonely and deserted as only a summer resort can be in the chilly off season. But Reles need not fear the perils of loneliness. He had plenty of company, courtesy of the three fellow prisoners and six police guards barricaded with him behind a fortified steel partition in the sixth floor's east wing.

At that moment, Abe Reles was the most wanted man in the nation. Wanted dead, that is. The New York Mafia had a contract on his life, one that had been in force for several years now. The bounty on

Reles's head was enormous, a princely sum. Louis "Lepke" Buchalter had put up a $50,000 bounty on Reles and Charlie "Lucky" Luciano had matched him. A legion of top killers was gunning for him, both the local lifetakers and some imported talent. The out of towners hailed from such locations as Cleveland, Chicago, Detroit, and St. Louis.

Reles was talking. Talking to the law, that is. Never before had so highly ranked a mobster spilled his guts about the syndicate, nor so damagingly. Kid Twist had put a hurting on his one-time friends and confederates.

His testimony had decimated Murder, Inc.'s varsity squad of elite killers. Lepke himself was now on trial for murder in part because of Reles's pointing the finger at him for a kill.

Lepke's boss, volatile Albert Anastasia, mobdom's Lord High Executioner, had also been directly implicated in a murder thanks to information from Reles. Anastasia had turned fugitive and vanished from the sight of the law.

To the New York mob, it was as if the world had turned upside down. But the situation in the fall of 1941 had been a long time in the making. It began in the aftermath of the Dutch Schultz assassination.

The big six gang chiefs ruling the city were minus one—the Dutchman—leaving the Mafia bosses of the five families in control. All should have been well, but with Schultz gone, Special Prosecutor Thomas E. Dewey turned his attention to other targets, zeroing in on the most powerful mobster of all: Lucky Luciano. Dewey empaneled another grand jury to probe Luciano's doings, unleashing a swarm of investigators with subpoena powers to expose the underworld empire.

Now that he was on the receiving end of a Dewey probe, Luciano was learning in 1936 what Schultz had known a couple years earlier when he'd first bemoaned that the prosecutor was his nemesis.

Schultz's proposal to hit Dewey had been seriously considered by the Commission, with some mob bosses in favor of the proposition.

Two of its most determined opponents were Luciano and Lepke—ironic, the way things turned out.

From the time he'd assumed de facto command of the New York Mafia (and by extension the national crime syndicate), Luciano had sought to insulate mob bosses like himself from the daily routine of dirty doings down on the street level and so protect them from the hazards of arrest and conviction. To a large extent he'd succeeded, but certain gaps remained in the strategical hierarchy of Mafia infrastructure.

Luciano had a piece of all Mafia operations at city, state, and national levels. He was into everything: labor-industrial racketeering, gambling, narcotics, protection, and so on. It was the business of prostitution that proved to be his undoing. As boss, he was in charge of prostitution no less than any other racket. In his personal life, he was a frequent user and client of whores.

The trouble was that some of them were around when he talked business to his various associates and subordinates. A handful of whores who were regular hangers-on at his parties and private entertainments told what they knew to Prosecutor Dewey.

A jury believed them and in 1936 convicted Luciano of racketeering in prostitution. He was hit with a massive thirty- to fifty-year sentence and incarcerated in the Clinton State Prison in Dannemora, New York. It seemed that his luck had run out—but had it?

He was still the boss, the one to whom the other members of the Commission looked for direction, the final arbiter. He continued to run his criminal empire from behind bars, shaping strategy and tactics for the organization and transmitting his orders through a series of go-betweens, such as lawyers and visitors who made the long trek upstate to seek his counsel and hear his decree. He pulled the strings as always and waited for the inevitable opportunity to come knocking at his cell door. It did, but not for another eleven years.

His lieutenant, Vito Genovese, was next to feel the heat. A potential murder rap hanging over his head caused him to flee to Italy, where he would remain until after the war.

That put Frank Costello in the slot of acting boss in Luciano's absence. Costello was a smooth article whose poise, smarts, and heavyweight political connections had caused the underworld to title him the "Prime Minister." He was a bootlegger and gambler with a lucrative line in slot machines and other rackets in New Orleans, where his interests were overseen by his sideman, Dandy Phil Kastel.

Costello's network of Tammany Hall political connections made him the go-to guy in New York City for those who needed an accommodating politician to do them a favor. He also had plenty of powerful connections at the state and national levels. He and Luciano had shared hotel rooms with powerful New York politicos in 1932 in Chicago at the Democratic presidential convention. He was too slick for Dewey to get a line on.

Less insulated, however, was Louis "Lepke" Buchalter, lord of the garment center and chief of Murder, Inc., which he ran for his immediate boss, Albert Anastasia.

Lepke was born as Louis Buchalter in 1897 in Manhattan to Jewish parents. His three brothers became, respectively, a rabbi, a pharmacist, and a dentist, while his sister became a schoolteacher. Lepke, the affectionate diminutive of "Louis" by which his family called him, took a different path.

In the 1920s, he teamed with Jacob "Gurrah" Shapiro, a strong-arm tough whose oft-repeated phrase "Get out of here!" became in his gravel-voiced dese-dem-and-dose patois, Gurrah. Lepke was the brains and Gurrah was the muscle, the two becoming known as the Gold Dust Twins for their facility in reaping cash from their arm-twisting activities.

They moved in on a number of speakeasies and joints, but it was the garment industry strike of 1926 that showed them the way to wealth and power. The garment industry of that day was centered in midtown Manhattan, with an outpost in Brooklyn. During the labor troubles, Lepke and Gurrah sold their gang's strong-arm services to management and labor, sometimes at the same time.

Realizing the fabulous wealth generated by the industry, the duo set down roots for a long stay. It was Lepke's inspiration to realize that a few key unions were critical to the operation of the entire 50,000-person labor force. One such labor force was the garment cutters and another was the truckers. These unions were the first to be taken over by Lepke's stooges.

The garment district was milked for all it was worth. Strikes were costly and potentially ruinous to manufacturers. They could be settled or scuttled by hefty cash payoffs to Lepke and company. Then, too, there was the threat of industrial sabotage, of fabric slashed, production lines monkey-wrenched, stinkbombs set off, acid poured on merchandise, and untimely fires. It was the old protection racket amped up to industrial strength. Not to be neglected, of course, were the possibilities of theft of payrolls and/or merchandise, with a whole district ripe for the plucking.

Labor-industrial racketeering was the money machine; Murder, Inc. came into being as the enforcement arm charged with keeping that machine rolling. The gangsters used violence and murder to enforce their will. A squad of specialists in that line took form, a pool of talent among the killer elite. They devised and operated a system of murder that was smooth, efficient, and virtually foolproof. This ultra-professional apparatus excited the admiration and interest of other family chiefs, who contracted with the squad to do loan-out assassinations. The Murder, Inc. tag was hung on them some time later by *World-Telegram* newspaper reporter Harry Feeney.

The hit squad was owned and operated by Lepke, who answered to Albert Anastasia of Brooklyn's Adonis-Mangano family.

In 1937, the heat from Dewey's probe of the labor rackets caused Lepke to go underground and turn fugitive. Lepke was now not only Dewey's but also the FBI's most wanted. Lepke didn't go far; he spent most of his fugitive career in Brooklyn. He instructed certain key men and underlings to make themselves scarce and depart for points elsewhere, far from Dewey's investigators and process servers.

Lepke had a simple theory, chilling in its implications and lethal in practice: No witnesses, no indictments.

He inaugurated what Brooklyn's assistant district attorney would

label a "war of extermination" against those deemed to be too soft
and unreliable to withstand the threats and blandishments of the
law. In practice, this meant not only potential witnesses and other
civilians but also gang members, including even members of the
murder squad itself. Lepke lay low and months passed, each one
seeing a further diminution of the pool of persons classed by him as
a potential threat.

In 1938, Dewey was elected to the Office of District Attorney of
the County of New York. Democrat William O'Dwyer, a creature
of Tammany, was the district attorney of Brooklyn. He hired then-
political independent attorney Burton Turkus (later a Republican)
as assistant district attorney.

Turkus had his work cut out for him, as Brooklyn had an abun-
dance of tough crooks and gangsters. A lively zone of lawlessness
was the sector including Ocean Hill, Brownsville, and East New
York, prime recruiting ground for some of Lepke's frontline troops.
With Lepke himself unavailable due to his fugitive status, Turkus
kept things warm by rousting the hoods in the aforementioned
areas. The cops would harass them in the candy stores and street
corners, arresting them on charges of vagrancy or whatever and
generally making life tough for them.

Turkus never intentionally set out to investigate Lepke's murder
squad. He was unaware of its existence when he first set his racket-
busting legal apparatus into motion. He scooped up lots of small
fish and put the squeeze on them. Sure enough, some were weak
and inclined to unburden themselves to a sympathetic ear, even if it
belonged to the side of the law.

What Turkus soon learned was that Lepke's war of extermination
on possible weak links had backfired. Instead of terrorizing the living into silence, it terrorized them into switching sides and singing
to the law. Some of them were only too happy to fall into the hands
of the law, rather than of Lepke's executioners. They talked, giving
up their confederates in gangland murders.

Eventually, the separate pieces shaped themselves into a mosaic
revealing the existence of a top-level assassination squad being
largely run out of Brooklyn by Lepke for Anastasia. The whole

incredible story is told in Turkus's classic book *Murder, Inc.*, coauthored by ace crime writer Sid Feder. Though dated in some ways, particularly in the authors' insistence that the Mafia was virtually wiped out in 1931 and ceased to be a factor in organized crime—a measure of the mob's successful disinformation campaign, to be able to fool two such knowledgeable insiders—the book is still a dynamite read that any true crime buff is advised to acquire.

The boss of Brooklyn's Ocean Hill–Brownsville area was Abe Reles. Like Dutch Schultz, Reles was well known by a name belonging to another old-time yegg from the Gangs of New York era, in his case Kid Twist. The original Kid Twist had been a specialist with the knife who earned his handle by his practice of twisting the knife that he'd stuck in the belly of his victims to do more damage to their innards. Like his namesake, Reles was in his own way a specialist, too.

One of Turkus's lesser lights pointed the finger at Reles, tying him to a gang killing. Reles stewed in jail for a few months before sending his wife with a message to Turkus: he was willing to talk. Turkus was amazed at his good fortune. In truth, the case he had against Reles was far from ironclad, and there was a good chance that the gangster could beat the rap if he chose to contest it in court.

To his surprise, he found the offer was genuine—and Reles had a lot to offer. Kid Twist was no fool. He knew that New York state law mandated that a criminal prosecution requires corroboration from an outside source. That is, a person cannot be prosecuted for a crime simply on the word of an accomplice and confederate in that crime. What is needed is corroboration, testimony, or evidence generated by a person who was not a party to that crime. Otherwise, no case.

Reles had been in on plenty of crimes, most notably a mind-boggling chain of murders ordered by Lepke. What's more, in virtually every case he knew where to find outside corroboration to prove those crimes, be it a gas station attendant who'd sold a can of gasoline that was used to torch a corpse, an acquaintance who'd observed some of the principals on their way to committing a crime, and so on.

Turkus had Reles moved out of jail to a safehouse in a hotel guarded by police, where he conducted lengthy debriefing sessions of the hoodlum. Reles showed an amazing recall of detail involving the crimes he'd committed. Better, the details almost always checked out when Turkus had them verified out by independent investigators. Reles would also prove to be an effective witness when taking the stand in court: cold, unflappable, and sneering as he parried the efforts of top-flight defense attorneys to trip him up in cross-examination.

Reles laid out a pattern of murder. He admitted to committing eleven murders, ones in which he'd done the killing, whether by strangler's cord, knife, or gun. But he'd been along on dozens of other murders helping out.

He fingered the core cadre of Lepke's murder squad: Reles himself; his lieutenant and best friend Martin "Buggsy" Goldstein; bloodlusting Harry Strauss, aka Pittsburgh Phil but known to his fellows by the cheery cognomen of "Pep"; Harry "Happy Maione," so-called because of his perpetually dour expression; Frank "Dasher" Abbandando, named for the hustle he'd shown on the baseball diamond while playing on the Elmira Penitentiary team; and hulking Vito "Socko" Gurino.

All answered to Lepke, who in turn answered to Albert Anastasia, the underboss of the Adonis-Mangano Brooklyn Mafia family. Louis Capone, a restaurateur and no relation to Big Al, served as Anastasia's go-between to the killer elite.

Reles had personal involvement or direct knowledge of at least eighty murders committed by the squad. Turkus estimated the total of murders committed by the Brownsville bunch to number around 200. It may well have been closer to 1,000.

Who was killed? Those who were in the way. The murder squad began as an adjunct to Lepke's garment-center rackets, liquidating those in both management and labor who resisted the takeover. Potential snitches and even inopportune witnesses were also on the firing line. The executioners were so good at their job and their technique so effective that they began branching out, doing hits for the other families in town.

This then was the operation that gained infamy under the tag of Murder, Inc.

Dewey convicted Luciano of prostitution racketeering and sent him to jail, then started nosing around Lepke's garment-center interests. Lepke went underground, dropping out of sight to direct his war of extermination on all weak links who might talk. Again, his theory was no witnesses, no indictments.

That's when the murder machine went into high gear, in the years from 1937 through 1939. The tactic backfired, though, as bodies piled up, not only those of civilians and outsiders, but even close associates and friends of the killers who were thought to be bad risks, security wise. A number of those cooperating with Turkus did so only because they were on the kill list or thought they were and would likely not have talked otherwise.

Lepke's fugitive status put the heat on the New York mob and there was talk that maybe it would be best for all concerned if he surrendered. Standing solidly against the proposition was Albert Anastasia. He and Lepke were tight. He kept Lepke so well hidden that even though he was in Brooklyn for most of his time on the run, the law never got a line on him.

Albert A. didn't see what the rush was all about. The longer Lepke stayed at large, the safer he was. Witnesses could be eliminated and the survivors were more likely to have a memory lapse as time went on.

Lepke then fell victim to a classic double cross. One of his oldest associates and the one he trusted the most was gangster Moey "Dimples" Wolinsky. Wolinsky told Lepke that a possible deal was in the works. Lepke was wanted by the feds for a narcotics violation. The idea was that he would surrender to them, receiving in return a sentence of a few years in a not-too-tough federal prison, where he would be safe from the reach of Tom Dewey.

Lepke went for the deal. In a celebrated episode, on a hot August night he appeared by prearrangement on a street corner, where he was picked up by influential newshound, gossip columnist, and radio commentator Walter Winchell. Winchell drove him to a site where the director of the FBI himself, J. Edgar Hoover, waited, backed by a phalanx of G-men planted nearby. Lepke surrendered personally to Hoover and was whisked away. It wasn't very long, barely a minute or two, before Lepke realized that Hoover was unknowing of any such deal as the one that Dimples Wolinsky had described. By that time, though, it was too late for Lepke to change his mind. That train had already left the station, leaving him in custody.

Disillusionment deepened when he drew a fourteen-year sentence for narcotics racketeering and was sent to the federal pen in Leavenworth, Kansas—a tough joint to do time in. In 1943, a visitor told Lepke of the death by shooting of Dimples Wolinsky. The bearer of glad tidings said that after hearing the news, Lepke had never looked happier.

In 1940, though, the feds turned Lepke over to now-Governor Tom Dewey for prosecution by New York state for labor racketeering. Lepke drew a thirty-year sentence on that rap, to be served after he'd finished serving his fourteen-year federal term.

That same year Burton Turkus began to roll up a series of convictions of Murder, Inc. luminaries. On June 12, 1941, Pittsburgh Phil and Buggsy Goldstein went to the electric chair in the death house at Sing Sing Prison in Ossining, New York. February 19, 1942, saw the executions of Happy Maione and Dasher Abbandando. Charles "the Bug" Workman was turned over to Newark authorities for prosecution for the murder of Dutch Schultz. Workman's eleventh-hour plea of "no defense" resulted in his dodging execution to receive a sentence of life in prison with hard labor (though he was paroled after serving twenty-three years of this sentence).

At his trial, Buggsy Goldstein had tagged Assistant D.A. Turkus with the label of "Mr. Arsenic." Now, it was Lepke's turn to sample some of the toxic brand of legal poison that Turkus was so adroit at distributing to deserving hoods.

Back in 1936, Lepke's muscling into the trucking industry had left trucker Joseph Rosen embittered and impoverished, reduced to ekeing out a living at a tiny Brooklyn candy store. He put out the word that if he didn't see some money, he was going to have a chat with Dewey. That marked him for death. Lepke huddled with Louis

Capone, Emanuel "Mendy" Weiss, and a hood named Little Farvel to arrange Rosen's demise.

Reles provided some information, but the center of the case resided with labor activist Max Rubin and Murder, Inc. killer Allie "Tick-Tock" Tannenbaum.

The Brooklyn D.A. tabbed Turkus for the prosecution. Lepke was in the federal pen at Leavenworth, beginning to serve his sentence for narcotics dealing, and was therefore available for trial when needed. Louis Capone and Mendy Weiss were also arrested and jailed pending prosecution.

The Hit

The mob had at first simply refused to believe that Reles was talking. Buggsy Goldstein, Reles's right-hand man, persisted in this state of denial right up until the moment in his own trial when he saw Reles take the stand to testify against him. At that moment, Goldstein wept.

As the Turkus prosecutions began making inroads on the higher-ups, the mob went to Condition Red. Nothing was more important than shutting Reles up for good. Turkus was aware of the high stakes he was playing for. Jail was too unsafe an environment for this dangerous informer. Even if kept segregated from the rest of the inmate population, 99 percent of which would gladly have stuck a sharpened spoon or similar shiv into Reles to do him in, there was still the risk of his food being poisoned or gotten to by other devious ways.

Turkus moved Reles and three other, lesser (though still important) informers—Tannenbaum, Sol (Sholem) Bernstein, and Mikey Syckoff—to Coney Island's Half-Moon Hotel. They were kept in the east wing of the building's sixth floor, where extraordinary precautions were taken to further safeguard them. The wing was in an L-shaped corridor, the entrance to which was barred by a newly constructed steel wall with a door in it. No one would be admitted beyond that door without first being screened.

Reles and the three other informers each occupied a room of

their own. There was also a room used by the guards. There were eighteen guards in all, with six guards assigned per shift, for a total of three eight-hour shifts. Protection from gangland marauders was also supplied around the clock to the wives and families of the informers.

Tight security was also enforced inside and outside at the courthouse where the trials were taking place. Entrance to the courtroom was tightly screened and buttressed with a heavily armed police presence.

Reles and company were lodged in the heart of a police security cocoon. They were probably more heavily guarded during that period than the president of the United States. Which does not necessarily imply that they were better guarded.

Reles's testimony wreaked havoc among the Murder, Inc. apparatus, delivering a cadre of its frontline troops to the law. Reles was working his way up the organizational pyramid, jeopardizing the higher-ups, the masters who gave the orders to the murder squad.

He was slated to testify against Lepke at his trial. He had already put at some risk Benjamin "Bugsy" Siegel for his involvement in a West Coast kill. Worse, from the standpoint of the Mafia, he was the centerpiece in a pending investigation of Lepke's boss, Albert Anastasia himself.

The tie-up came from the 1939 slaying of labor activist Morris Diamond, a delegate of Teamster's Local 138. In the spring of that year, District Attorney Dewey began looking into the mob's incursions in the trucking industry. Diamond went to Dewey's office to tell what he knew, a capital crime that put him on the kill list. This was at the height of the "no witnesses, no indictments" war of extermination, and to be known to be cooperating with Dewey was the equivalent of a death sentence.

Ordinarily, Reles would have been a prime candidate to take the contract, but the luck of the draw found him uninvolved in the Diamond hit. However, he had just happened to be present when Anastasia and Mendy Weiss were discussing the planned action, with Albert A. chiding Mendy over the delay in taking care of the matter. Mendy said that his spotters were out on the street casing the hit, and as soon as they got Diamond's home address, he'd pass it along to Albert.

"When I get it, we will take care of him," Anastasia said. A short time later, Diamond was gunned down.

Now that Reles was talking, Anastasia was in a tight spot. It was the corroboration gimmick again. If Reles had participated in any way in the Diamond hit, he would have been an accomplice and his accusation would have no legal worth, uncorroborated by outside testimony. But since he was in the clear on this one, his testimony was permissible in a murder case against Anastasia.

Anastasia went underground, remaining at large through 1940 and most of 1941 while the case against him was in progress. He'd managed to successfully hide Lepke for several years when the latter was the most wanted man in the United States, and he was no less successful himself in evading the law.

Meanwhile, a grand jury investigated Anastasia's role in the Diamond hit. But for some unknown reason, Reles was not called before the grand jury to testify on the matter. The delay was beginning to look funny if not suspicious. The official line was that it was pointless to have Reles testify before Anastasia was apprehended. That sounded fishy to Turkus, who traced the obstruction to James Moran, a powerful chief clerk in the office of District Attorney William O'Dwyer and a longtime crony of O'Dwyer.

In November 1941, with Lepke and codefendants Louis Capone and Mendy Weiss on trial for murder, and the Anastasia grand jury probe holding fire, Reles was more unpopular than ever in mobdom. On the eleventh of that month—Veteran's Day—with Lepke's trial nearing its climax and Reles slated to testify, Turkus received an early morning phone call of stunning import.

At 6:45 A.M. of that day, bystanders in the vicinity of the Half-Moon Hotel reported hearing a crumping noise. A body was observed on the roof of a low-extension structure located below the sixth-floor room where Reles was lodged. The room was empty; the window open. The dead body was indeed that of Reles.

The public and press uproar that resulted from the event was slightly terrific. Here was Reles, the most important informer from the mob's top ranks to date, the man whose testimony had wrecked Murder, Inc., sent four ace killers to the chair, and threatened top bosses Lepke and Anastasia, a man ringed by a protective cocoon of police security, now lying dead under mysterious circumstances.

What happened? Found near the body was a rope made of knotted bedsheets strengthened by a length of wire. The implication was that Reles had made the rope, secured the wire end to a radiator, and climbed out the window with the purpose of using the rope to lower himself. The wire had not held, causing him to fall to his death some forty feet below.

Turkus (and many others) found this hard to swallow. The scene looked like Reles was making an escape attempt when he was undone by a poorly tied rope. Escape? Escape to what? On the street, he would have every man's hands against him, those of the underworld and the law. He occupied the top spot on the mob's kill list. He could count on the help of not a single friend or acquaintance in the criminal world. Anyone in that milieu who helped him would be destroyed. Not that they wanted to. To crookdom, he was a rat, the king rat of all time. His face, plastered daily across the newspapers, was immediately recognizable by a large portion of the public, crooks, and law-abiding citizens, who would be on the lookout for him the moment his escape was announced.

No, the safest place in the world for Reles, and the one spot from which he had a platform to positively affect his fate, was the sixth-floor room in the Half-Moon Hotel that he had so definitely quitted.

An alternate theory was that Reles had not gone out the window to escape, but had done it as a prank, intending to lower himself down to the fifth floor, let himself in by a window, and return upstairs to confound his captors by presenting himself to them. The idea was not without its merits, most of them based on the nature of the man himself. Apart from being a killer and racketeer, Abe Reles was also an obnoxious character, a smug, smirking know-it-all, sarcastic needler, always looking to one-up the other guy, no matter what the circumstances. There was no love lost between him and the guards who were supposed to protect him. He tried to boss them around. He played pranks on them, like tying a snoozing guard's shoelaces together to trip the unsuspecting fellow when he got up, or making crank calls to them at their homes in the dead of night. It was possible, barely, that Reles might have intended such a stunt, showing his guards he could escape if he wanted to, showing them up, taking the play away from them and aggrandizing himself.

But there's a big difference between giving a guy a hotfoot and essaying the difficult and dangerous maneuver of lowering oneself by a rope to the next floor down, just for the sake of a prank. Reles was abrasive, but he was neither crazy nor stupid.

The rope of knotted bedsheets happened to be only long enough to reach down to the next floor and no lower. The wire that had been used to reinforce it had been supplied to Reles by his keepers some months earlier to be used to repair his radio.

The wire was another factor that didn't fit. Reles knew his way around ropes, having wielded the garrote in a number of murders and having trussed up hog-tied victims with a sliding noose that caused them to strangle themselves as they struggled for freedom. Had he rigged the wire-bedsheet combination, logic says that he would have secured the end anchored to the radiator in such a way that it would have held under his weight.

A third, even weaker "solution" was the suggestion that Reles had committed suicide. If that was the case, why bother to go through with the rigmarole of the knotted bedsheets? Most suicides leave notes, but he didn't, quite an omission for one like Reles, who loved to sound off and hog the limelight no matter what the occasion. It's hardly likely that he would have chosen to make his grand exit from the stage of life without leaving behind a note with a few choice sentiments for the world to remember him by.

Suicide doesn't gibe with his emotional state at the time. He was doing as well as a man in his circumstances might be expected to do. From the moment he first began talking, he showed no remorse at betraying his friends and associates and paving their way to the death chamber. His attitude was that they would have done the same to him, only he talked first and beat them to the punch. He had the sociopath's lack of conscience when it came to his own crimes; he regarded the murders he'd committed with as much indifference as if he'd been swatting flies instead of taking human lives.

Once he started talking, he took a positive pleasure in it, showing off his ability to remember names and details. He thrived on putting his one-time crime pals and bosses on the spot. Going to court to testify against them was always a big event for him, a day at the fair. Once more he would be the focus of all eyes and ears, the court-room hanging on his every word, the defendants glaring at him with murder in their eyes.

No, suicide just wasn't in the makeup of the man.

Rule out a fatal accident while trying to escape or while pulling a prank, and what's left? Murder.

That's where the calculation became really sticky, because Reles had been sealed in a secure wing of the hotel with only three fellow informers and police guards to keep him company. The guards were detectives, six to a shift. On the morning when Reles died, though, only five guards had been on duty.

Another sticking point was that the guards were supposedly all asleep when Reles went out the window. Apart from any depart-mental rules against sleeping while on duty, that was quite a coinci-dence.

Could it have been one of the other informers? There were three of them sharing the east wing with Reles: Sol Bernstein, Allie "Tic Toc" Tannenbaum, and Mikey Syckoff. Of them, Allie was the most accomplished killer, having actively participated in a number of Murder, Inc. killings. Bernstein had mostly done things like steal getaway cars and run errands for the big killers. Syckoff was a loan-shark and less facile in the arts of applying muscle or murder.

Reles had little use for any of them, and all three had come to hate his guts. Tannenbaum was there because Reles (and Bernstein) had fingered him to Turkus for a couple of Murder, Inc. kills. Bernstein had taken a swing at Reles in response to a crack he made about Bernstein's wife, and police had had to pull them apart.

It can't be ruled out that one or possibly two of them might have done in Reles. The same applies to the police guards.

The official cause of Reles's death was ruled to be a fractured spine, the injury sustained when he had hit the extension roof below in a sitting position. There were no other obvious injuries or marks on him than those inflicted by the fall. No evidence of poison or drugs were found in his system. Turkus noted that the autopsy report made no mention as to whether any alcohol had been found in Reles and was unable to determine that important point. By the time he wrote his book, he wondered aloud in print if there had been any knife or bullet wounds that had also escaped mention—a measure of his distrust of the official line on Reles's death.

So who did it? Some of the police guards? The prisoners? Or a combination of the two?

One person could have done it while the others slept, but it would have been a tough job. Reles knew how to take care of himself and would have put up a terrific fight if he'd been attacked. The clamor would have alerted the others, at the very least. But there was no clamor, no alarm given.

It was the middle of November, not the time to open a window. A murder-minded individual, guard, or prisoner might have tried to lure Reles to the window, possibly by pretending that some nonexistent event was going on outside at street level and saying, "Hey, take a look at this."

But the kill-wise Reles would have been justly wary of even a friendly invitation to draw too near to an open sixth-floor window.

His body lay about twenty feet away from the building wall, a fair distance, and the autopsy showed that he landed in a sitting position. This would accord if two men had cradled Reles in their arms and pitched him out the window.

What would Reles be doing while this was going on? Nothing, if he'd somehow been rendered unconscious or otherwise incapacitated before the kill. This could have been done by a knockout blow on the head or the administration of drugs or poison. The autopsy stated that no evidence of a blow, poison or drugs were observed on Reles. Considering that Turkus came to wonder at the factuality of the report, such negative evidence need not be taken as established fact. Turkus didn't take it that way and ultimately said so in print and on the record.

The Reles death was officially ruled as accidental. A departmental trial later cleared all five police guards of charges of neglect of duty. They went back to work and no other administrative or legal action was taken against them. No charges were ever filed against their immediate supervisors.

On the street, the wags delivered the one-liner that would serve as the tag line for Abe "Kid Twist" Reles: "The canary could sing— but he couldn't fly."

Handicapping the Reles Hit

STRATEGY

Abe Reles had to die. But he was a hard man to get to. He was too well guarded for even a suicide squad of cowboy killers to get to, and too well screened to offer a possible shot to a marksman with a scoped rifle. No mob executioner could get to Reles from the outside. The only way he could be gotten to was from the inside.

That was difficult but not impossible. The hotel's sixth floor was fortified, with access restricted. Still, visitors were admitted, such as family members and law enforcement agents. Inside were four prisoners and a rotating three-shift staff of eighteen police guards. Money talks, and with the fabulous sums available for a Reles hit, there was much to tempt even a relatively honest but low-paid cop.

The hard part was the getaway, or rather the lack of it. In a closed system like the hotel's east wing, all present would become suspect should Reles die as a result of foul play.

That's where the suicide angle came in. The hit would be framed to look like an accident. Reles died either while trying to escape or as the result of a failed prank—that's how the scene was supposed to look. It would give those present at the site a measure of deniability. No less important, it would provide deniability to the authorities charged with guarding and protecting Reles.

Kid Twist's death would raise a big stink, no matter what. But as long as there was some ambiguity, some clouded circumstances that allowed the argument that it was all his own fault, the incident would fade sooner rather than later. The accident angle was a whole lot less provocative than an out and out hit. Had he been the victim of an obvious and clear-cut assassination plot, had he been shot, stabbed, or strangled, the outcry would have been deafening. An outraged public would have clamored for more and tougher action against the mob.

An accidental death, however, offered the possibility of quick closure. No one need be held responsible, because it was Reles's own damned fault.

Certain politicians and higher-ups in the justice system were also eager to see the end of Reles, not only to accommodate their mob buddies but also to ensure that the ever widening dragnet would not encompass them in its meshes. The same ones, perhaps, who had let the Anastasia probe go on for almost two years without once bringing in Reles to be deposed and get his statement on the record.

Political pull and clout would be useful in containing the aftermath of a Reles death and keeping the details from being examined too closely. The mob had the hit wired inside and out. The rest was in the hands of the assassins.

Still, it was risky. The deed had to be done in the heart of the enemy stronghold. There was only a limited amount of time to do what had to be done. If the hit went sour in some way and Reles managed to survive, there would be some deniability possible, since it would be the word of the would-be killers versus Reles. They could claim he attacked them, was trying to escape, or something to that effect. But the opportunity to get Reles would be lost, and a failed attempt would goose the authorities to increasing his security and making him an even tougher target. It might also goad the law into moving harder and faster in the grand jury probe of Albert Anastasia.

Deduct 2 points for the killers' high risk of exposure with no getaway.

STRATEGY: 3

TACTICS

The Kid Twist kill is a kind of black-box situation. We don't know what went on inside the black box of the Half-Moon Hotel's sixth-floor east wing, and we have to reason by inference as to what really happened.

However the hit went down, it came to Reles as a fatal surprise. He was gutter-tough with a pronounced survival instinct, but there is nothing to indicate that he apprehended any danger from those on his side of the hotel's protective barrier, neither fellow prisoners nor police guards. Whatever was in the air, he didn't smell it, or he'd have squawked long and hard until the perceived threat was neutralized.

In *Murder, Inc.*, Turkus describes how when Reles would enter a courtroom, his eyes would be in constant motion, scanning the scene, searching for anyone who might have been a danger for him. He felt safe in the Half-Moon Hotel—as safe as anyone in his position as the underworld's number-one rat could feel.

He had been held in the hotel for over a year before the end came, time enough for him to grow comfortable in the familiar surroundings. That was more than enough time for an interested party to clock the routine of guards and prisoners.

An inside man was needed for the hit. There were several possibilities in place. Any of the other three prisoners, Allie Tannenbaum, Sol Bernstein, or Mikey Syckoff, were all in place and could have served as spotters, casing the situation and relaying the information to a go-between, such as a guard or visiting family member. They were all on the mob's kill list, so what better way than to get back in its good graces and maybe buy themselves a chance at staying alive than by cooperating? Also, any police guard could have furnished the information, passing it along to mob planners.

The pool of available suspects narrows to those who were actually present at the time of Reles's death: the five guards and three other informers. It's possible that at least one of the guards was gotten to.

The knowledge that guards and prisoners (the ones who weren't in on the hit) would all be asleep at the same time in the early dawn hours provided a window of opportunity.

It's highly unlikely that all the guards were suborned by the mob; with so many paid off, the odds were huge that one would make a slip or talk out of turn, upsetting the apple cart. One guard would have sufficed, but evidence indicates the participation of more than one man. Reles fell twenty feet away from the wall of the building, in a sitting position. One man would have had his hands full heaving Reles out the window by himself. The sitting position in which he fell could have been very easily accomplished by two men, cradling the body in their arms and pitching it out the window.

Playing the probabilities, it might have been tougher to find a police guard willing to turn killer than it would to find one who would be willing to play a secondary role. A high-profile target like Reles would be a pretty big assignment for a crooked cop turned killer.

All the police guards on the shift were cleared of charges of negligence in the mishap, and none were ever charged or prosecuted for any alleged involvement in Reles's death. So all of this is mere speculation, of course. But for those who refuse to believe in a verdict of accidental death or suicide, the only other alternative is murder. If it was murder, some one had to commit it. What follows is only a theory, but one that fits the facts as to how the Reles kill was worked.

Apart from Reles, there was at least one other highly skilled professional killer in the east wing at the time of death. That was Allie Tannenbaum, who'd been in on many a Murder, Inc. hit. Bernstein was a car thief and glorified errand boy and Syckoff was a loanshark and not a lifetaker. But Allie was a stone pro. Besides, Reles had fingered him to Turkus, providing an additional grudge motive.

A plot could have been worked out using Allie and at least one of the police guards.

Inside intelligence showed that guards and prisoners were usually all asleep at the same time in the dawn hours. Like the other prisoners, Allie had his own room, with no roommate who might have stirred when he slipped outside into the hall. The guards shared one common room, and a wakeful guard could have slipped past his sleeping fellows.

It would be well to work the hit as a two-man operation, with Allie taking the active role and the guard serving as a lookout. Had something gone awry, like one of the guards not in on the plot waking and prowling the scene, a crooked guard would have been in the best spot to allay any suspicions.

Next comes the tricky question of the approach to Reles. Kid Twist was a survivor with jungle instincts, and he'd have put up a major battle if he caught or even suspected anybody was making a move on him. But he was silent, making no such fuss or outcry.

He was either taken by surprise and despatched before he could make a sound, or he was immobilized before the approach was made.

Two possibilities suggest themselves. In taking the second one first—that he was immobilized—it must be noted that the autopsy report found no traces of drugs or poison in his system. Which may or may not be true. But that's what the report said.

Still, any foreign substances could have been present in traces too subtle to be detected; or the postmortem tests themselves could have been sabotaged, cooked, or gimmicked at any number of places along the way.

No mention was made as to whether any alcohol was present in Reles's body. Reles liked a drink but was no big drinker. It's not impossible that he could have had access to a bottle or two while inside the fortified east wing. One of the killers (most likely a guard, whom he'd be more inclined to trust than, say, Allie) could have gotten him drunk, leaving Reles in a drunken stupor when they later came for him. Drunks have a way of waking up at the most inconvenient times, though, and there was a lot that had to be done to frame the scene.

Another possibility: Reles was slain as he slept. One of Murder, Inc.'s signature ways of dealing death was with an icepick, resulting in instant death when shoved into the base of the skull where it joins the spine. Other fatal strikes with the icepick are in the mastoid nerve junctions behind the ears and above the hinges of the jaw, or through the ear directly into the brain.

Allie Tannenbaum was no novice to an icepick kill. Assume that the wayward guard with whom he's working has already slipped him an icepick. Allie enters Reles's room while the guard keeps watch in the hall. Allie sneaks up on Reles and shoves the pick in behind the ear or through it into the brain, either one a swift, sure death blow.

The wound would be small, about the size of a bee sting. If Reles was stabbed through the ear, there might not have been any external wound showing. Also, the needlelike shape of the instrument would leave little more than a few drops of blood, if that.

If Reles had been drunk and sleeping it off, it would have been easy for Allie to approach and make the strike. If Reles had been only sleeping, it still could have been done. In the latter case, it would have made sense to hedge against Reles's awakening at the last seconds by having the guard close at hand, ready to clap a hand or pillow over Reles's mouth and help hold him down until Allie finished the job.

The icepick puncture might well have been masked or screened by the traumatic injuries Reles sustained in the fall. An honest yet careless autopsist might have missed it; a less honest one could have been paid to overlook it. Or the police hierarchy might have buried it, to keep from opening the can of worms that would have been generated by a verdict of foul play rather than suicide.

Or maybe it wasn't there. Maybe Allie or the guard knocked Reles on the head with a blunt instrument, the evidence of which went undetected.

In any case, Kid Twist was almost certainly unconscious or dead when the killers set to work framing the scene. It didn't take much, merely knotting a couple of bedsheets together, reinforcing it with wire, and rigging it so it looked like it had been tied to the radiator and come off.

The window was opened. The killers picked up Reles, cradling

him in their arms in an upright position, and at 6:45 A.M. heaved
him out the window, producing the crumping sound heard by several bystanders. All that remains is for them to slip back to their respective rooms unobserved and wait for the inevitable hue and cry.
If an icepick or blunt instrument was used to subdue Reles, be sure
that there was in place a foolproof method of putting it where it
would escape the eyes of investigators.

Speculation? Absolutely. A scenario and nothing more. Yet, it fits
the facts as we know them. And there is one piece of provocative
later data that tends to add some solidity to the thesis.

Abe Reles's death was ruled accidental and the books closed on it.
Lepke's trial moved along without him.

The main witnesses against Lepke were Max Rubin, who through
a million-to-one freak occurrence somehow survived being shot in
the back of the head by a Murder, Inc. gunman and lived to testify
against the gang boss, and Allie Tannenbaum.

Allie, who openly acknowledged at least six kills to his credit,
with many more no doubt going unacknowledged, fulfilled the rest
of his duties for the prosecution and was ultimately released free
and clear, serving no additional jail time.

He dropped into no doubt welcome obscurity for some years,
surfacing about 1950 when he was discovered living in Atlanta,
Georgia, where he was gainfully employed as a lampshade salesman.
The story of the reformed murder man got a quick but wide play
in the press.

The mob's penalty for informing is death. Allie had informed on
the mighty Lepke himself, his testimony helping send Lepke, along
with Lou Capone and Mendy Weiss, to the electric chair. Such action would hardly endear Allie to the Mafia, which has a long memory in such matters.

But they did nothing. Nothing! Allie Tannenbaum continued to
live his life undisturbed and unmolested. Not for him was there the
inevitable fate of informers ("rats" in mob parlance): sudden dooms
such as a bomb under the hood of the family car, a shotgun blast
roaring out of a darkened alley, a knife in the back, or any of the
even far less pleasant ways to die.

The significant factor is the negative template of what did not happen. Allie did not die by mob revenge. Which is funny, because if anybody had it coming, he did. Great efforts have been made to take down renegades whose offenses were far less than his. Even if he'd managed with government help to change his identity and start a new life in Atlanta, once the news went public about his new, law-abiding life, the mob could have found and liquidated him with no trouble at all.

But they didn't, and one has to ask why. Why did Allie Tannenbaum escape the sure swift sword of Mafia retribution? Had he won reprieve from the death sentence decreed by his crime of informing, and if so, what had he done to buy back his life?

If he had been instrumental in eliminating Abe Reles, full pardon for all his sins would have been a small price to pay. By killing Reles, Allie would have saved himself.

It's only a theory, of course. Pure speculation and presented as such.

A final note on the tactics of the Reles hit: they were so smooth and well accomplished that we are still in the dark as to what exactly did happen that early morning in the east wing of the Half-Moon Hotel. A masterpiece of tradecraft and finesse, doubly impressive when considering the pressure of the high stakes and the limited window of opportunity.

TACTICS: 5

RESULTS

A lot of people in the underworld and the overworld had reason to celebrate when Reles went out the window. Lepke wasn't one of them.

Kid Twist was scheduled to be a star witness at Lepke's trial for the murder of Joe Rosen, but he was not the only witness. Even without Reles's testimony, on December 1, 1942, Lepke was found guilty of murder one, along with codefendants Louis Capone and Mendy Weiss. All three were sentenced to die in the electric chair at Sing Sing Prison.

The execution was set for thirty days after the sentence was passed, but it was not to be. Not so quickly, anyhow. Lepke still had several options to play, legal and otherwise. The legal maneuvering took a curious turn. Lepke had been in federal prison serving a fourteen-year sentence for narcotics when he was turned over to New York state, which prosecuted him for labor racketeering and sentenced him to thirty years.

Now he'd been found guilty of murder and would be executed by the state. Legal procedure required the feds to relinquish their control of Lepke and render him to the state. Legal protocol required that Lepke receive a federal pardon so he could be delivered free and clear to state authorities.

In the event, though, there was nothing free and clear about it. Month after month passed by without the Justice Department putting through the necessary paperwork. New York complained to the head of justice, Attorney General Frances G. Biddle, but still nothing was done. Assistant D.A. Turkus was not alone in noting that Washington seemed curiously reluctant to release Lepke into their custody.

Lepke surely could not have been pleased by a message relayed to him by his former partner Gurrah Shapiro, himself doing time in prison for labor racketeering. When Dutch Schultz had argued in favor of assassinating Tom Dewey, Gurrah had been strongly in favor of the proposition, which was defeated by the antiassassination faction whose two most voluble proponents were Luciano and Lepke.

Gurrah's message to Lepke?—"I told you so."

Dewey was now the governor of New York, who with the power of commutation was the one man who held Lepke's life or death in his hands.

More papers were filed and more hearings were heard, but it was not until the election year of 1944 that Lepke was finally handed over to New York state. He, along with Mendy Weiss and Louis Capone, were penned in the death house. They'd held off the executioner for two years but now their time had come.

The execution was set for Saturday, March 4, 1944. As the clock ticked, Lepke seemed breezily confident. In the last day or two left to him, he met with Governor Dewey's man, New York D.A. Frank Hogan.

Was it possible? Had the unthinkable occurred, with Lepke about to go the Reles route and turn state's evidence?

Lepke played a very careful hand. He had a specific something to trade, his knowledge of the collusion of a highly placed national political figure with gangsters. A number of well-placed sources hold that the key to Lepke's ploy lay in certain earlier incidents in the career of Sidney Hillman, the one-time head of the mighty Amalgamated Clothing Workers Union (400,000 strong) and now head of the powerhouse War Procurement Office in Washington, D.C. It is believed that Lepke wanted to trade what he knew about Hillman's alleged involvement with the mob to buy himself a pass out of the electric chair.

There were some interesting political angles here. Hillman was a big in the administration of President Franklin D. Roosevelt, a Democrat. Dewey, the Republican governor of New York, made no secret of his presidential aspirations. And 1944 was a presidential election year, with Roosevelt angling for an unprecedented fourth term. Dewey might go far by exposing FDR stalwart and high-profile administration member Sidney Hillman as having used the mob to iron out labor troubles way back in his Amalgamated Clothing Workers Union days.

The bait was not taken. Hogan never revealed the specifics of Lepke's offer, but he went on record as stating that Lepke had been elusive and cagy, never offering specifics and refusing to implicate or inform on any of his mob associates. It was a limited offer, iffy at best, and it was refused.

That confirmed Lepke's date with demolition.

The prison warden determined the ordering of the three condemned men's executions. It was felt that Lepke was the toughest and therefore would go last. Louis Capone, with a heart condition, would go first. It was feared that he might have a heart attack and so disrupt the proceedings, possibly even being so unsporting as to die on his own and thus cheat the hangman. Mendy Weiss was handed the number-two slot.

On Saturday night at around eleven o'clock, Louis Capone took a seat in the electric chair. He had no last words. Mendy Weiss followed, professing his innocence and sending his love to his family.

Last came Lepke. The gaze of his soft brown eyes was described as hard and unyielding. He had nothing to say. Twenty-two hundred volts hit him, rendering his silence permanent. He left behind a statement read after death by his wife, declaring that he had not offered to inform and give information in return for a commutation of his death sentence, but only that a commission be formed to investigate any information he had given and that he live or die on the basis of that commission's findings.

Decoded, he seems to have been sending a signal to his mob pals that he hadn't talked about them, but only about certain politicians. A point of something not unlike honor, that, if one of nice distinction.

Lepke was the first of the big-time modern American mob bosses to be executed for his crimes. Executed by the state, that is, and not by other mobsters. He was also the last such mob chief to be executed in the United States.

It was a fate that Albert Anastasia had been spared, thanks to the timely demise of Abe Reles.

RESULTS: 10

Murder Meter Box Score
    STRATEGY: 3
    TACTICS: 5
    RESULTS: 10

TOTAL: 18

6

Going Hollywood: Bugsy Siegel

On the evening of June 20, 1947, in a mansion in Beverly Hills, bigshot gangster Benjamin "Bugsy" Siegel sat on a living room couch reading the *Los Angeles Times*. His back was to a window. The drapes were not drawn, contrary to household custom, but had been left open, a matter that would soon take on a life-and-death significance.

Siegel's swift ascent and storybook career was an only-in-America saga of social mobility. He'd come a long way since the 1920s, when he'd been a bootlegger, extortionist, racketeer, gangland enforcer, and first-rate killer. He was about to go a lot farther.

Benjamin Siegel was born on February 28, 1906, in the Williamsburg section of Brooklyn, New York, to a poor but honest Jewish family of which he was destined to become the shame and scandal. He had a brother and several sisters, all of whom grew up to be respectable, law-abiding citizens. Nothing in his family history indicated the propensity for crime that young Siegel was quick to evince.

Like Louis "Lepke" Buchalter, he had a mental twist toward the lawless side of the street, as well as an inborn dislike for anything approaching honest work. He was unlike Lepke in the matter of temperament. Lepke generally maintained a soft-spoken, even-tempered disposition, while Siegel was prone to explosive outbursts of rage and aggression, a tendency that led to his being tagged at an early age with the nickname of "Bugsy." It was a name to which Siegel took violent exception, as those who were careless or unfortunate enough to use the name to his face would learn to their dismay.

Siegel grew up in the Jewish enclave of Manhattan's Lower East Side, where he followed the standard pattern of the era's young punks, starting with truancy, vandalism, and petty theft, followed by membership in a street gang with all the attendant brawling, assaults, and inevitable escalation into serious crime and violence.

He was known to have held one "honest" job in his life, that of taxi cab driver. But even there, he had an angle. He worked the theater district at night, driving ticketholders to the big Broadway shows. That gave him a chance to case his riders and see which ones looked well heeled, which wives were wearing expensive jewelry or furs, and so forth. He knew where the marks lived because he'd picked them up at their homes. Their tickets meant that they'd be out of the apartment and safely placed in the theater for some hours, giving Siegel and his thief associates time to burgle the residences at their leisure. Siegel eventually lost the job when a female rider accused him of rape. She later dropped the charges, no doubt having been persuaded to see the light by Siegel or his emissaries.

During his earlier formative years, he made several important lifelong friendships. One was with a lad who came from Manhattan's Hell's Kitchen district, west of midtown. Born George Ranft, he would later change his last name to Raft and go on to Hollywood and indeed worldwide stardom. George had to have been quick and slick to run with a hell-raising young hooligan like Ben Siegel.

The central friendship of Siegel's life, though, was with Meyer Lansky. Lansky, like John Torrio and a few others, is generally regarded as one of the true masterminds of modern crime. He was born Maier Suchowljansky to Jewish parents in 1902 in Grodno, Poland, then under the domination of Russia. His family immigrated to America in 1911 and settled on the Lower East Side.

The youth, who'd Americanized his name to Meyer Lansky, went as far as the eighth grade in school, a fact that fails to convey the power of his calculating, Machiavellian intellect. He was gifted with an aptitude for mathematics and mechanics.

Lansky also had a penchant for crime. His analysis of the world convinced him that a life outside the law was the quickest and surest way to amass wealth and power. He was small and slight but appropriately ruthless when the situation called for it.

Early on, in boyhood days, he partnered up with Ben Siegel. They were a well-balanced duo, thanks to the combination of Lansky's brains and Siegel's brawn. The dynamic was more subtle and complicated than that, of course; Lansky could handle the rough stuff as needed and Siegel was possessed of a native insight and shrewd cunning, but essentially, Lansky was the thinker and Siegel the muscle.

Together with their followers, in the early 1920s they formed the Bug and Meyer mob, a viciously effective and profitable strong-arm unit. They hired out to other mobsters as antihijacking guards on truck convoys of bootleg booze. From there, it was a small stretch for them to get into bootlegging themselves and to pressuring speakeasy owners to carry their brand of hooch.

They were into whatever would turn a crooked buck: gambling, narcotics, robbery, and labor violence. A specialty was stolen cars, which the mechanically minded Lansky then souped up into fast and anonymous crime machines for resale to other criminal gangs.

Another specialty was murder. The Bug and Meyer mob fielded an elite squad of professional killers who sold their guns to other mobsters (not least of them, Lepke). They were a forerunner of what would ultimately become Murder, Inc.

One of Lansky's earliest arrests had been in 1918 for brawling with another up-and-coming crook Salvatore Lucania, later known as Charlie "Lucky" Luciano. Luciano would remember Lansky a few years later and form an enduring and effective alliance with him that would determine the shape of modern organized crime. They were much alike, cunning and ruthless men who preferred to make money and use murder as a last resort. They would overcome their ethnic differences—Lansky was Jewish, Luciano Italian, to form a crime syndicate that endures to this day.

Siegel, though, was different, possessed of a hair-trigger temper that could erupt in an eyeblink and result in raw, vicious ultra-violence. He liked the action, the kick of breaking the law. He was an accomplished triggerman who took pride in killing and continued to do so long after his high rank should have caused him to recuse himself from the rough stuff.

In 1927, he married Esther Krakower, the sister of Whitey Krakower, one of his gunmen. He and Esther had two daughters. He was an amiable and doting family man when he was home, which was less and less often, due to the long hours he spent working his rackets and the time he put in romancing a string of showgirls and similarly attractive femmes. He was a handsome man and a sharp dresser. He took long daily showers and had his hair trimmed and nails manicured every day. He had a liking for houndstooth-checked sport jackets, expensive shirts and slacks, and custom shoes. He was a real gangland dandy.

Luciano's links with the Bug and Meyer mob would prove crucial in the watershed year of 1931, as the Mafia's Castellammarese War (a Mafia conflict between two stubborn mob bosses, Joe "the Boss" Masseria and Salvatore Maranzano) neared its climax. One of Luciano's major points of dispute with his chief, Masseria, was Masseria's aversion toward cooperative ventures with other mobsters outside their gang. Joe the Boss, unable to cooperate with rival Sicilian mobsters (as his feud with Don Maranzano had so disastrously demonstrated), was even less inclined to combine with Italian, Jewish, or Irish gangs. Luciano had already profited from co-ventures with Lepke and the Lansky-Siegel mob. He figured he stood to make a lot more money working with them than he would as Masseria's underboss.

On April 15, 1931, Luciano neatly arranged the assassination of Joe the Boss. The shooters who did the deed at Scarpato's Restaurant in Coney Island have been identified by some sources as future mafia bosses Albert Anastasia, Vito Genovese, Joe Adonis, and Bugsy Siegel.

Six months later saw the liquidation of would-be Boss of Bosses

Maranzano, in a hit ramrodded by Bo Weinberg, Dutch Schultz's top gun, and seconded by several shooters from the Bug and Meyer gang.

A new era began when Luciano put into operation Maranzano's blueprint for the Mafia, recognizing the five families' overlordship of organized crime in New York and, through the establishment of the ruling Commission, over the prime principalities and territories of Underworld, USA.

On the night of November 12, 1931, a routine roust by police of a gathering of nine suspicious characters in a New York hotel resulted in one of Bugsy's few arrests. The roster of those present for the meeting was a real rogue's gallery, including not only Siegel but also Lepke and Lepke's brutish partner, Jacob "Gurrah" Shapiro; as well as other future Murder, Inc. star performers such as Harry "Big Greenie" Greenberg, narcotics dealer Curly Holtz, and gambler and gangster Joseph "Doc" Stacher. The arrest was a Mickey Mouse affair and one that was easily shrugged off by the participants, against whom no charges were filed.

More worrisome was a gang war in 1934 that pitted Siegel and company against Philadelphia-based gangster and dope czar Irving "Waxey" Gordon and his lieutenant "Chink" Sherman.

Siegel wasn't so lucky with his recent meetings. One November night, he was in conclave in a room with some of his men when a bomb was dropped down the chimney. The infernal device snagged somewhere in the chimney and blew before falling into the fireplace, causing Siegel to escape the blast with a relatively minor scalp injury.

He was treated for his wound at Gouverneur Hospital in downtown Manhattan, checking into a private room for some recuperation. He learned that the man behind the bomb plot was Tony Fabrizzo, two of whose brothers had been slain in the dope war. Coincidentally, Fabrizzo was part of the two-man team that in 1932 had eliminated Vincent "Mad Dog" Coll on behalf of Dutch Schultz.

The following night, after visiting hours at the hospital were over and the nurses had finished making their rounds, Siegel got dressed and slipped unobserved through the corridors and out of the building. Standing nearby was a car with two of his gunmen in it.

They drove across the Brooklyn Bridge to the Fabrizzo family house. The two gunmen got out while Siegel waited in the car. They rang the front door bell. The door was opened by one of Fabrizzo's older male relatives. The strangers identified themselves as detectives. The relative went back inside and got Tony, who came to the door. The gunmen shot him to death, got back in the car, and drove away.

The vehicle dropped Siegel off near the hospital, and he sneaked back in, remaining unseen and unnoticed. He went to his room and climbed back into his hospital bed, secure in the knowledge that he now had an ironclad alibi for the Fabrizzo kill.

Siegel was pals with Bo Weinberg, Dutch Schultz's top gun. When the Dutchman was in upstate New York fighting his tax trials, Siegel had been one of those who'd urged Bo to grab Schultz's rackets while the getting was good. Weinberg had no reason to suspect Siegel of treachery or even of harboring any ill intentions against him.

What he didn't know was that Siegel had taken a contract from Schultz to kill Weinberg. This element of trust made Siegel the ideal choice to hit Bo, according to the cruel and remorseless logic of mob murder.

Sometime in September 1935, when the car in which they were out riding around together was safely pulled over on a dark side street, Siegel made the strike, stabbing Weinberg to death and then dumping his body, wired with weights, into the East River.

Another version is that Siegel delivered Bo alive to Schultz, who had Weinberg's legs encased in cement and then dropped him alive into the river. Schultz himself was later liquidated by another "buggy" shooter, Murder, Inc.'s Charles "the Bug" Workman.

The underworld was turned upside down in 1936, when District Attorney Thomas E. Dewey successfully prosecuted Luciano for bossing the city's prostitution rackets. Luciano was convicted of "extortion and direction of harlotry" and sentenced from thirty to fifty years in prison. He was incarcerated at Clinton State Prison in Dannemora, a site so remote from New York City as to make far-distant Albany seem accessible by comparison.

Meyer Lansky reportedly swore that he would somehow succeed in springing Luciano from prison. The prospect seemed doubtful but if anyone could accomplish it, the Commission reasoned, it would be the wily and capable Lansky. In the meantime, Luciano continued to exert his rule from behind bars, his will carried out first by his underboss Vito Genovese and later, Frank Costello. The strength of the organizational infrastructure Luciano had estab-lished became clear as the five families and Commission continued to operate uninterruptedly in his absence.

Dewey's assault on the mob was far from done, as he now turned his sights on Lepke, who went into hiding. Witnesses and persons suspected of being potential weak links were murderously purged to prevent their testifying for Dewey.

A number of gangsters left town in 1937, removing themselves from the reach of Dewey's subpoenas. One such voluntary exile was Ben Siegel, who was not only leaving but also going places.

He was on a mission to consolidate and expand the Commission's West Coast operations. Home base would be the city of Los Angeles, California. Siegel was excited about going to Hollywoodland. He memorably quipped, "There may not be many virgins out there, but it's virgin territory for us."

If by "us" he meant the New York combination, he was right. The five families had yet to begin properly exploiting the assets of the Golden State. California was hardly without organized crime, however.

The Mafia had been established throughout the state since the start of the twentieth century. Los Angeles had its own Mafia boss, a tough one, the grimly efficient Jack Dragna. Born Anthony Rizzoti in the town of Corleone near Palermo, Sicily, he'd made his way through the California underworld, acquiring a well-earned reputa-tion as a deadly and inexorable gang killer and enforcer.

The Commission made it clear that Siegel was to be in charge, with Dragna taking on a kind of subsidiary or secondary role. He may not have liked it, but Dragna wasn't the type to sound off about it. His supreme allegiance was to the Mafia, and when its ruling board decreed that he relinquish the top spot to the man from New York, he followed those orders in his usual stolidly efficient, tight-lipped manner.

Once in California, Siegel wasted no time in battening on to boyhood chum George Raft, now a genuine movie star who specialized in playing raffish gangster types. Raft was happy to serve as Siegel's entrée into Hollywood society, introducing his pal Ben as a "big man from back east." Siegel preferred to refer to himself as a "sportsman."

Siegel made a big splash with the Hollywood elite, cultivating the acquaintance of such folk as studio boss Jack Warner, heiress Barbara Hutton, actors Cary Grant and Gary Cooper, and "platinum bombshell" Jean Harlow, among others.

It was a classic case of what's now called "gangster chic," a phenomenon with a long history. Siegel fit right in, with his movie-star good looks, athletic physique, and breezy manner. The dark side of his personality was kept hidden, except during those times when someone called him "Bugsy" to his face, triggering violent outbursts.

He leased a spectacular Beverly Hills mansion for his wife and daughters. He joined a gym, where daily workouts helped keep him in shape. He bedded a succession of starlets and other beautiful women. He took to the lifestyle like he'd been born to it. Los Angeles was his kind of town.

His Hollywood sojourn was not all fun and games, though. There was work to be done. He looked around to see where to first put the bite.

Labor racketeering was always surefire. Los Angeles was a company town. The company was the motion picture industry. Unhappily for Siegel and the East Coast interests he represented, the real action at the studios had already been sewn up by the Mafia's Chicago branch, widely known as the "Outfit."

The Chicago mob had taken over the International Alliance of Theatrical Stage Employees and Motion Picture Operators (IATSE), gaining a stranglehold over movie theaters nationwide. The threat of a crippling strike was used to extort vast sums of protection money from the studio heads. The Outfit's man in Hollywood, gangster Willie Bioff, worked hand in glove with IATSE union boss George Browne.

There's more than one way to skin a studio head, though. Siegel fastened on to the stage extras' union. The extras were bit players, those faces in the crowd in the background. They were in every movie, and all the studios used them. Siegel put the squeeze on them, forcing them to pay for the opportunity to go before the cameras. He used Dragna's boys to supply the infrastructural organization and muscle.

He was not yet done. A job action or strike by the extras' union could send studio productions grinding to a very expensive halt. Siegel shook down the studio bosses for protection money against such an eventuality, working up an extortion racket that netted him a very respectable $400,000 a year.

Proving that all was grist for his mill, Siegel also wangled a series of so-called loans from a number of his male and female movie star chums. These sums, totaling many thousands of dollars, would of course never be repaid.

The Commission had charged Bugsy with expanding opportunities in gambling and narcotics. Siegel acquired a piece of an offshore gambling ship and a dog track. A prime source of funds was the wire service business, a key component of offtrack gambling and bookmaking operations.

At that time, it was legal to bet on a horse race only at the track. Offtrack bets made with bookmakers were illegal—a minor technicality that scarcely impeded gamblers and bookies.

A wire service was a business that leased telegraph lines and used them to transmit up-to-the-minute information about everything that could affect the betting odds at various race tracks holding a race on a given day. This included the rapidly changing last-minute odds on the races, scratches, jockey substitutions, track conditions, and so on. This information was vital to bookmakers, allowing them to adjust the odds and to lay off much of the risk of a heavy favorite coming in and decimating their bankroll. It also protected against the scam of past-posting, in which chiselers took advantage of the time lag between the real time in which a race was held versus the delay in finding out the winner, allowing them to bet on horses that had already successfully run the race. Though subject to periodic pressure and scrutiny from the authorities, it was legal to run a wire service operation.

When Siegel was in California, the leading nationwide wire service was the Continental Press Service. The Continental operated out of Chicago, where it had a fitful and troubled working relationship with the Outfit.

The Outfit lusted to take over the service, lock, stock, and barrel, but so far had allowed itself to be placated by vast sums of protection money paid yearly by Continental. Always willing to tighten the screws another turn, the Chicago mob organized its own competing wire service, the Trans-America Press Service. It pirated its information from Continental and sold it to bookmakers. Mafia ownership of Trans-America presented a persuasive sales element to survival-minded bookies.

Siegel was responsible for pushing Trans-America in the West. The Siegel-Dragna combine hammered the bookies into dropping Continental and taking the mob wire. Stubborn holdouts were beaten or shot as a warning to others.

This was serious business. It has been estimated that during the period of the 1940s and 1950s, wire service–related killings accounted for 50 percent of all gangland murders.

Another moneyspinner was narcotics. It generated big money that was tough to resist, despite the risk of heavy federal prison terms for trafficking. In Hollywood, the dope racket was as old as the film colony itself. Drugs were much used and craved by talent on both sides of the camera, and in the administrative offices and executive suites, too. A Lansky associate and veteran narcotics racket hand established a new drug pipeline connecting Mexico to Los Angeles. Siegel babysat the pipeline, nursing it and watching it grow.

All work and no play was for chumps, not for Ben Siegel. A notable conquest was socialite Countess Dorothy di Frasso, an heiress who'd married an Italian count. She described Siegel as "a perfect gentleman . . . a charming, delightful young man." He accompanied her on more than one tour of Italy's chicest watering holes and pleasure spas.

They became involved in a bizarre treasure-hunting scheme along with Marino Bello, the manipulative and scheming father-in-law of the recently deceased movie sex goddess Jean Harlow. Bello claimed to have a treasure map indicating the location of $90 million in loot, buried on an island off Costa Rica.

He, Siegel, and the Countess all set sail for their destination on a yacht stocked with gangsters, rogues, and seadogs—and plenty of booze. The ship made a rowdy, lurching sea cruise into stormy waters. Brawls, binges, and a near mutiny marked the trip, which culminated in the spectacle of a sorry bunch of hungover hoodlums digging up the island beaches in a vain search for treasure, only to collapse prostrate under the tropical heat.

Siegel's Hollywood idylls received a rude awakening in 1939 courtesy of the ongoing Dewey probes in New York and of the wayward conduct of one of his old Murder, Inc. cohorts. The irritant was Harry "Big Greenie" Greenberg, a veteran killer who'd been part of the same exodus a few years earlier that had sent Siegel out west.

Big Greenie had gone north to Canada. With his funds running out, he'd sent a dunning note to the boys back in New York, demanding that they send him some money and intimating that if they didn't, he might have a thing or two to tell Tom Dewey.

Lepke had eliminated men for much less. He wanted very much to be rid of Big Greenie. Greenberg stayed a step or two ahead of the hunters, slipping back into the United States and eventually surfacing in, of all places, Los Angeles, California. He was marked for death and Siegel would be only too happy to oblige. Through Dragna's organization, Siegel had the town wired, and it wasn't long before he'd turned up the locale of Greenberg's hideout.

New York sent out an emissary to help with the hit, none other than the redoubtable Allie "Tick-Tock" Tannenbaum, then in his heyday as a well-respected professional killer.

That wasn't enough for Siegel. He wanted to handle the hit himself, to demonstrate that he still had the stuff to do the big job. Taking charge of the mission, he more or less relegated Allie to the backseat.

The hit went down on the night of November 22, 1939—Thanksgiving Eve. The participants were Siegel, rising hoodlum Frankie Carbo, Harry "Champ" Segal, and Tannenbaum. Whitey Krakower, Siegel's brother-in-law, stole a vehicle that would be used as the murder car.

Hard logic and good sense mandated against Siegel's taking part in the hit. A mainstay of Luciano's overhaul of the Mafia was the insulation of the top bosses from direct involvement in the down and dirty routine lawbreaking of underworld street soldiers. Let the underlings take the risk and the jail terms, securing the higher-ups from arrest and conviction.

The Jewish Siegel was no mafioso, of course, nor were Lepke or Lansky, but all three were subject to Commission rule. The bottom line, though, was that results trumped risk. If a gang boss's participation was necessary to carry out a Commission-approved hit, then so be it.

Siegel liked the action. And there was another calculation involved. By demonstrating his continuing and ready ability to kill, he proclaimed to any potential challengers or usurpers that he remained a tough and dangerous adversary.

Big Greenie had found a hole to hide in near Hollywood and Vine. He laid low for most of the night and day, often emerging only to pick up the day's paper. The killers caught him out in the open, sitting in his parked car and reading a newspaper. They put the blast on him. Frankie Carbo, in later years to gain infamy as the mob's top crooked promoter of fixed boxing matches, is believed to have done the actual shooting.

Siegel's boys-night-out on the Greenberg kill would return to plague him a year later in 1940 with the onset of Abe "Kid Twist" Reles's exhaustive aria on Murder, Inc. doings to Brooklyn's Assistant District Attorney Burton Turkus.

Reles helped put the finger on Tannenbaum, who turned himself and also began singing in the choir. Allie told of the Big Greenie hit and Siegel's participation in it. Siegel was potentially out on a limb, more dangerously exposed to the law than he had been in years.

In June of that year, Whitey Krakower was killed in a drive-by shooting in Brooklyn. That was one less loose end for Siegel to worry about. Krakower's demise was cause for sincere grief by George Raft, who'd loaned Ben's brother-in-law several thousand dollars a month earlier.

Turkus's boss, Brooklyn D.A. William O'Dwyer, had Tannenbaum and Reles secretly flown out to Los Angeles under heavy guard to testify before a grand jury about the Greenberg kill.

The jurors handed down an indictment for murder against Siegel, Carbo, and Segal. Siegel was arrested and jailed, but apparently his confinement was none too onerous. Besides receiving VIP treatment in the Los Angeles County Jail that included catered meals brought in from fancy eateries, Siegel was also observed dining with actress Wendy Barrie in a Hollywood restaurant when he was supposed to be behind bars. The scandal triggered a big publicity splash but not much came of it.

The same could be said of the investigation. When Los Angeles investigators went to New York to interview Tannenbaum and Reles, they were stalled and given the runaround by the Brooklyn D.A.'s office until they gave up in disgust and returned home.

O'Dwyer was deadset against sending the two star witnesses on another trip to California, offering as a reason his fear that they would not be as well protected as they were under his stewardship. He flew west to confer with the Los Angeles district attorney. A short time later, the charges against Siegel were dropped. No corroboration was the reason given.

The episode was matched by another curious case of obstructionism from O'Dwyer's office, namely the delay in bringing Abe Reles before the grand jury to testify on the record against Albert Anastasia.

Many found the delay suspicious, not least of them Assistant D.A. Turkus, who in his memoirs a decade later expressed the feeling that there had been something funny going on with his boss.

Reles was thrown out the window of Coney Island's Half-Moon Hotel on November 11, 1941, effectively killing the Anastasia investigation along with its star witness (Reles's murder was never solved).

In California, a new grand jury again charged Siegel and Frankie Carbo with Big Greenie's murder. The death of Reles had taken a lot of the heat off them, nullifying his testimony that Murder, Inc.'s Emanuel "Mendy" Weiss had ordered Greenberg's murder.

Allie Tannenbaum was flown out for the trial in the early months of 1942, testifying to no effect whatsoever, especially when Siegel's defense counsel, famed Hollywood lawyer Jerry Geisler, had finished his blistering cross-examination of the Tick-Tock man. The case was thrown out, and Siegel was a free man again. Frankie Carbo beat the rap, too, but went down for other, unrelated criminal offenses and wound up doing some prison time.

The World War II era was a bonanza for organized crime. Scarcity breeds corruption, and a black market flourished in such wartime-rationed commodities as tires, gas, and red meat. The mob could supply that demand.

Then as now, in wartime national security issues trumped local concerns. A prime area of military interest was the New York waterfront, one of the world's great ports and a rich target for enemy spies and saboteurs. The security issue was underlined with the burning of the *Normandie*, an ocean liner that had been converted to a troop ship and was consumed in a suspicious dockside blaze.

From this incident developed one of the most shadowy and obscure affairs in twentieth-century American history: the formation of an alliance between U.S. military intelligence and the Mafia. This military-intelligence mission was labeled "Operation Underworld." Its existence was a closely guarded secret and even today, over sixty years since it first began, many critical details of the alliance remain hidden, buried in sealed, classified files. Naval

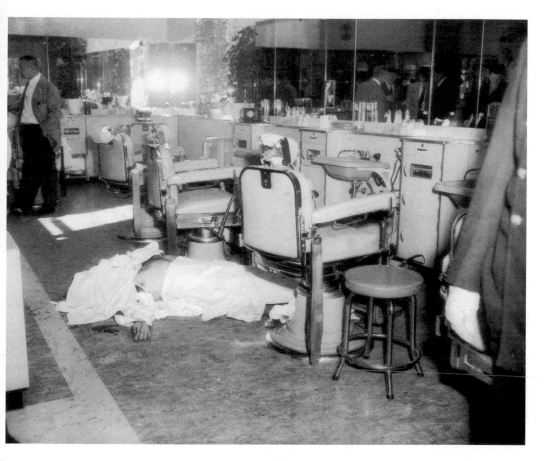

"I SAID JUST A LITTLE OFF THE TOP!"
The body of Mafia boss Albert "the Mad Hatter" Anastasia on the floor of the
barbershop at New York's Park Central Hotel after his murder in October 1957.
Anastasia's murder was engineered by Vito Genovese and Carlo Gambino, paving the
way for Gambino to take over the Mad Hatter's *borgata*, or crime family. Half a century
later, the Gambino family is still a major presence in organized crime.
(AP Wide World Photos)

LAST EXIT IN BROOKLYN

Mourners gather at the grave of Albert Anastasia as curious rubberneckers line the gates of Greenwood Cemetery to view the funeral on October 28, 1957. Anastasia was also known as the "Lord High Executioner" for organizing and supervising the mob's in-house hit team in the 1930s, which came to be known as Murder, Inc.

(AP Wide World Photos)

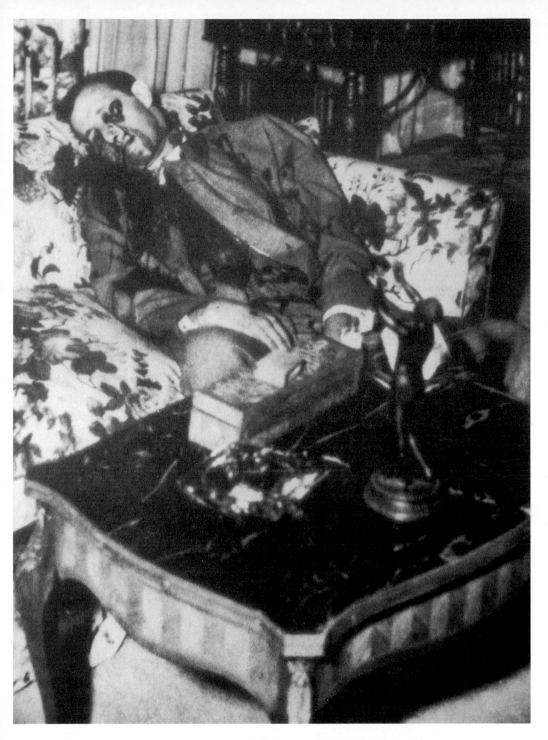

"ANYBODY SEEN AN EYEBALL?"
Benjamin "Bugsy" Siegel shortly after being gunned down in the living room of the
home belonging to his girlfriend, Virginia Hill, on June 20, 1946, in Beverly Hills.
(AP Wide World Photos)

"CHECK, PLEASE!"
The bloodied body of Mafia boss Carmine "Lillo" Gigante, the cigar still clenched
between his teeth, lies on the floor of the backyard garden of Joe and Mary's Restaurant
in Brooklyn, on July 12, 1979. Carmine was threatening to kill rival mob bosses Tommy
Lucchese and Carlo Gambino among others, but they beat him to the punch.
(AP Wide World Photos)

"BUT I LEFT A 25 PERCENT TIP!"

New York's Finest carry the body of Carmine "Lillo" Gigante from the murder scene,
July 12, 1979. In a bold example of truth in advertising, note the bottom of the
restaurant's sign: "We give special attention to outgoing orders." *(AP Wide World Photos)*

"IT'S OKAY, I CAN WALK TO THE CURB FROM HERE."
The bodies of Gambino family crime boss Paul Castellano (*right*, next to pole) and his bodyguard Thomas Bilotti (*left*, covered by sheet) lie next to the limo from which they were emerging on December 16, 1985, when they were gunned down in midtown Manhattan. The hitters were all members of John Gotti's crew. Castellano's death paved the way for Gotti to become boss of bosses of the Gambino family.
(AP Wide World Photos)

URBAN SPRAWL
Paul Castellano's bodyguard Thomas Bilotti lies dead on the street after being gunned down on December 16, 1985, outside Sparks Steak House on East 46th Street. Sparks' business tripled after the hits, prompting a neighboring restaurant owner to comment, "If I'd known how famous Sparks would get after this, I'd have dragged Castellano's body in front of my place." *(AP Wide World Photos)*

GALLO WHINE
Pallbearers carry the body of Joey Gallo into St. Charles Church in Brooklyn on
April 10, 1972. Gallo declared war on the Profaci crime family. He lost.

Intelligence and later, elements of the Office of Strategic Services, a wartime civilian intelligence agency that became the forerunner of the Central Intelligence Agency (CIA), worked the operation, communicating primarily through go-betweens to their contacts in the mob.

Because of the ultra-secrecy that surrounded it, the origin and background of the alliance are obscure, and what information that is on the record may or may not be salted with disinformation, half-truths, and lies. The basics are these: Someone in Naval Intelligence got the idea that the Mafia could do what law enforcement couldn't; namely, police the sprawling and strategically vital New York waterfront and protect it from spies and saboteurs. They may have gotten this idea from Meyer Lansky and his lawyer, who were both present at the creation and at the center of the alliance throughout its run.

Naval Intelligence first made covert arrangements with Fulton Fish Market boss Joseph "Socks" Lanza to tighten up dockside security. But Lanza complained that he was stretched too thin and that he was unable to command the respect and influence needed to get the various waterfront gangs to cooperate in the great patriotic venture. Such influence could be commanded only by one man, the boss in all but title. Lucky Luciano.

At this point, a cynic might well be forgiven for wondering if the *Normandie* was torched not by Axis agents, but by Luciano loyalists trying to sell the navy on the reality of a sabotage threat. Did the Mafia burn the *Normandie*? In his autobiography, Luciano claims that this is the case. The mob would have done a lot more than that to get Luciano out of jail, but the identity of the arsonists remains unknown.

Luciano was contacted in prison and agreed to cooperate with the intelligence agents. Soon after, he was moved from the Dannemora site ("Siberia," the inmates called it) to confinement in an Albany prison, where he was more accessible to Naval Intelligence officers and their go-betweens, as well as to his lawyers and selected mob associates.

The arrangement proved to be of mutual benefit to both parties. Spies and saboteurs were absent from or at least neutralized on the

New York docks for the duration of the war. Also of value to the war effort was Luciano's delivering of the cooperation of Sicilian mafiosi when American troops invaded the island to liberate it from the Nazis.

After the war, in 1946, the seemingly impossible became a reality. Tom Dewey, the man who'd sent Luciano to prison and who was now the governor of New York, paroled Luciano by commuting his sentence to time spent.

Dewey's motivation for the release remains a question. Was it because of large campaign contributions made to him by Frank Costello, as underworld insiders alleged? Was it through the influence of military intelligence, paying off its part of the bargain for Operation Underworld by having Luciano set free? Was it a combination of both. Or was it some other, as yet unknown factor?

The fact was that Luciano was out of prison and immediately due to be out of the country, too, for good. That was part of the package, the sting in the tail of his release.

The Sicilian-born Luciano had never become a citizen of the United States. The U.S. government was therefore deporting him back to his home country of origin. This was a strategy that had been successfully used on other foreign-born gangsters who'd neglected to become U.S. citizens.

Luciano was deported to Sicily, soon winning permission from the authorities for him to live on the Italian mainland. He was still the boss. Mobsters from the States visited him regularly, delivering suitcases full of money and returning home with his orders for the organization.

In a return to his dope-peddling roots, Luciano helped orchestrate the rising heroin trade, funneling raw opium to clandestine refineries in Italy, Sicily, Corsica, and Marseilles, where it was processed into white powder and transshiped to the United States.

Operation Underworld had ended—officially—with the war's end. In reality, the dangerous liaision between U.S. government spy agencies and the Mafia would continue for decades more.

*   *   *

In 1941, as part of his mandate to push the Trans-America Press Service, Ben Siegel had spent some time in Las Vegas, Nevada, "persuading" local bookies to take the service. This visit saw the birth of the germ of an idea that would eventually grow to such titanic proportions as to possess the mind and soul of Ben Siegel, becoming an obsession that drove him to make history and in the process, seal his own doom.

Not until 1945, however, was he ready to make that dream a reality. One of his first confidantes on that score was Meyer Lansky, his childhood buddy and the man who would be instrumental in lining up the financing to actualize that dream.

Siegel envisioned a first-class casino-hotel to be built in Las Vegas, Nevada, something chic, swank, and expensive, something along the lines of an American Monte Carlo.

The town itself already had a gambling district with a Wild West, sawdust-on-the-floor flavor. Siegel planned to build his edifice outside of town, on a piece of land along Highway 91 outside the city limits: the genesis of the future Las Vegas Strip.

The concept did not actually originate with Siegel, but was the brainchild of one of his nonmob chums, Billy Wilkerson, the publisher of the *Hollywood Reporter*. Wilkerson had actually bought the land for the site several years earlier but was unable to capitalize on it. Siegel acquired the property as the tract on which to build his pleasure dome.

It would be a class joint, top-shelf all the way. A monument to Ben Siegel and to the new lady in his life.

She was Virginia Hill, a lusty call girl, mob courier, go-between, and one of the world's "great lays," as she unblushingly described herself in later years while testifying under oath before the U.S. Senate's Kafauver Committee investigating organized crime.

Ginny Hill was born in Alabama in 1916, one of ten children of a marble polisher and his wife. It was a hardscrabble existence, one she was quick to leave behind. She matured early and showed no hesitation in using what nature had given her as her ticket to a better life.

A redhead with a beautiful body and a master of sexpertise, she wound up in Chicago, where she became the longtime girlfriend of mobster Joseph Epstein, a financial wizard and paymaster for the Outfit. Ginny refused to let her relationship with Epstein tie her down to one man; many top mobsters enjoyed her favors, most notably Joe Adonis, the sinister and powerful "Mr. A." of the Brooklyn mob.

It was perhaps inevitable that sooner or later she would cross paths with Ben Siegel. Sparks were struck and little time was wasted on preliminaries before beginning their epic copulations. For the rest of her life, she maintained that the sex she'd had with Siegel was the best of her life.

They were a good match for each other, so good that Mrs. Siegel was provoked into filing for divorce from her wayward spouse. She'd stood for plenty, but enough was enough. Siegel readily acceded to her terms, paying generous monthly alimony support. With his wife shucked, he could devote all his amorous attention to Virginia.

Her red hair and long legs had given her the nickname of "Flamingo." The gangster planned to name his gambling showplace "Ben Siegel's Flamingo Hotel." In the end, it was called the Flamingo Hotel.

Lansky readily grasped the potential, using his clout with the Commission to secure several million dollars' worth of building funds. He and Frank Costello set up an intricate financial structure whereby the mob's investment in the casino would be hidden from the state, as well as from legitimate investors who held a noncontrolling minority share.

Siegel began building in 1946, but he couldn't have picked a worse time for construction. In the immediate postwar environment, there was a shortage of necessary building materials, supplies, and skilled laborers. Much of the raw materials had to be trucked in from out of state. He demanded the finest stone, timber, and marble and paid top-dollar for it. He also paid top wages to keep masons, electricians, plumbers, and suchlike crews working at top speed to finish the job.

Yet delays mounted. Supplies were stolen. Costs escalated, spiraling. The Flamingo was a sponge soaking up money. Mob money.

Lansky knew that one had to spend money to make money and arranged for another major infusion of Mafia funds.

Problems continued to multiply. Money pressures forced Siegel to open the casino prematurely. He'd planned to open the casino-hotel simultaneously, harvesting big bundles of cash through the rental of pricey rooms to high-rolling gamblers. Instead, he opened the casino before the rooms were ready for occupancy.

A gala premiere had been planned for the grand opening on December 26, 1946, with planeloads of Hollywood celebrities being flown into Las Vegas for the occasion. But a storm squall over the mountains grounded the planes and only half of the celebrities ultimately showed up, after first having endured the rigors of a lengthy train ride. Siegel loyalist George Raft was present, to be sure, and entertainment was provided by stellar attraction Jimmy Durante, but despite that, the opening was widely and fairly accurately described as a flop by the Hollywood and showbiz press.

Discontented rumblings began to be heard from the Commission as ill luck continued to dog the Flamingo. Now, improbably, the casino was losing money, its funds decimated by lucky gamblers. This, in a business where the house has the edge or it has nothing. Against all the odds, the gamblers were winning and the house was losing. Or so Siegel said.

His claim was met with no little skepticism by the increasingly dubious members of the Commission. They had trouble believing that a steady run of bad luck at the tables was what was putting the Flamingo in the red. Even if the dealers and croupiers had been larceny-minded and working with the big winners, it was tough to picture them ripping off Ben Siegel in Ben Siegel's casino with impunity. The suspicion was that the so-called shortage was probably a Siegel scam designed to rip off the mob's money.

The delays and cost overruns associated with the Flamingo would have driven to distraction a more even-tempered individual than Bugsy Siegel, whose increasing public displays of rage and violence were making waves and generating bad publicity.

*　*　*

Siegel met his Waterloo not because of the Flamingo, but primarily because of his stance on the Trans-America Press Service.

In 1946 in Chicago, the Outfit's troubled hands-off policy regarding the Continental Press Service came to an end, as mobsters pressured owner James Ragen to sell. They were not minded to take no for an answer. They offered to buy him out completely or buy in at a 40 percent stake.

Ragen argued that their direct involvement with the Continental would bring the wrath of J. Edgar Hoover and his FBI down on their heads, ultimately destroying the service on which nationwide illegal bookmaking depended. Unimpressed, the Chicago mob made it clear to Ragen in no uncertain terms that he'd better play ball.

Instead, Ragen went to the FBI, offering to cooperate. Top Cop Hoover generally steered clear of organized crime cases for a number of reasons, not least of which was the difficulty of making headway and getting convictions, which would damage his G-men's reputation for crimebusting efficiency. Ragen's dilemma was too good to resist.

The Outfit moved hard against Ragen, eventually trapping him on June 24, 1946, in a streetside ambush. Ragen, while driving his car, was being tailed by a second car containing his bodyguards. A tarpaulin-covered truck pulled up alongside him. Beneath the tarp lay a trio of mob executioners, who emptied shotguns into Ragen's vehicle. Ragen's bodyguards returned fire, but the truck got away. When it was found later, it was discovered that the rear of the truck had been equipped with a sheet of bulletproof armor as protection against Ragen's defenders. Ragen crashed his car but survived the shooting, though critically wounded.

The shooters were identified as the frontline extermination team of Dave Yaras, Lenny Patrick, and William Block. All three were stone killers who specialized in Mafia hits.

Yaras was an enforcer for old-time Capone associate and political payoff czar Jake "Greasy Thumb" Guzik. A crony of International

Brotherhood of Teamsters boss Jimmy Hoffa, Yaras was later instrumental in founding the union's Local 320 in Miami, Florida.

Lenny Patrick has been described as a "Chicago mob execution expert" and high-ranking nonmember Mafia associate. Like Yaras, he was also linked to the Teamsters and to Chicago Mafia chief Sam Giancana.

William Block's background is more obscure, but it's certain that he was a veteran pro hitman and contract killer.

Yaras, Patrick, and Block were high-level hitmen at the top of their profession. Ragen was lucky to survive their assault. He lingered for some weeks in a hospital bed surrounded by a police guard stationed there to protect him. He rallied, seeming to recover, only to swiftly fail and expire.

An autopsy revealed that he'd died from mercury poisoning, with which someone on the staff had been surreptiously dosing him. The poisoner was never found. The case against Yaras, Patrick, and Block ceased to exist.

With Ragen dead, the Outfit took over the long-desired Continental Press Service. Now that they had the real thing, there was no more need to run the competing Trans-America service. In fact, there was every reason for closing it down, as it was costing them money for every moment it continued in operation.

On the West Coast, Ben Siegel didn't see it that way and kept Trans-America in business, collecting a lion's share of the profits. He needed the money, every cent, to offset the Flamingo's hemorrhaging of funds.

The Outfit vehemently protested. Siegel countered, arguing that Trans-America was a valuable going concern and offering to sell it for a cool $2 million. This at a time when he'd already sunk millions of mob money in the red ink-spilling Flamingo project with no slightest signs yet of return.

Even more than the financial funny business at the Flamingo, it was Siegel's machinations with the wire service that put him in the wrong with the rest of the syndicate. That, and his insulting and aggressive responses to mob bosses Lansky, Costello, and Adonis when called to account for the ever mounting financial debacle.

Rumors flew. One story had it that Siegel planned to sell out his interest in the Flamingo for big bucks, quit the mob, and go off to live in luxury somewhere overseas in Europe with Virginia Hill.

A special meeting to address the problem was convened in December 1946 in Havana. A number of Commission members attended, but the motivating force of the conclave was the presence of Lucky Luciano. The terms of his deportment mandated that he stay in Italy, but Luciano was unwilling to let a minor detail like that hamper his freedom of movement.

Ben Siegel was high in the ranks of Mafia associates. Any action taken against him would have to be a board decision. The Commission looked to Luciano for guidance.

Siegel flew in to meet Luciano, who demanded that Siegel repay $3 million in mob money. Siegel flew off the handle, telling Luciano where to get off. Ben Siegel was afraid of no man. But he wasn't bucking a man, he was bucking an organization, one that held no man indispensable. Nonmade guys such as Siegel were even more expendable.

Meyer Lansky, who by all accounts loved Siegel like a son, tried to intercede on behalf of his longtime partner. It was a measure of the respect in which Lansky was held by the Commission in general and Luciano in particular that Siegel had lasted as long as he had.

Lansky's intercession bought Siegel some more time, but if Siegel was aware that the clock was running out, he didn't show it. He remained as stubborn, greedy, and intransigent as ever.

After the disastrous December opening, Siegel closed the Flamingo for several months, while construction continued on the hotel. He reopened in March 1947. Business began to improve, and in May the casino turned a $300,000 profit. Ben Siegel's big gamble was paying off after all.

The Hits

Siegel and Virginia Hill had always been a fractious couple, alternately boozing, brawling, and loving. They fought like cats and dogs and then made up by going at it like a couple of tigers in heat.

In early June 1947, things got out of hand and Siegel walloped Ginny more violently than usual, beating her so badly that she would require plastic surgery to repair her face. She followed that up by swallowing too many pills—not her first botched suicide attempt. She and Siegel made up a week or so later, but there was still plenty of strain between them.

Ginny had been in the habit of shuttling back and forth between Las Vegas and California. When she was in Los Angeles, she stayed in a rented mansion, a Moorish castle located on 810 North Linden Drive in Beverly Hills. Now, she told Siegel that she had to get away for a while and that she was going to Europe. She offered to let him stay at her house while she was away. On June 16, she departed.

Siegel was in Las Vegas on June 20, flying into Los Angeles in midday. He went to the house on Linden Drive. With him was Allen Smiley, a self-styled "movie director," marginal Hollywood character, and hanger-on.

Staying at the house at that time was Virginia Hill's younger brother, Chuck Hill, and his girlfriend, Jerri Nason. They planned to leave the next day to get married in Las Vegas.

Siegel, Smiley, Hill, and Nason went out for dinner, returning to Linden Drive at about 11:00 P.M. Hill and Nason went upstairs to their room to pack. Siegel and Smiley lounged around downstairs in the living room.

The living room drapes were open, affording a clear sightline into the house. Normally, they were closed. Siegel sat on a couch, reading the *Los Angeles Times*.

Shots erupted. So did Siegel's head. The first round blew out his right eye. The next two ventilated his skull. Four more shots were fired, harmlessly hitting the wall.

Ben Siegel was dead, slain by a shooter armed with a 30-30 carbine, a high-velocity rifle with a short stock and barrel. The killer was a marksman, placing the three slugs in Siegel's head closely together.

With skills like that, it may be assumed that if he'd wanted to shoot Allen Smiley, too, he wouldn't have missed. Possibly the four extra shots were made to sow confusion in advance of the killer's getaway.

It was ironic that Siegel, so vain of his good looks, should have had them shot to pieces. Or perhaps it was a message from the mob, an insulting one of the poetic justice variety.

Also ironic was that Siegel had gotten it unexpectedly while reading a newspaper, just as Big Greenie Greenberg had been doing when Ben helped put the chill on him.

Within minutes of Siegel's shooting, mobsters Moe Sedway and Gus Greenbaum barged into the Flamingo's casino offices and announced that they were taking over.

The following day, June 21, saw the arrival at the Flamingo of Joe Epstein, the Chicago Outfit's paymaster and, perhaps not so coincidentally, the solicitous sugar daddy of Virginia Hill. Ahead of him lay the big job of making sense of and straightening out the Flamingo's tangled financial accounts.

Virginia killed herself in 1966, at age fifty, depressed over being broke and lamenting her fading good looks.

STRATEGY

Not since Dutch Schultz had so high ranking a mobster as Ben Siegel acted with such reckless disregard for his own neck. Siegel's behavior near the end was not only erratic but also suicidal. He'd always had a high opinion of himself, but in recent years his delusions of grandeur had ripened into a dangerous megalomania.

His antics with the Flamingo and the Trans-America wire service were the last straw. He had refused the Mafia's dictate that he relinquish the wire service. Such defiance was a deadly affront to the Commission's authority. A cardinal sin. He might as well have tried to unilaterally secede from the law of gravity by jumping off a building.

Maybe Bugsy really was crazy, because a crazy man is unafraid. The only solution to such a man is death.

The Commission issued the order of execution. Most sources agree that the hit was handled out of Chicago. The Outfit, after all, was the offended party in the wire service beef. The high-powered hit team of Yaras, Patrick, and Block—the assassins of Regan—were given the contract. That was a strategic decision. Chicago was sending its killer elite to handle the big job.

Siegel was a dangerous man, but he lacked steady application. Some sources say that he knew the net was closing in on him, had been closing in on him for some time, and that on June 20, 1947, he'd left Las Vegas in fear for his life. Yet, during the day and that evening, he had no bodyguard in attendance.

The plotters' ace in the hole was Jack Dragna. Dragna was Mafia all the way. When the Commission had told him to vacate the top slot and back Siegel all the way, he'd done so without murmur. Now the wheel had come full circle, and Siegel was on the outs.

Dragna's organization was essential to Siegel's mastery of Los Angeles and the West Coast rackets. Without that support, Siegel would be critically handicapped. He would not even know that he'd been put on the spot until the moment of the final, fatal betrayal.

The plan was to hit Siegel hard and fast and at a time and place of the executioners' own liking.

STRATEGY: 5

TACTICS

The Chicago murder trio were inventive and not restricted to the classic mob tactic of shooting the mark at close quarters with a handgun. The Ragen kill with its drive-by shotgunning had proved that.

Yaras, Patrick, and Block were a top hit squad, cunning and adaptable to field conditions. They were sheltered and assisted in Los Angeles by the power and influence of the Dragna mob. This invaluable asset gave them a secure home base from which to operate. They had Dragna's organization's extensive resources working to monitor Siegel and keep track of his moves. They were aware of his comings and goings.

An interesting question is what if any foreknowledge of the hit was held by Virginia Hill.

Siegel was in Virginia's house when he was killed. She'd left for Europe four days earlier. The timing of her leave hardly seems coincidental. She was no dummy. She'd known for some time that Siegel's head was on the chopping block.

Was it intuition that prompted her to make herself scarce, or had she been tipped by an insider, someone like, say, her old friend from Chicago, Joe Epstein? It's unlikely, though, that she would have let her brother Chuck and his girlfriend remain in the house if she'd known that the hit was going to go down there. In any case, when the deed went down, she was out of the line of fire.

A number of cigarette butts were found on the ground outside the house, indicating that the shooter or his spotter had smoked them while staking out the site. This might have been done during the hours when Siegel and the others were away from the house eating dinner.

The smoking was a procedural error, since at night the tip of a lit cigarette can be seen from a long way off, while the smell of tobacco smoke drifting the wrong way could also have betrayed the lurkers' presence to chance passersby or the foursome returning to the house. This was clearly a slip up.

An interesting detail is the matter of the drapes. The custom of the house was for the living room drapes to be closed at night. They were open on the night of the murder. This can hardly be by sheer chance. It wasn't the killers who opened them; no evidence exists that they were ever in the house.

They could have been opened by any of the foursome inside the house at any time during the day and left that way into the night. Careless of Siegel not to have noticed it, though.

Had the drapes not been opened, providing clear sightlines and firing lines through the window at Siegel, the night's outcome might have been dramatically different. The kill might even have had to have been postponed for another time. But they were open, and that made all the difference.

The killers made their hit and got away clean. Nothing to fault in their tactics there.

Deduct 1 point for smoking on stakeout and leaving behind butts as possible clues.

TACTICS: 4

RESULTS

No great urgency on the part of the mob inspired the execution of Bugsy Siegel. It wasn't like the Maranzano slaying, a case of kill or be killed; it wasn't like Dutch Schultz's demise, a race against time to hit the Dutchman before he hit Tom Dewey and so triggered a reaction that would bring down the organization; and it wasn't like the timely elimination of a prosecutor's star witness as with Abe Reles.

Siegel was simply a high-up Mafia associate who forgot his place and paid for it with his life. His liquidation was a matter of internal policing and disciplinary example. If he could defy the Commission with impunity, others would inevitably follow his example, imperiling the whole monumental edifice of the national crime syndicate. Not even Lansky, Siegel's powerful and influential friend, could dispute the justice of the verdict.

Ben Siegel had outlived his time and had to go—and he went. He was killed and it was remarkable how little of lasting importance accrued to his passing.

It was a spectacular hit and generated massive press coverage but in the end it all blew over without too much official fuss. Despite the gaudy trimmings and Hollywood tinsel, the Siegel kill was basically a solidly planned and expertly carried out gangland execution: swift, brutal, and inexorable.

Jack Dragna, a man who shunned publicity and personal flamboyance as much as Ben Siegel courted it, reclaimed his position at the top of the Los Angeles mob. Siegel's bodyguard and enforcer

Mickey Cohen and several sidemen would dispute for mastery with Dragna but never posed any real threat to his supremacy.

Siegel burst on the West Coast underworld skies like a meteor, blazing bright and burning out fast. Dragna, built for the long haul, lasted.

As it turned out, for all its gaudy glitter, Los Angeles never really was Bugsy Siegel's town after all. It was Jack Dragna's.

RESULTS: 5

Murder Meter Box Score
    STRATEGY: 5
    TACTICS: 4
    RESULTS: 10

    TOTAL: 19

7

The Mad Hatter: Albert Anastasia

In February 1952, amateur crimebuster Arnold Shuster stumbled onto a lead that was the most wanted equivalent of a winning lottery ticket.

Shuster was twenty-four years old, an ex-Coast Guardsman, and a Brooklyn resident who worked as a pants presser in his family's tailor shop. His real passion, though, was law and order. He was a police buff, continually engrossed in true crime and detective magazines and radio programs.

On the wall near the stand where he pressed pants, he kept a number of FBI wanted circulars where he could study them by the hour. Prominently featured among them was Willie "the Actor" Sutton, bank robber extraordinaire and one of the nation's most wanted fugitives.

Lo and behold, on February 18 when he was riding the subway, who did he notice sitting in the corner of a crowded train car but Willie Sutton himself?

Shuster was sure that the slight, quiet fellow seated nearby was Sutton, a professional heist artist bank robber who'd been at large for the last two years since his most recent prison break. Sutton who, when once asked why he robbed banks, famously replied, "Because that's where the money is."

Sutton carried a gun on his bank jobs but worked things so he didn't have to use it. No law enforcement personnel or civilians had been hurt during any of his smooth, swift stickups. Yet here he was, right out in the open, riding the Brooklyn subway during rush hour like anybody else, just as if he weren't a chart-topper on J. Edgar Hoover's Most Wanted List.

When the suspected fugitive got off at a stop, Shuster got off, too, tailing him from a distance. His quarry climbed the subway stairs and made his way to a car parked on the street. He raised the hood and peered at the engine, indicating that he was experiencing some sort of car trouble.

A safe distance away, Shuster flagged down a passing police car and told the officers that he thought he'd spotted Willie Sutton.

The lawmen may be excused for not becoming overly exercised by the news. For the last two years, ever since he'd broken out of jail, Willie Sutton had been spotted dozens of times in locales scattered all over the United States. Inevitably, once the sightings were investigated, the parties in question proved to be anyone but the notorious bank robber. So, when Arnold Shuster delivered the news that he'd spotted the most wanted fugitive in the country, the odds were that he was another well-meaning but mistaken amateur with an overeager imagination.

Still, the cops decided to investigate. The patrol car rolled alongside the car parked at the curbside where the man Shuster had ID'd as Sutton was busy removing the car battery. The cops asked him who he was and what he was doing. They were casual about it.

The man gave them a name that wasn't Willie Sutton and produced some identification that backed him up. It looked okay, so the cops drove off.

A short time later, a second cruiser came along. This one carried a plainclothes detective in it. The detective picked him up and brought him to the station for a "routine check" that included fingerprinting. Sure enough, when the fingerprint check came back, it positively identified the suspect as Willie Sutton.

The cops couldn't believe their luck in bagging the nation's most wanted. They had no idea how lucky they really were, but they were about to find out. Nobody had bothered to search him and while he was sitting where he was under the scrutiny of only one police officer, he'd had a handgun in a hideaway holster concealed under his clothes. Had he wanted to, he might well have made yet another spectacular getaway—or gone down in a blaze of gunfire.

But the Actor had had enough of the limelight. He was tired of running. His run was done.

It was a matter of luck, bad luck, he later told investigators. His car battery had gone dead—the first time it had ever happened to him—and he was in the process of taking care of it when Shuster had spotted him. He'd been unaware of Shuster eyeballing him, and he guessed it was because he'd been preoccupied about the car trouble and getting it fixed. He hadn't noticed Shuster tailing him to his stalled car. He'd been about to take the battery out and get it replaced at a garage when the police had happened along the first and then the second and final time.

All in all, it was a kick in the head, proving that when fate puts the finger on a guy, there's no escape from destiny.

Sutton's capture was a media sensation. Initially, the New York Police Department tried claiming full credit for making the arrest, leaving out Shuster's role and chalking it up to wide awake police work. Shuster got the mistaken idea from the newspapers that the finder of Willie Sutton was in for a $70,000 reward and surfaced himself as the key man in the capture.

Shuster enjoyed what would nowadays be called his "fifteen minutes of fame." His picture and story were in all the papers. He appeared on a number of television shows. One featured a watch company awarding him a gold watch for his good citizenship. That was about all the recompense he got, because the rumors about a hefty reward for Sutton were just that—rumors.

The story would have played itself out and dropped Arnold Shuster back into the obscurity from which he'd come had not the story taken a sudden, shocking twist. A month later, in March, Shuster was walking home at about nine o'clock at night when a gunman suddenly jumped out of an alley and shot him four times, killing him.

The development was as brutal as it was unexpected. Except for Shuster's kith and kin, no one felt worse about it than Willie Sutton himself. He knew he was sunk.

Until then, because of his nonviolent bank heists, part of the public had been sympathetic to him, getting a kick out of his larcenous exploits. But now, the man who'd fingered him to police was dead, executed gangland style. Arnold Shuster had been a straight arrow, a young veteran who'd only been trying to do his civic duty, and he'd been gunned down for it. What else was the public to think but that Sutton had been behind the heinous act?

There was even a readymade suspect to fit the bill for the job. When Sutton had last broken out of jail, he'd been accompanied by fellow convict Frederick Tenuto, a mob soldier and hitman known as the Accommodation Killer for his willingness to take a murder contract.

Insiders weren't so sure. They knew that arrested crooks generally don't have the kind of friends who'd burn down a public-spirited citizen to avenge a pal's arrest. Crooks look to the main chance and there's no percentage in a showboat play like that. In fact, it would only make things worse for Sutton by linking him to a brutal murder by proxy. That was something a judge would be sure to take into account when passing sentence on the Actor.

Two hundred investigators fanned out across Brooklyn searching for leads. A break of sorts came when the murder gun was found by chance in an out-of-the-way locale. The weapon was part of a load bound for Japan that had been stolen off the Brooklyn docks. Police arrested the nine longshoremen who'd been on the work site the night of the theft and held them for questioning.

The docks in question were part of the territory of mobster and waterfront labor racketeer Anthony "Tough Tony" Anastasio. Despite the slightly different spellings of their last name, Tough Tony was the brother of still-tougher Albert Anastasia, once Lord High Executioner of Murder, Inc. and currently head of Brooklyn's Mafia family. Tough Tony called a work stoppage on the docks to protest what he called an attempt to frame the Shuster kill on his people.

The stolen gun was traced to Chappie Mazziota, a local hood and bookie who'd disappeared around the same time that Shuster was killed. The trail ended there.

A judge handed down a hefty prison sentence to Sutton. Years passed, with the Shuster kill remaining one of the most puzzling questions in the history of modern organized crime. Not until eleven years later, in 1963, was an answer provided to the question: Who did it?

The solution was provided by a unique source: Mafia turncoat Joe Valachi, then in the process of providing law enforcement with the most authoritative and detailed picture of the workings of the Mafia to date.

Valachi was at the height of his career: a midlevel soldier in the Genovese crime family who'd never been able to get on the gravy train where the real mob money was generated. He was married to Mildred Reina, the daughter of the gang boss whose killing back in 1930 had been one of the inciting incidents of the Castellammarese War. Vito Genovese himself had been the best man at Valachi's wedding, but that was long ago.

A narcotics bust in 1958 had sent Genovese to the federal prison in Atlanta on a fifteeen-year term. A few years later, a dope bust had sent Valachi to the same pen. Valachi made the disconcerting discovery that, for no good reason he could possibly discern, he was on the outs with Genovese. Don Vitone suspected him of disloyalty. It didn't take much to get on the wrong side of the perpetually paranoid and suspicious Genovese, and those who got there generally didn't live too long.

It was as easy for Genovese to order someone killed inside prison as out—easier, since in prison you knew exactly where the mark was at all times.

Jumpy, Valachi felt Genovese's assassins closing in. He tagged a fellow inmate for being a potential murderer and got to him first by beating his brains out with a lead pipe. Only it turned out he'd killed the wrong guy. Now he was facing the death penalty in an open and shut case.

It was here that Joe Valachi made a conceptual leap that would have previously been unthinkable for him, as it had been for legions of mafiosi over the generations. He decided to break the omerta code of silence and talk to authorities, to tell all he knew about his life and times in the Mafia.

Keep in mind that at the time Valachi began testifying in 1963, the official position of the FBI and most other law enforcement experts was that there was no such thing as the Mafia; or at best that there had been a Mafia, once upon a time in America long ago, but that it was all old hat and had gone out with Blackhanders and the Unione Siciliane. This, even after the mob conclave at Apalachin, New York, in 1957 had gone public in a spectacular debacle. The Federal Bureau of Narcotics, whose head Harry J. Anslinger had long been FBI Director Hoover's most detested rival, knew better and had maintained for some time the official position that the Mafia existed outside the overheated imaginations of tabloid headline writers and Hollywood crime dramas.

Valachi provided groundbreaking information regarding the history and tradition of the Mafia, as well as a wealth of detail about its workings going all the way back to 1930 and beyond. Not least of his nuggets of data was the fact that its members never referred to the organization as the Mafia, but referrred to it as "la Cosa Nostra," literally, "this thing of ours" or "our thing." The phraseology may have originated with Don Salvatore Maranzano during his bid to reorganize the Mafia and establish himself as its boss of bosses. To this day, FBI reports refer to the organization by the initials LCN: La Cosa Nostra.

Mafiosi were aghast at Valachi's unprecedented tale-telling, seeming to resent most of all his perfidy in revealing the details of the traditional initiation into the society, with its ritualized oath-taking. Wiretapped conversations recorded at that time among mobsters in different parts of the country note their dismay at Valachi's letting the cat out of the bag.

Valachi wasn't privy to the inner workings of the Commission and rarefied world of the higher-ups, but he provided a comprehensive picture of the daily routine and workaday world of a Mafia street soldier. Along the way, he filled in a lot of gaps in the history of organized crime, including a solution for the murder of Arnold Shuster.

According to Valachi, it had been the work of Brooklyn crime boss Albert Anastasia. Albert A.'s hair-trigger temper and violent rages—and the murderous consequences of those eruptions—were well known and equally feared by those who knew him best.

Pinpointing the moment when the mob boss had gone ballistic, Valachi said that it had been when Anastasia was watching the television show where Shuster had received the gold watch to reward his good citizenship.

Albert exploded, saying, "I hate squealers. Hit him!"

The Lord High Executioner's decree was law, and the deed was done. Valachi said the killer was none other than Sutton's prison break partner, Freddie Tenuto, who was hiding out in Brooklyn at the time that Sutton was nabbed. Anastasia picked Tenuto because he was Sutton's pal and because he was expendable. Tenuto slew Shuster and was liquidated for his pains, with Anastasia having the killer hit, too, thereby tying up loose ends.

Why had Anastasia hit Shuster? There was method to his seeming madness. An investigating commission was sniffing around Albert's territory, probing corruption on the docks. The Shuster kill sent a message to all in the Executioner's domain: No squealing, on pain of death.

Valachi's version may not necessarily be the gospel, because it was based on hearsay. But like much of what he said while spilling his guts to the authorities, it seems to have held up and is widely believed to be the truth. Certainly, there's nothing in it that contradicts the relentless brutality that was the hallmark of Albert Anastasia's criminal career. Even Commission law proved no barrier to his hard-charging ambitions; he defied it with impunity to make himself head of the Brooklyn crime family.

But when he finally locked horns with the devious and serpentine Vito Genovese, ah, that was a different story.

He was born Umberto Anastasia in 1903 on the Italian mainland. His early years are obscure until 1917, when he abandoned a job as a deck hand and illegally jumped ship in New York, establishing himself on the waterfront. A number of his brothers including Tough Tony later followed suit, also jumping ship to set foot in New York.

No longer Umberto but now Albert, the burly young Anastasia quickly established himself as a violent, physical enforcer of the most primordial sort. Murder was an art he soon mastered, becoming expert in the use of gun, knife, and strangling cord.

Hatmakers had traditionally worked with mercury-based compounds whose fumes they breathed day in and day out, until finally the mercury poisoning caused them to go out of their heads. Thus the saying, "Mad as a hatter." It is indicative of the repute that Albert already enjoyed that caused his fellow gangsters to name him the "Mad Hatter."

At age nineteen, he was arrested and convicted for the slaying of dock worker George Turello. Sentenced to execution in the electric chair at Sing Sing, he spent 1921–1922 on death row until a technicality in the case led to his release from prison. Before a second trial could be held, all the key witnesses had been murdered. Therefore, no trial. Albert was off the hook and back in business. He is believed to have been one of the assassins of Joe the Boss Masseria in 1931 at Scarpato's, along with Vito Genovese, Joe Adonis, and Bugsy Siegel.

He served as underboss of the Brooklyn Mafia family headed by Joe Adonis, and continued in that post when legal troubles and too much publicity caused Adonis to recede into the shadows and make way for new head Vincent Mangano, sided by his brother, Phillip, another Murder, Inc. gun.

Anastasia and Louis "Lepke" Buchalter worked hand in glove establishing and operating Murder, Inc. Anastasia was the boss of nonmember Lepke and is believed to have personally committed over sixty murders himself, besides ordering many, many times more. The death toll racked up by Murder, Inc. through the early 1940s is conservatively believed to number about a thousand, and may be greater.

In 1937, when Lepke turned fugitive, Anastasia oversaw the murders of over a dozen gangsters thought to be possible "weak links." For two years, while Lepke was the FBI's most wanted fugitive and the object of a nationwide manhunt, Anastasia hid him in Brooklyn.

Albert was ready and willing to keep on hiding Lepke indefinitely. He believed that the longer Lepke stayed at large, the less chance the government had of convicting him. Witnesses would be whacked and those who weren't would find their memories growing hazier with each passing day.

Anastasia told Lepke not to give himself up, but Lepke had bought in to the deal that Moey "Dimples" Wolinsky had told him was in place, guaranteeing that Buchalter would draw a minimum sentence on his federal narcotics rap. Even though Anastasia was against it, he was the one who drove Lepke across the river to rendezvous with columnist Walter Winchell and through him, to surrender to J. Edgar Hoover. There was no deal, as Lepke learned too late.

Albert would have known all too well what the other was enduring on Sing Sing's death row, but there was no similar reprieve for Lepke, who was executed in the electric chair.

Wolinsky was an associate of Meyer Lansky, who Albert disliked anyway, largely because of the respect and influence that the money-spinning nonmember had with the members of the Commission. Any suspicion that Anastasia had that Lansky had helped set up Lepke (though it could only have been done with the full knowledge and authorization of Charlie "Lucky" Luciano) would hardly have futher endeared Lansky to him.

Anastasia did maintain close relations with Frank Costello, the acting boss in Luciano's stead. They were an odd couple, the brutish Mad Hatter and the suave Prime Minister, but each supplied something the other lacked.

Costello was held in universal respect for his financial smarts and heavyweight political clout, and Anastasia would hardly be immune to the ego-gratifying regard and warm fellowship in which Costello held him. Costello, ever smooth and eager to prevent the rough stuff from lousing up profits, was secure in the knowledge that if and when the rough stuff was required, few could dish it out like the fearsome Albert A.

Born Francesco Castiglia in Italy in 1891, he arrived in America in 1895, his family settling in the Italian enclave of East Harlem. The family house was a block away from the infamous 107th Street "murder stable" operated by Lupo the Wolf. In 1908, young Costello was arrested for robbery and assault. In 1915, he spent a year in jail for carrying a gun. In 1920, he teamed with the king of the bootleggers, Big Bill Dwyer (not to be confused with William O'Dwyer, later Brooklyn district attorney and mayor of New York).

A few years later, Costello hitched his rising star to the wagon of Joe the Boss Masseria. More important alliances were forged between Costello, Lucky Luciano, and Meyer Lansky. Costello also established a depth of heavyweight connections with the Democratic political bosses of Tammany Hall, extending his influence deep into the workings of New York City government. He had a quick financial mind and a facility for setting up lucrative rackets and deals that enriched himself and the Commission members.

With the repeal of Prohibition, Costello got into the slot machine business, using Mafia enforcers to get his machines in the neighborhood gin mills and candy stores and muscle out the competition. New York mayor Fiorello LaGuardia took extralegal measures to stymie the racket, ordering police to confiscate Costello's machines, break them up with sledgehammers, and dump them in the river.

Costello recovered by going into business with Louisiana governor Huey Long, who was willing to take all the slot machines Costello could send him. Costello's man in New Orleans was gambler and fixer "Dandy" Phil Kastel, who ensured that the city was chockful of Costello slot machines. It was a bonanza moneymaker until Long was assassinated under mysterious circumstances on September 8, 1935. Long's successors thumbs-downed the slots, so Costello moved the machines to parish districts outside the New Orleans city limits, where he also set up some lucrative Gulf Coast gambling casinos.

With Luciano jailed and Luciano's underboss Vito Genovese

having fled to Italy, Frank Costello became the first among equals of the Mafia Commission, acting as Luciano's proxy. Costello was more interested in making money than in killing people; he preferred to order murder done as a last resort. He dressed conservatively in dark blue pinstripe suits, presenting the image of a businessman or corporate executive. He was a power in both New York and the nation.

Perhaps it was Costello's clout with Brooklyn D.A. William O'Dwyer, ambitiously looking ahead to a future mayoralty race, that caused O'Dwyer to stall on bringing Abe Reles before a grand jury to testify about Anastasia's role in the killing of labor activist Morris Diamond. The case went out the window when Kid Twist did likewise at the Half-Moon Hotel in 1941. It had been a close one for Anastasia. O'Dwyer later ran for the Office of Mayor of New York City and, with Costello's help, won election to the post.

War's end saw the freeing from prison of Lucky Luciano and his almost immediate deportation thereafter. On February 10, 1946, Luciano prepared to sail for Italy on the ship *Laura Keene*. Frank Costello and Meyer Lansky visited him on shipboard, delivering a suitcase with a half-million dollars in cash as a going-away present.

Departure time arrived and the ship sailed away, taking the boss with it. Costello continued to serve as Luciano's key lieutenant. Costello's key allies were Brooklyn's Albert Anastasia and Joe Adonis; Meyer Lansky; Costello's longtime friend and New Jersey crime boss Willie Moretti; Phil Kastel; and financial expert and bookmaker Frank Erickson.

Luciano's leave-taking coincided with Vito Genovese's return.

Born in 1897 in Naples, Italy, Vito Genovese at age sixteen arrived in America with his family, settling in Greenwich Village, Manhattan's downtown district that housed both a bohemian and Italian American populace.

A story is told of Vito early in his crime career as a young punk, how when he was caught pilfering items from a pushcart, he told the peddler, "Don't touch me. Call the police but don't lay a hand on me. I'll kill you if you do."

Growing into thuggish manhood, he became part of the Joe the Boss's crime family and was later one of the assassins who gunned down Masseria. Lucky Luciano became head of the family and Genovese became his underboss.

Genovese was married in 1925, his first wife dying of natural causes in 1929. Vito then met the love of his life, Anna Petillo, who was married to another man. Vito wasn't going to let a small thing like that stop him.

In March 1932, Anna's husband, Gerard Vernotico, was found dead on a rooftop. He'd been hog-tied with a slip noose, so that as he struggled against the ropes, he slowly garotted himself. A second man who'd been in the wrong place at the wrong time was also found dead on the scene. Vito and Anna were soon wed.

When Luciano went to prison in 1936, underboss Genovese was next in line to head the family and arguably the Commission. He was also next in line on Special Prosecutor Thomas E. Dewey's list of top targeted hoods. Genovese decided to make himself scarce by going to Italy. He left Anna behind to keep an eye on his business interests, and by all accounts she made a good job of it.

It seemed an unlikely destination, given Italian dictator Benito Mussolini's relentless hammering of the Mafia in his campaign to extirpate it, but times had changed. Il Duce welcomed Vito and the abundant cash with which his friends and associates in New York kept him supplied. Anna made regular trips, bringing him suitcases full of cash.

Genovese's reach extended back to New York, where he arranged the murder of Mussolini's foe, Italian antifascist writer and publisher Carlo Tresca, assassinated by Vito's man Carmine Galante. Genovese made himself so agreeable to the regime that he was awarded the most prestigious medal that the *fascisti* could bestow on a civilian.

Mussolini's later wartime reverses failed to affect Genovese, who near the end of World War II turned up in Naples in time to befriend the liberating U.S. Army. Vito soon became the kingpin of a black market empire in which everything—jeeps, nylons, liquor, foodstuffs, everything that could be plundered from army warehouses—was available to those who could pay for it. Top army brass were gifted with choice selections of contraband to remind them what a fine fellow Vito was.

Army investigator Orange Dickey arrested Genovese and held him in confinement for months while trying to track down his identity. Someone finally recognized him from his picture in a true-crime magazine. Dickey made inquiries, learning that Vito was wanted in the case of a double murder that had occurred back in New York almost a decade earlier in 1934.

Back then, a gangster named Ferdinand "the Shadow" Boccia had steered a well-heeled businessman and prime pigeon to a crooked big-money card game operated by Genovese and his lieutenant Michele "Mike" Miranda, who plucked the chump of $160,000. Boccia demanded a third of the take as a finder's fee for steering the sucker for the fleecing. Vito had no intention of paying Boccia, and when the other's demands became more strident, Genovese had him hit.

A local hood named Willie Gallo knew too much about the hit, so Vito had him hit, too. The killer in the Gallo hit was Ernest "the Hawk" Rupolo, so-called because of his beaklike nose. Rupolo soon after took a fall for another, unrelated crime, doing a long stretch of prison time.

Not long after being released in the mid-1940s, the hapless Rupolo pulled another kill and was picked up for it. Having had enough of hard time, he decided to cooperate, cutting a deal to give up Genovese on the Boccia-Gallo kills.

Corroboration being the rule, Rupolo's statement was no good in court unless it could be backed up by the evidence of another party who had not been involved in the crime. Corroboration existed in the form of gangster Peter LaTempa, who coincidentally had once knifed Genovese soldier Joe Valachi in a prison brawl. LaTempa was placed for safekeeping in protective custody in a Brooklyn jail.

The state of New York's case was short lived, as was Peter LaTempa. Suffering from gallstones while in jail, he took a daily painkilling medicine. Someone tampered with the pills, making a substitution of more lethal pellets. On January 15, 1945, LaTempa took his daily dosage and promptly dropped dead. The autopsy found there was enough poison in him "to kill eight horses."

Retribution waited another two decades until 1964 before finding Ernie the Hawk. Rupolo's body surfaced in the river, shot and stabbed. It was not a case of Genovese reaching out from his then-prison cell to have Rupolo done in; rather, it seems that some of Rupolo's associates had become convinced that he was an informer (which he was) and taken drastic steps to staunch the leak.

In 1945, though, LaTempa's liquidation put Genovese feeling on top of the world. Free of a murder charge looming over his head, he was returned to the United States. A slight smile showed on his face as he heard himself being denounced from the bench by Judge Samuel S. Leibowitz, frustrated because he had to order Genovese's release. Back in 1932, then-defense counsel Leibowitz had displayed equal passion and energy while winning the release of his client, Vincent "Mad Dog" Coll, on charges of machine gunning a street full of civilians in a botched attempt at killing Joey Rao.

The return to New York of Vito Genovese was a destabilizing element in the smooth workings of the five families and beyond that, the Commission. The question could not help but arise: Who was the boss?

Lucky Luciano was technically still in charge, but he was in Italy, a long way off. Frank Costello was Luciano's man, running things for him. Genovese had been Luciano's underboss, and it was unclear who outranked whom between Vito and Frank Costello.

Costello was in the power position, well respected and politically connected. He was popular with the Commission, whose members were enriched by participating in his financial schemes. He could call on the services of Anastasia and his deep ranks of stone killers, a potent deterrent. Beneath those rarefied heights of mobdom, though, there was a pervasive feeling in the middle and lower ranks that Costello was remote and unapproachable, divorced from the concerns of the street soldiers.

Genovese was displeased on his return to discover how much his following and assets had shrunk during his years abroad. He could rely mainly on his two principal lieutenants, Mike Miranda and

Anthony "Tony Bender" Strollo. Tony Bender protested that Vito had told them all to keep a low profile during the time he was away.

Vito growled, "I didn't tell you to bury yourselves!"

Costello was careful to make a show of great respect for Genovese during occasions when they were seen together at family meetings and social events. Vito was getting the respect but not the power.

The destabilizing effect of Vito's return must have made Albert Anastasia restless enough to shoot a big move of his own.

In 1951, Brooklyn crime family head Vincent Mangano vanished or more accurately was disappeared. Brother Phillip Mangano had little time in which to flail around impotently before being slain gangland style. Vince was never found.

Anastasia took over, making himself head of the Brooklyn family. It was a bold stroke. He had taken out a Commission member and he hadn't asked anyone's permission to do so. The other members knew, even though they couldn't prove it, that Anastasia had hit the Manganos. That was a gross violation of a key organizational tenet prohibiting the hitting of Commission members, but nobody called him on it or so much as said boo to him. He'd calculated on that particular outcome and guessed right.

What was happening was that the organizational infrastructure that Maranzano had envisioned and Luciano had made a reality, was starting to come undone. Peace between the five families heads had existed for over a decade. But violent change and upheaval had come and the pace would soon accelerate.

The infant phenomenon of television was now about to turn its cyclops eye on the mob, thanks to the Senate Investigating Committee on Organized Crime, whose televised hearings were fascinatedly devoured by an audience ranging from 20 to 30 million viewers, a ratings share that networks and sponsors would kill for today, where ten million viewers is the cutoff point between a show's living or being canceled.

The committee chair was Senator Estes Kefauver, a Tennessee Democrat who turned the hearings into a traveling show, holding sessions in a chain of big cities. What fun when the roadshow finally reached New York in March 1951. Most of the mobsters called to testify before the Committee took the Fifth Amendment, refusing to answer on constitutional grounds against self-incrimination.

Frank Costello was in a tight spot. His power base depended in large part on his political pull. He was a well-known public figure who was frequently featured in the tabloids. He had once told a reporter, "If you say I'm a gambler, you'd be right. But I'm an uncommon gambler. I accommodate common gamblers."

He had always presented himself as a sportsman and gambler. Now, his thinking was that if he refused to answer questions by taking the Fifth, he would be lumping himself in with the other gangsters who'd done so. That would shake up his political connections, throwing a scare into them and weakening his influence over them.

Costello's lawyers extracted this concession from the Committee: when Costello was testifying, the television cameras could not show his face, but only his hands. As it turned out during the next three days of grueling grilling for Frank, this was a mistake of the first order. The audio of his gravelly, rasping voice combined with the visual of his hands with their well-manicured fingers nervously tapping, created an iconic image of the hands of a secret empire reaching out to pull the strings on wise men and fools alike.

The ploy backfired even more when Costello got fed up and stopped answering questions he didn't like, leading to his being cited and penalized for contempt of Congress.

The hearings were not without their lighter moments, however. Al Anastasia lived in a fortresslike mansion in Fort Lee, New Jersey, on the Palisades overlooking the Hudson River with a superb view of the Manhattan skyline. When asked how he'd paid for the hefty upkeep on the property, Anastasia stated flatly, "I don't remember."

New Jersey mob boss Willie Moretti was a big hit with the television viewers at home, a real-life Damon Runyon character with an opaque line of doubletalk that baffled yet bemused the committee probers.

It wasn't funny. Like Al Capone, Moretti suffered from an advanced case of syphilis on the brain, subjecting him to spells of disorientation and delusion. Frank Costello had had to hide him for a time until his latest spell had passed and he had once more returned to a state of lucidity. He'd handled himself ably during his appearance before the committee.

A cunning intriguer like Vito Genovese knew how to exploit such an opportunity. He set a whispering campaign in motion among the mob. Yes, poor old Willie had managed to get through the committee probe without suffering one of his recurring attacks. But who could say he'd be that lucky next time? There were no guarantees. The man's mind was going. He was a menace not only to himself but also to the whole organization. Better that he be humanely put down before he could do any real damage. Vito piously concluded that if he, Don Vitone, were ever to be in such a way as Moretti, he could only hope that someone would be good enough to put him out of his misery.

He was playing a deep game, uninterested in Moretti except only as a way to strike at Frank Costello. Moretti was a close ally of Costello's. Vito was poisoning the well against Frank through his guilt by association with the unreliable, dangerous Moretti. Costello would also lose prestige if he were unable to keep Moretti alive. Vito moved to make Moretti dead, putting an open contract out on him. And he didn't go to the Commission first for an okay, either.

On October 4, 1951, Moretti was shot and killed in Joe's Restaurant in Cliffside Park, New Jersey. Joe Valachi later described it as a kind of "mercy killing." Nobody had a beef with Moretti, everybody liked him, but he had to go.

Costello's problems multiplied. His dismal performance at the committee hearings had had a chilling effect on his contacts and connections. His political pals couldn't help but be less chummy, with Costello in the spotlight for the foreseeable future.

Worse, he had to serve a fifteen-month prison term for contempt of Congress for clamming up and refusing to answer any more questions during his grilling. He did his time and went back to doing business.

In 1952, Vito Genovese encountered a rough patch of marital woes, when Anna divorced him. She knew plenty about his illicit financial dealings and in court she told plenty. Vito suffered a major embarrassment and loss of face among Mafia members, who assumed that he would retaliate against the now ex-Mrs. Genovese with his customary venom. He left her unmolested, satisfying himself by ordering the execution of her friend and business partner, Steve Franse. The kill served as a reminder to Anna to keep her mouth shut, and in all future encounters with the law, her memory went blank in regard to the life and times of Vito Genovese.

Years later, when Joe Valachi and Genovese were both in the Atlanta federal pen, Valachi observed Genovese shed real tears while reminiscing about Anna. She really was the love of his life— second only to himself, that is.

On the night of May 2, 1957, Frank Costello was returning home to his apartment on Manhattan's Central Park West, then and now an ultra-fashionable and expensive address. Earlier, he'd met friends (among them Tony Bender, Genovese's lieutenant) at Candler's cocktail lounge, moving on to a haute cuisine dinner at L'Aiglon, and from there to Monsignore, another chic watering hole.

Costello returned alone to his apartment building, entering the lobby. A voice shouted, "This is for you, Frank!"

It belonged to a gunman, a hulking three-hundred-pound shooter with a bowling pin shape and odd, waddling gait.

Costello whirled, turning toward the intruder just as he fired one shot. Costello sank to the floor, bleeding from a head wound. The easily panicked shooter fled, botching an easy opportunity to administer the coup de grâce of a couple of bullets in Frank's head.

Costello was not dead, nor even seriously wounded. The bullet had just grazed him, plowing a furrow along his scalp and spilling a fair amount of blood that made it look worse than it really was. Costello himself was unsure of how badly he'd been hit; the amount of blood spilled made him assent to being taken to the hospital. While he was there, a police search of his pockets turned up a slip of paper on which was written the sum of $651,284—not so coincidentally, the amount of the take at the Tropicana Hotel in Las Vegas, Nevada. Mobsters were not allowed to hold casino interests in Vegas, so the paper trail was of great interest to federal investigators and tax agents.

Someone had made a try on the great Frank Costello himself. Had it succeeded, it would have been the first public execution of a Commission member in New York. Its failure succeeded only in generating a blizzard of headlines and news copy on the Prime Minister's narrow escape from assassination.

Who would want to kill Frank Costello? Or dare to try?

In his mansion in Atlantic Highlands, New Jersey, Vito Genovese summoned all his capos to him, forting up with them in his domicile and prepared to repel all boarders. Forty of his men responded in the affirmative; one, Anthony Carfano, better known as Little Augie Pisano, failed to respond to the imperial summons.

That signaled his finish. Two years later, Little Augie received a telephone call steering him to some kind of meeting. He was excited about going to that meeting, as shown by his energetic demeanor. Suspecting no foul play, he went to the rendezvous with his girlfriend. Their dead bodies were both found later in his car.

Genovese awaited a murderous response from Costello, or more specifically from Albert Anastasia. Anastasia impatiently awaited marching orders from Frank, which never came. Costello had no stomach to play guns any more. He expressed his willingness to get out, to surrender his position at the top of the heap in exchange for a comfortable and secure retirement. Genovese breathed easier.

A suspect was arrested in the assault on Costello, an ex-boxer and strong-arm enforcer for the Genovese family named Vincent Gigante, whose oversized chin had landed him the nickname "the Chin." When he surrendered to authorities some three months after hiding out since the May shooting, he'd dropped a hundred pounds.

In court, Costello failed to identify Gigante as the man who'd shot him, while a doorman who'd made a positive ID had his credibility called into question along with his eyesight. Gigante was acquitted.

The remarkable fact was that Chin hadn't been hit by Vito Genovese for bungling the Costello action. Don Vitone was not the forgiving type. Joe Valachi said of him, "If a guy was doing wrong and you told on him, Vito would have him hit. Then he'd have you hit for telling on the guy."

Possibly, Genovese held his hand to avoid confirming by execution that Gigante actually had been gunning for Costello. This way, there was still some deniability.

Joe Bonanno, original Commission member and longtime head of one of the five families, intruded himself into the dispute in a self-aggrandizing attempt to play peacemaker, brokering what he described as a mutual nonaggression pact between Genovese and Costello. With customary modesty, he labeled it the "Pax Bonanno."

One in whose savage breast no peaceful urges had arisen was Albert Anastasia, who was red hot and raging over the turn of events. He took the attack on Costello harder than Frank did, possibly because Frank had already mentally thrown in the towel and was looking forward to getting out. Albert was in and he meant to stay in. He wasn't going anywhere. So he thought.

The Hit

Roughly six months had passed since the abortive attempt on Costello. On the morning of October 25, 1957, Albert Anastasia was driven to the Park Sheraton Hotel in midtown Manhattan. He entered Grasso's Barber Shop in the lobby of the building. He was a steady customer and well known to the staff.

One of the barbers asked him if he wanted a shoe shine and he said yes, but he'd have it later. He seated himself in a barber chair, where his face was wrapped in hot towels preparatory to getting a shave.

Two men entered the shop. In one version, they were both wearing dark, wraparound sunglasses that hid the upper halves of their faces. In another, they wore bandanas covering the lower halves of their faces. Possibly, they were wearing both.

They brandished handguns, motioning the barbershop staffers to silence. They took up a position in front of the chair, facing Anastasia.

Under the hot towels, Anastasia sensed something was wrong. He pulled the towels off his face, seeing the guns in the hands of the two men, guns that were pointing at him.

He remained true to his nature to the last, not recoiling but attacking. He hauled himself out of the barber chair and had enough time to throw his hands up in front of his face in a futile defensive gesture.

Two guns blazed, pumping five slugs into his head and chest. Anastasia reacted violently, kicking away the chair's footrest. At that, he still made it out of the chair to his feet, charging even as he ran out of life, lurching sideways and crashing into a mirrored wall whose glass racks were filled with ranked bottles of barbering compounds and lotions, sweeping them down to the floor with him as he collapsed.

The two killers slipped out the door and away.

The Mad Hatter had dropped through the rabbit hole: Albert Anastasia was dead.

Oddly, in an eerie echo of an era gone by, the Park Sheraton was the hotel into which in 1928 Arnold Rothstein, the big bankroll of the New York underworld and the man who had fixed the 1919 World Series, had stumbled after being mortally wounded in a shooting.

It is said that on learning of Anastasia's death, Frank Costello wept.

STRATEGY

In the words of a Western movie, the town wasn't big enough for Vito Genovese and Albert Anastasia. Frank Costello was neutralized, no longer a threat. But Genovese could never enjoy a moment's peace while the unpredictable Albert A. was alive and kicking. Just because Costello had lost his stomach for a fight didn't mean that Anastasia had. With his volatile nature and sudden, slashing assaults, Anastasia was a deadly foe.

Yet already the axis of power had shifted, realigning toward the odds-on favorite. That was Genovese. Costello's power had been fatally weakened by the Kefauver Committee hearings. His public profile was such as to destroy the stealthy effectiveness needed to pull the strings behind the scenes. He was in the spotlight at center stage, no place for a veteran clandestine operator.

Luciano's sentiments on the transfer of power are unknown, but no matter where they might lay, he himself was in Italy, a long way off from being able to influence the action. Lansky was moving away from Costello and gravitating toward Genovese. Anastasia hated Lansky, and the feeling was mutual. Recently, Anastasia had made several lurching moves toward muscling in on the lucrative Caribbean and Cuban gambling interests held by other Commission members. Florida Mafia boss Santos Trafficante Jr. had been in New York, meeting with Anastasia not long before the latter had stepped into the barbershop for a final trim.

Genovese had an inside: he'd entered into a covert alliance with Carlo Gambino, Anastasia's underboss. Gambino had reason to fear that he might fall victim to one of Albert's arbitrary and murderous flareups. Besides, with Anastasia gone, he'd be in position to occupy the top spot at the head of the family. That was a masterful stroke by Genovese, undoing his foe by suborning Gambino, Albert's number-two man.

The identity of the killers remains a mystery, although a strong school of opinion holds that they were two of the Gallo brothers (no relation to Willie Gallo): Larry Gallo and Joseph "Crazy Joey" Gallo, a couple of hotheaded renegades from the Profaci family.

Alluding to the Anastasia kill, Larry Gallo is alleged to have said of himself and his brothers and sidemen, "Let's just say you can call us the barbershop quartet."

The selection of the Gallos as assassins was a chancy call. They were a lot more high profile than other more anonymous professionals. As Larry's remark shows, they liked to shoot off their mouths almost as much as their guns. They were cowboys, in Charlie "the Bug" Workman mode; they'd get the job done or go down shooting. With a wild bull like Albert A. for a target, it might make sense to send a couple of shooters with more balls than brains to take his scalp. They were old school in the sense that if captured by the law, they could be relied on to keep their mouths shut.

Still, their hiring was an unnecessary risk, especially with the depth of gun talent available in and out of town.

Deduct 1 point for hiring the erratic Gallo brothers.

STRATEGY: 4

TACTICS

The strike was swift, bold, and cunning. Its success was empowered by subverting Anastasia's bodyguard, Tony Coppola. In the finest tradition of double-crossing bodyguards, he made himself absent at the right time, clearing the way for the killers. Most likely he was recruited for the plot by Carlo Gambino or a go-between. Coppola was eating breakfast in a restaurant across the street when his boss was ventilated. Try as they might, the cops couldn't budge his story. Coppola denied that he even was a bodyguard, implying that he was just a pal who liked to buddy up with Albert.

Coppola's likely involvement with the plot also indicates the possibility that he could have been the finger, the inside man who alerts the killers that the mark is en route to a particular destination at such-and-such a time.

The hit was both slick and basic, no frills. The killers were pros enough to keep their faces hidden and not shoot any of the innocent bystanders. A slaughtered civilian or two would have spun the shooting into a whole other world of negative press and still more intensive police heat.

Albert was stretched out in the barber's chair, face swathed in hot towels, as vulnerably exposed as he was ever going to be.

Enter the killers, who had him just where they wanted him.

This was no amateur night like the May 2 flop try on Costello. These killers put the blast on Anastasia and kept it there until there could be no question of his survival. The getaway was clean, too.

TACTICS: 5

RESULTS

Albert Anastasia's death removed the final obstacle to Vito Genovese's assumption of supreme power on the Commission. Unlike Luciano, who craved the power of the boss of bosses but not the title, Genovese craved both the power and the title. His return to the United States in 1946 had ushered in a destabilizing decade for the Mafia, culminating in the coup against Frank Costello and the kill that nullified Anastasia.

But Vito's reign was to be an inauspicious one.

Genovese wanted to call a meeting of the top mafiosi to proclaim his authority over them. A conclave was called. Sam Giancana suggested Chicago as the meeting place but Vito vetoed it. Genovese had a better idea. The gathering would be held in an obscure town in New York state near the Pennsylvania border, a town called Apalachin. Limousines and big black Lincoln Continentals (a favorite of mid-twentieth-century mob bosses) began arriving from all corners on November 13, 1957, to converge at this obscure rural locale.

State troopers became suspicious when learning that Joseph Barbara, a shady local character with a criminal record, was buying large amounts of steaks, veal cutlets, cold cuts, and other oddments, indicating that he was hosting a big meeting. Surveilling his home, troopers noticed carloads of strangers unloading at the site. The strangers were mostly middle aged and elderly men dressed like businessmen, garb that made them stand out in this rugged rural area.

Somebody at the house spotted the state boys on stakeout and gave the word, sparking an exodus of visitors from the Barbara estate. Some fled by car; others tried to get away on foot. Police detained some fifty or so individuals. A check of their identities revealed them to be the nation's top mobsters. In the event, there was nothing they could be charged with and they were all released.

Vito Genovese, whose own sense of self-aggrandizement had caused the conclave to be called to formalize his coronation with the coveted title of boss of bosses, suffered a loss of prestige as a result of the debacle. The massive publicity caused the federal government to turn the big heat on the mob.

Little time remained for Genovese to savor his place at the top of the greasy pole. In 1958, he was nailed on a federal narcotics rap and sentenced to fifteen years in prison. While there, he was reunited with soldier Joe Valachi.

Genovese's well-deserved reputation for treachery and murder was such that Valachi, in fear of his life, committed the panicky wrong-way killing that ultimately resulted in his revealing the Mafia's secret to the world. Call it Genovese's ultimate legacy to the mob.

Genovese's successful assassination of Anastasia resulted in his assuming the Mafia's top spot, setting in motion a chain of events that swiftly encompassed his downfall.

Vito Genovese died in 1969 of a heart attack while in prison.

Frank Costello died in 1973—as a free man.

RESULTS: 5

Murder Meter Box Score
   STRATEGY: 4
   TACTICS: 5
   RESULTS: 5

   TOTAL: 14

8

The Man Who Would Be Kingmaker: Sam Giancana

The 1960s was an era of unprecedented American affluence and power, a time when old ways were crumbling and new ones were racing to take their place. A mood of "anything goes" was in the air. Anything was possible, anything: the CIA and the Mafia could team up to plot the assassinations of foreign leaders. A Chicago mobster could determine the outcome of a presidential election. That same mobster and the president he helped put into office could share the same mistress.

All this could happen and did. The events and players involved changed the course not only of national history but also of world history, and we are still living with the consequences.

Al Capone's conviction in 1931 on tax fraud charges moved Chicago down a notch to the position of Second City of the American underworld, ceding the top spot to New York. Capone's successors were mafiosi Paul Ricca, Anthony Accardo, and Frank Nitti; sided by high-ranking nonmembers Jake Guzik and Murray Humphreys.

Born in Naples in 1898, Paul DeLucia early on in his crime career took the name Paul Ricca and was tagged with the nickname the "Waiter." A one-time bodyguard for Capone, he became the top man in the Chicago outfit after Big Al went away.

Enforcer and killer Anthony Accardo had been given the nick-name "Joe Batters" by Capone himself, Al being favorably impressed by Accardo's slugging abilities. It is said to be Accardo who invented the ploy of hiding a submachine gun in a violin case.

Ricca and Accardo held the real power, though they preferred to stay in the shadows and let Frank "the Enforcer" Nitti operate in the spotlight as the Outfit's titular head. Jake "Greasy Thumb" Guzik went back to the early days of the John Torrio–Al Capone combination and continued to serve their successors as the Chicago mob's paymaster and fiscal comptroller. Murray (born Llewellyn) Humphreys was the only major American gangster of his day to be of Welsh descent; he was a strategist, councillor, and master schemer.

The repeal of Prohibition affected the Chicago mob the same way it did all its other criminal brethren throughout the land, causing the Outfit to take up the revenue-producing slack by diversifying into narcotics, protection, labor racketeering, jukebox and coin-operated vending machine monopolies, and the like.

Two lucrative rackets that the Outfit marked out for special attention were the racing wire service and the movies.

During the 1930s, the Outfit was willing, if not entirely content, to allow the main Chicago wire service to operate independently of its control, in return for receiving continuing payoffs that totaled many millions of dollars.

The mobsters took control of the IATSE, the theatrical stage workers' union, using it to get a stranglehold on the Hollywood studios and squeeze them for millions of dollars to avoid labor trouble. It was a sweet racket while it lasted, but it soured in 1943 when the hoods tried to squeeze the motion picture industry for another million-dollar shakedown. Instead, the studios cooperated with Washington to stop the extortion, prompting a series of federal investigations and prosecutions that decimated the upper ranks of the Chicago underworld.

An early casualty was boss Frank Nitti, found dead under mysterious circumstances; his body lay near some railroad tracks, clutching the gun with which he apparently killed himself.

Prison terms were handed out to Willie Bioff and George Browne, the workhorses of the Hollywood shakedown scheme; Johnny Rosselli, the Outfit's unofficial ambassador to Tinseltown; and even mob chief Paul Ricca himself.

Ricca's jailing led to Tony Accardo's assumption of the top spot. A useful tool in gaining and holding the number-one slot was Sam Giancana, Accardo's top enforcer.

Giancana's parents were both Sicilian; he was born Salvatore Giangana in America in 1908, a true native son. He and his family lived in the tough Chicago slum district of the Patch. His mother died when he was a child, so the streets became the major formative influence on his life. He fell in with a street gang, taking the name Sam Giancana. Other aliases included Sam Gold, Sam Flood, Momo, and Moe. Crookdom had another name for him: "Mooney," as in lunatic or crazy; just a different way of saying "Bugs."

He had a wicked temper and a sadistic streak that let him enjoy dealing out violence and murder. He was one of those glandular types of gangsters, a volcanic hothead in the mode of Dutch Schultz, Benjamin "Bugsy" Siegel, and Albert Anastasia.

He became a pillar of the Forty-two gang, a training ground for some of Chicago's most vicious criminals, not least of whom was himself. Superior driving skills and an ability to evade police pursuit marked him for distinction and made him a much-desired wheelman and getaway car driver.

He was of average physical attributes, compensated for by a mercurial viciousness and a talent for ultra-violence. He also racked up numerous arrests for assault, robbery, bootlegging, and other crimes, not least of which were three separate arrests (and no convictions) for murder, all before he was twenty.

During his crime career, he racked up a total of over sixty arrests for various crimes. His driving skills won him a job as Paul Ricca's driver and later as the driver for Tony Accardo. He was close to Ricca. He somehow found time to get married and have three daughters.

After serving a prison term from 1939 to 1942, he was required like all other male citizens of a certain age to report to the local draft board—this being wartime. The examiners marked him as unfit to serve, classifying him as a "psychopath."

Giancana approached some of Chicago's top mobsters, offering to deliver for them the Chicago policy banks in the African American neighborhoods, a similar setup to Harlem's numbers game. Like their New York counterparts in the early 1930s, the Outfit bosses had been oblivious to the millions generated by the nickel-and-dime daily numbers game. Giancana opened their eyes to the potential profits, a subject he was well schooled in, having been up until then a partner of Eddie Jones, the black boss of a leading policy wheel.

Sam turned on his erstwhile associate, kidnapping and holding him for six days and releasing him only on payment of a $100,000 ransom and Jones giving up his policy bank to the mafioso. Jones turned over his business and moved with his family out of Chicago—to Mexico.

His bosses were well pleased with Giancana, who continued to move up in the organization.

In 1946, the Outfit knocked off James Ragen and took over his Continental Press Service, then knocked off Bugsy Siegel when he refused to turn over the Trans-America Press Service to them. That same period saw Chicago consolidate its takeover of the Teamsters' union, through its control of Teamster boss James Riddle Hoffa.

Short, squat, and powerfully built, Hoffa had allied himself with the mob to counter gangsters hired by management interests to terrorize and intimidate union organizers and members. Chicago mobster Paul Dorfman was a key link between Hoffa and the bosses of the Outfit.

The Teamsters were one of the nation's most powerful unions, holding a vital position in the transportation industry that directly affected commerce and the economy. A juicy bonus for the mob was access to the bulging coffers of the Hoffa-controlled Teamsters Central States Pension Fund, which was able to make tax-free loans of millions of dollars to well-connected gangsters.

Many of these loans were used to finance construction of a number of casino-hotels that sprang up on the Las Vegas Strip. Bugsy Siegel's dream had become a reality.

During the 1950s, Vegas enjoyed boom growth, becoming with its gambling, neon-lit glitz, and legalized prostitution a kind of Disneyland for adults and an ever more popular vacation and tourist spot. Las Vegas became an open city for the American Mafia, with crime families from coast to coast holding pieces and points and, in some cases, control of most of the major casino operations, through intricate fiscal arrangements and front men.

A major allurement of casino ownship was "the skim." Casinos deal in an all-cash basis and must accurately account for the precise amount of the daily take, for tax purposes. The skim took a piece of that cash straight off the top, each and every day, pocketing it for the gangster owners. The yearly skim from a single casino could add up to millions.

Las Vegas was a gang goldmine, yes. But why stop there? Casinos in other countries were beyond the reach of active U.S. law enforcement and free from the costly harassment of constant probing by tax auditors and agents.

Cuba beckoned as a second front in the gambling industry. An island located ninety miles south of the tip of the Florida, it was conveniently located for easy access by American tourists. It had a balmy tropical climate and picturesque scenery, for those who should chance to wander outside the casinos.

More important, its government was warm and friendly, especially to American gangsters and gamblers who paid for the privilege of operating free and untrammeled on Cuban soil.

It was a time of major mob growth tempered by complex and often intense internal and external stresses: internal, from plots and subterfuges within the Commission itself; and external, from high-profile congressional hearings probing the workings of organized crime.

The Senator Estes Kefauver hearings of the early 1950s generated some light and more heat on the mob. A similar battering was inflicted in the mid-1950s and the latter half of the decade by the McClellan Committee. Named for the senator who chaired it— John L. McClellan—its mission was to investigate the mob's hold on the labor movement.

One of McClellan's staffers was Robert "Bobby" Kennedy, whose brother was Senator John F. Kennedy of Massachusetts; their father, Joseph P. Kennedy, was one of the richest men in America and a former ambassador to Britain on the eve of World War II.

Bobby Kennedy's front and center role as a hard-nosed prober and investigator afforded him a comprehensive overview of the extent to which organized crime permeated the nation's economic structure from top to bottom.

In 1956, he conducted a memorable questioning of Sam Giancana, baiting him about murders and other crimes he'd allegedly committed. For once keeping his head and not rising to the bait, Giancana started laughing at young Kennedy's histrionics, prodding an enraged Bobby to accuse the mobster of "giggling like a schoolgirl."

More primal was Kennedy's obsession with Teamsters boss Jimmy Hoffa, which established a lifelong feud with deadly consequences. Kennedy made it clear during his questioning of Hoffa before the committee that he thought the labor leader was a corrupt mobster who battened on the hard-earned wages of honest working men.

Hoffa, with a rough and ready pugnacity, had no hesitation in expressing his view that Kennedy was a spoiled rich kid who'd never held a real day's work in his life. Hoffa managed to slip the nets of the investigators that time, but Bobby Kennedy had already marked him in his own mind for destruction.

Joseph P. Kennedy—"Old Joe"—the family patriarch, was less than thrilled with Bobby's probe of mob-labor ties, perhaps with good reason. President Harry Truman once said of Joe Kennedy, "There's not a bigger crook anywhere in the country." Frank Costello once stated that he and the senior Kennedy had been partners in several bootlegging ventures.

Mobsters generally seek to aggrandize themselves by inflating the importance of their connections with prominent politicians and legitimate businessmen. Costello, however, was a genuine political

powerhouse with a kind of flinty integrity in matters not directly relating to Mafia interests, giving his remarks a kind of credibility not
readily granted to lesser gangsters.

While the nature and extent of Kennedy's possible bootlegging
business remains an open question, in any case it is certain that he
was not without some firsthand knowledge of the gangster breed
through his dealings with them during his involvement in the motion picture industry and the liquor-importing business.

Old Joe had plans for postwar America, big plans. He'd cherished
the dream of becoming president once himself, but his unsavory
business reputation had been compounded by his pro-Nazi ap-
peasement during his tenure as ambassador to Britain, a tenure that
had been prematurely cut off by President Franklin D. Roosevelt,
who called him back to Washington and pressured him to tender his
resignation from the diplomatic post.

His first-born son, Joseph Kennedy Jr., had been groomed for a
political career culminating in White House tenancy, but the dream
died in midair over England during wartime when young Joe's plane
exploded, destroyed by high-explosive armaments it was carrying
on a dangerous bombing mission.

Kennedy Senior's remorseless dynastic ambition ensured that his
second son, John F. Kennedy, moved into the position left vacant by
the death of young Joe. Jack Kennedy's seat as senator from Massachusetts was only a way station toward his eventual, presumably irresistible advance toward the presidency itself.

With a presidential election coming in 1960, the Kennedy clan's
hour of power seemed to have arrived.

A major issue in that campaign would be Cuba, which had been
transformed from a tourist playground run by a friendly dictator to
a communist dictatorship that took its cues from the Kremlin in the
Soviet Union.

What happened? Fidel Castro.

In earlier days, Castro, a ballplayer of some skill, tried out for a
spot on an American baseball team but failed to make the cut. It's
interesting to speculate how different the course of the mid-twentieth

century would have been had he made the team, instead of returning home to Cuba and making a revolution.

With his brother, Raoul Castro, and his sideman Ernesto "Che" Guevera, Fidel spearheaded a revolt against dictator Fulgencio Batista, who was so wonderfully pliant and agreeable to U.S. mob gambling interests. Castro assembled a small but effective fighting force in the mountains in the interior, waging from there in the late 1950s an ever escalating guerilla war against the Batista regime.

To some, the bearded, cigar smoking Castro, habitually clad in olive-drab army fatigues, was a "romantic" figure and freedom fighter for his oppressed island nation. This opinion was shared in a certain quarter of the CIA, which provided covert arms and assistance to Castro's guerilla army.

January 1, 1959, saw a triumphant Castro take power in Cuba after having ousted Batista, who had fled the country. It was not long before some of those who'd been most vocal in hailing Fidel's assumption of power found themselves bitterly regretting it.

It was the old Trojan Horse ploy. During his rise, Fidel had been careful to conceal his true nature and convictions from outsiders, the Cuban people, and all but a handful of his most trusted inner circle, a well-disciplined cadre of like-minded revolutionists. Shedding the mask of moderation once he was master of the country, Castro revealed himself to be a hard-core, dedicated Marxist-Leninist. A member of the international communist conspiracy, for real— a Commie!

Fidel ruthlessly suppressed dissents, jailing as political prisoners thousands of men and women who objected to having their country turned into a communist state. Finally, even Washington got the message loud and clear when Castro nationalized U.S. interests in Cuba, taking them over lock, stock, and barrel without a penny in compensation to the owners.

Among those pirated interests were the American Mafia's gambling holdings, as expressed in the form of a handful of glittering casino-hotels sited in Havana. Such mob citadels as the Sans Souci casino and the Tropicana, Meyer Lansky's own pleasure dome, were dispossessed of their American operators and staffers, many of whom were thrown into Castro's prisons and held for months before being released.

It was a bitter blow, negating at one stroke a power role and principal profit source that generated hundreds of millions of dollars a year for the American Mafia. That put Fidel at the top of the mob's hit parade.

Castro was equally unpopular in Washington with President Dwight D. Eisenhower and his administration. His takeover in Cuba of assets and properties such as soft drink bottling plants, hotels, sugar refineries, and such that belonged to American corporate titans set the blood of capitalists and anticommunists to boiling.

Vice President Richard M. Nixon took a particular interest in the matter, coming early to the conclusion that there was no living with Fidel Castro and that it was better that he be removed as soon as possible. Removed from office certainly; removed from life if feasible; in any case, removed with dispatch. Fidel was already making wooing noises to the Soviet Union and Red China, both of whom were eager to exploit this Red beachhead in the New World.

Nixon and some military and intelligence advisers devised Operation Pluto, tasked with the overthrow of Castro and his regime. Nixon was mindful of the U.S. election coming up in 1960, since he would be the Republican Party's standard-bearer in the presidential tilt. But the man's bedrock anticommunism would have guaranteed that Fidel would have been anathema to him in any case.

Someone somewhere in the corridors of power came up with the bright idea of using the Mafia to assassinate Castro. Striking though it was, the concept of the U.S. government allying with gangsters and killers to assassinate the leader of another country did not spring forth full grown from a vacuum.

Its roots lay in Operation Underworld, the wartime alliance between Naval Intelligence and the New York underworld to secure and protect the waterfront. The link between U.S. clandestine intelligence services and organized crime could only grow in the post–World War II period, when the Soviet Union gobbled up

Eastern Europe while Western Europe became the battleground for communism and capitalism.

Elements of organized crime in other countries were engaged by U.S. spymasters to battle and suppress communist labor agitation, strikes, demonstrations, and marches. The Unione Corse, the Corsican syndicate in the south of France; the Mafia in Italy; and Yakuza gangsters in Japan, used violence and thuggery and sometimes murder to squash their opponents.

The CIA used a middleman to broach the offer to the Mafia, operating through Robert A. Maheu, a true international man of mystery. Maheu, a former FBI agent turned CIA operative, had officially left the agency to form his own private detective and corporate security firm. It was a good cover to carry out dirty tricks and morally ambiguous operations that the CIA would not care to be publicly linked to.

Maheu considered his options. If you wanted to hire the Mafia to knock off Fidel Castro, he knew a good place to start. In September 1960, he first approached Johnny Rosselli, that Hollywood gangster and "patriotic" mobster.

Filippo Sacco was born in Italy, arriving in America with his family in 1911. Early in his criminal career he was associated with New Jersey mob boss Abner "Longy" Zwillman and Al Capone. Joining Capone's crime clan, he changed his name to Johnny Rosselli, picking the last name at random from an encyclopedia entry on Rennaissance artist Cosimo Rosselli.

The post-Capone Outfit sent him out to the West Coast to promote its interests, much as New York would send Benjamin "Bugsy" Siegel west on a similar mission. Like Siegel, Rosselli took to Hollywood like a duck to water.

He was good looking and athletic, with an easygoing charm. He dated and bedded a plethora of attractive young women. He was a gambler, sport, and man about town. He was good buddies with Harry Cohn, the boss of Columbia Pictures. For some years, Cohn proudly wore a star ruby ring that Rosselli had given him.

Mainly, though, he was a gangster, gambler, and killer. In Los Angeles, Rosselli worked closely with Mafia boss Jack Dragna.

Rosselli was one of those caught up in the Willy Bioff–George Browne IATSE investigation, arrested and sent to prison. He and other Chicago mobsters in the case were paroled in 1947, sparking a parole board scandal that went nowhere.

Rosselli returned to his Hollywood haunts, incredibly wangling a post with a film company. "Incredibly," because Rosselli had gone to prison for extorting protection money from the studios. But that's showbiz.

Eagle-Lion, which employed him, was a minor studio but one whose films were usually slick, lively entertainment. Rosselli's exact duties remain unknown, but he was associated with three crime dramas that are well regarded by fans of the genre: *He Walked by Night*, *Canon City*, and *T-Men*.

Woes returned in the form of the Kefauver Committee, which called Rosselli before it, dredging up into the spotlight yet again the tale of his complicity in the Bioff-Browne affair and publicizing his long and close association with top mobsters. In the aftermath of the hearings, Rosselli found his Hollywood contacts turning on him. There were no lucrative studio posts to be had. Harry Cohn turned him down for a job, claiming the company stockholders wouldn't let him hire someone the Kafauver Committee had labeled a hood. Rosselli told Cohn what he could do with himself. But that was how it was. The territory was burned up for Rosselli; it was time to move on.

He went to Las Vegas, where he occupied high managerial positions in various Mob-owned casinos. He lived well, dressed sharp, ate and drank in high style, and enjoyed the attentions of a string of good-looking women.

This then was the man chosen by Maheu to make the Castro contract work.

Maheu and Rosselli had a meeting, during which Maheu made it clear that the government wanted the mob to make Fidel dead. Rosselli thought it was a great idea, for several reasons.

First and foremost was the alliance itself. An "in" with the CIA on so sensitive a matter as this had plenty of exploitational potential. One could never have too many friends in high government circles, especially when they were indebted to you. Then, too, the Mafia wanted Fidel dead as much as the government did. With Castro dead and the regime toppled, the mob could get its casinos back, not to mention paying Fidel back in the universal currency of blood and woe. Another factor worth mentioning is that Roselli figured it would be a patriotic gesture to knock off Fidel.

Rosselli went to Chicago to pass the word along to the now-acting head of the Outfit: Sam Giancana.

Tax troubles continued to bedevil the Outfit. In the late 1950s, federal tax probers targeted mob boss Anthony Accardo. Feeling the pressure, Accardo decided to turn active leadership of the Chicago mob over to someone else, freeing himself to devote his full energies toward beating the government's looming tax case.

Next in line for the throne was underboss Sam "Mooney" Giancana. Mooney had made it to the top slot the hard way as a stone killer and top moneymaker. He was old school, a street animal, brutal and direct. His reign as Chicago's acting mob boss began in 1957.

Giancana gave his approval to the idea of doing a deal with the feds to do in Castro. Wiretap transcripts and tapes from the period document that Rosselli was really gung-ho to get the job done, while Giancana adopted a more relaxed (some would say realistic) attitude toward the project.

The next critical meeting was held in Miami, Florida, at the Fontainebleau Hotel, where five men met at poolside. Present for the government were Maheu and CIA Operations Support Division head James O'Connell, the latter going by the name "Jim Olds." The mob was represented by Rosselli, Giancana, and Florida crime boss Santos Trafficante. Giancana went by the name "Sam Gold," while Trafficante was simply "Joe."

Trafficante was present for several reasons. The meeting was taking place in his territory and Mafia protocol demanded his attendence. Also, he had taken a major financial beating when Castro had taken over the casinos. But he had other fish to fry: specifically, a narcotics pipeline he'd set up in Cuba during the Batista regime. Trafficante might well find himself in a conflict of interests down the road.

Nobody at the meet was fooling anybody, with mobsters and spies each knowing the others for what they were.

O'Connell pitched the idea of taking out Fidel in a machine gun–type assault on his car when he was riding in a motorcade. The hoods thumbed down such a hopeless suicide mission. The parties came to an agreement on the idea of giving Fidel poison, a delayed-effect toxin that would allow the assassin to make good his escape. On this mutually agreeable note, the meeting broke up.

Later, Maheu delivered some poison pills that had been made up at the CIA's Technical Services Division lab. The pills were supposed to be passed through Rosselli to his contacts and ultimately to a conspirator close to Fidel who would administer them to the dictator when the time was right.

Several attempts were made, or at least said to be made, but the fact was that Castro lived on, the picture of health, continuing to taunt and enrage Washington with his strident anti-West rhetoric and increasing intimacy with Moscow.

Years later, Trafficante told his lawyer that he'd thought the idea was crazy and had flushed the poison pills down a toilet.

Strange currents were astir below the surface of the 1960 presidential campaign, which pitted Republican candidate Vice President Richard M. Nixon against Democratic Party candidate Senator John F. Kennedy.

Old Joe Kennedy, never one to leave things to chance, was also not minded to overburden sons John and Bobby with the dirty details of what it took to get business done. So it is unlikely that the candidate or his younger brother were aware of some of the machinations undertaken by their father to secure JFK's election.

Old Joe had his covetous eye set on the key state of Illinois, whose big block of electoral votes might prove the deciding factor in the election. He wanted the Outfit's support in helping to make his son president. He extended feelers to Giancana.

The Mafia was unsure of which candidate to support. A solid block of top mobsters was leaning toward Texan Lyndon Johnson, who had strong union backing. The unions were an area where the mob had control. Not to mention the fact that Johnson didn't have a racket-busting younger brother.

Old Joe's ambitions coincided with those of an unlikely but ultimately pivotal player: Frank Sinatra, the New Jersey–born songster turned Oscar-winning superstar.

Gifted with a big vocal talent and cursed with an ego to match, Sinatra was driven by an all-consuming need for respect and a sensitivity to slights, real or imagined, that would cause him to lash out vindictively when he thought he was being crossed. In this he was not unlike Sam Giancana, with whom he maintained an uneasy friendship for some years.

Sinatra had longtime mob links. A native of Hoboken, New Jersey, he came under the wing of area mob boss Willie Moretti. He was also on good terms with Frank Costello and other prominent mobsters, including Giancana, whom he seems to have known since the mid-1950s, if not sooner.

Sinatra was known to the underworld as a Mafia wannabe and a hanger-on of the syndicate set. He was pals with actor Peter Lawford, married to one of the Kennedy sisters, and brother-in-law to Jack and Bobby. A liberal Democrat at the time, Sinatra went ga-ga over JFK, putting himself to work for Kennedy's presidential campaign. The singer used his stardom and showbiz clout to persuade other big-name entertainers to participate in fund-raising galas for the cause.

Sinatra also exerted himself in more subterranean channels, as when he sought to convince Sam Giancana to help elect Kennedy. Giancana was dubious, mindful of how Bobby Kennedy had hammered the Outfit and its important client Jimmy Hoffa, the Teamsters boss. The Teamsters were rock-solid in the Nixon-for-president camp.

Sinatra assured Sam that JFK was nothing like his narrow-minded, mob-bashing brother. He, Sinatra, would have John Kennedy eating out of the palm of his hand. Sinatra's assurance on this score was

buttressed by the fact that for some time now, he'd been function-
ing as a kind of pimp for JFK, providing him with a succession of
gorgeous starlets and call girls on numerous occasions.

John Kennedy liked women, of that there can be no doubt, and
he wasn't going to let a few minor technicalities like being married
or running for the highest political office in the land deter him from
the steady diet of quick, casual sex with complaisant beauties that he
continually craved.

His reckless indifference to the source of some of these femmes
would in the future put him out on a limb and seriously compro-
mise his administration.

In February 1960, at a party in Las Vegas at the Sands casino-
hotel following one of Frank Sinatra's shows there, Kennedy was in-
troduced to a stunning brunette named Judith Campbell Exner.
The introduction was handled by Johnny Rosselli. JFK bedded Judy
Exner and continued a sexual relationship with her throughout the
campaign and into his presidency.

Sinatra pitched Sam Giancana that a Kennedy win would be a
good thing for the Mafia, which could call on his gratitude for helping put him in office. He would owe them. Giancana bit, getting behind the candidacy and lining up his fellow mob bosses for the
effort.

Old Joe Kennedy put the touch on the mob for big-money campaign contributions in May 1960 for the Democratic primary contest in West Virginia. The contributions were good, old-fashioned,
under-the-table, in-a-suitcase money. Rival Hubert Humphrey was
coming off a Wisconsin primary win that had dispirited the Kennedy
camp. The large infusion of cash from Vegas through Chicago was
spread around the state where it would do the most good, buying a
sizeable victory for John Kennedy over Humphrey, who then with-
drew from the race.

The real payoff came on election night in November 1960.
Returns showed Kennedy and Nixon running virtually neck and
neck. The outcome hung in doubt. The electoral totals were more

or less even, with the state of Illinois shaping up as the decisive battleground where the contest would be won or lost.

Then, as *Washington Post* editor Ben Bradlee stated JFK once told him, Kennedy was on the phone with Chicago mayor Richard Daley, who assured him that "with a bit of luck and the help of a few close friends, you're going to carry Illinois."

The "friends" must have been the gremlins in Chicago's West bloc who waited until the last moment to produce a big block of Democratic votes, enough to clinch the state for Kennedy and swing the election to him. The source and provenance of those deciding votes was smelly, so much so that more than a few of Nixon's closest advisors were telling him to contest the outcome of the election.

With the cold war raging, Nixon felt unable to throw the presidential leadership of the nation into doubt and chaos at such a critical time, so he conceded the election—much to the surprise of Jack Kennedy, who expected Nixon to make a fight of it.

The White House had fallen to John Fitzgerald Kennedy, the next president of the United States.

Mobdom's initial joy at Kennedy's win lasted less than a month, until December, when JFK announced his pick for U.S. Attorney General: brother Robert Kennedy.

This was a real kick in the teeth to the Mafia. Had they known or even suspected that their nemesis Bobby Kennedy was going to be the attorney general, they'd have done their damnedest to get Nixon elected. Bobby had been making things plenty hot for the mob as a McClellan committee man; now, he was boss of the federal government's Justice Department and all its assets, including the FBI. Though there was sure to be trouble on that last, since Bureau Director J. Edgar Hoover, long used to operating with virtual autonomy, was unwilling to voluntarily cede any of his authority to his nominal boss, Robert Kennedy, or to the president of the United States, for that matter.

The selection had an immediate practical benefit for the

Kennedy clan. The Justice Department wouldn't be investigating any complaints of vote fraud in the election, not with the president's brother at its head. Instead, it would devote the lion's share of its resources toward seeking out and destroying "the enemy within," which was the title of Bobby's book about his fight against organized crime.

The Mafia now learned to its distress what it was like to be on the receiving end of the really big heat that was coming down from the Kennedy Justice Department. Bobby beefed up the organized crime division, unleashing hordes of investigators on mob bosses and their crime families nationwide. The use of government wiretaps against mobsters multiplied tenfold, a hundredfold. Tax probes and IRS scrutiny increased in frequency and intensity.

When it came to hammering organized crime, Bobby Kennedy wasn't overly particular about how things got done. He had federal agents apprehend New Orleans Mafia boss Carlos Marcello and put him on a plane for Guatemala, illegally extraditing the nonnaturalized crime boss. Marcello managed eventually to get back into the United States, but not without difficulty.

Outrage swiftly turned to just plain rage on the part of afflicted mafiosi around the country, whose wiretapped telephone chatter began crackling with ominous threats and rumblings of violence against the Kennedy brothers.

Sam Giancana himself was a prime target of investigators, marked for what the FBI called "concentrated intensified action." He'd taken a big hit to his prestige due to the course of events. He'd been a leading, high-profile advocate among his brethren for a JFK win. Now, his associates blamed him for what they called the Kennedy double cross, though not to his face. Not yet. But there was a chilling effect; he could feel mob sentiment distancing itself from him.

Giancana held Sinatra to blame in no small part for his ongoing humiliation, and it was touch and go for a while there as to whether he would have Frank hit in retaliation. Ultimately, he decided against it, but for a while things were mighty iffy for the crooner.

One of the first casualties of Giancana's disaffection was the CIA's Kill-Castro plans, which he now decided to let hang fire until doomsday. He refused to bestir himself toward making the plans work, while he kept on taking the agency's money for plans that were doomed to disuse.

In July 1961, FBI agents intercepted Giancana and his companion, singer Phyliss McGuire, at Chicago's O'Hare International Airport, where they very publicly detained the couple and served McGuire with a subpoena. If the purpose of the exercise was to push Giancana's buttons, it succeeded. He blew his top, launching into a profanity-strewn tirade directed at G-man William Roemer, Giancana's nemesis in Chicago, telling him that he had a message for his boss (Attorney General Robert Kennedy) and his "superboss" (President John F. Kennedy). "I know all about the Kennedys, and Phyliss knows a lot more, and one of these days we will tell all," Giancana fumed. He told Roemer, "You lit a fire tonight that will never go out."

The thing was, Giancana did know plenty: about the mob's illegal cash donations in the West Virginia primary, about the Chicago vote theft and padding that nudged JFK over the line into the winner's circle on election day, and not least, about the parade of comely call girls and highline hookers with which Frank Sinatra plied Jack Kennedy.

On top of that, there was the deal with the CIA for the Mafia to knock off Castro. Giancana had a right to feel betrayed. He'd practically put JFK in the White House, and what did he get? A muscular assault by the Justice Department against the Mafia on all levels, accompanied by what he could only regard as humiliating and personally insulting harassment of himself. By the mob's standard, JFK didn't even meet the prime criterion of an "honest" politician; that is, one who stays bought.

Giancana's woes multiplied with the inauguration of Operation Lockstep, where Chicago G-men blanketed Giancana with surveillance teams night and day, wherever he went. No stealth operation this, but blatant harassment, as teams of G-men dogged Giancana on his daily rounds, making no attempt to conceal themselves, but following him as closely as possible, with the goal of unnerving him and making him lose his cool. They even crowded him on the golf course, throwing off his strokes and game with their intrusive presence.

Giancana had a sulphurous temperament that habitually exposed itself in electrifying episodes of verbal and frequently physical violence. This time, though, he played against type, going to court to complain that the too-obvious surveillance was a violation of his civil rights. The court found in his favor, ruling that the G-men must maintain a certain amount of distance between them and their subject. The publicity attendant on the case did not endear Giancana to Outfit boss Accardo and planner Humphreys, already disenchanted by the Kennedy double cross and increasingly disgusted by Giancana's high profile in the media.

It was only a matter of time before something had to give, and it did, in the form of a reality check named J. Edgar Hoover.

Jack and Bobby Kennedy had no love for the long-serving bureau director, and it was an open secret that they wanted to replace him with a more pliant Kennedy appointee.

Bobby Kennedy in particular used his position as attorney general to torment Hoover with a psychological warfare campaign of calculated slights and affronts to the director's authority, partly to give him a push to hurry him out of his job and partly because he was a bully with a mean streak.

The organizational chart said that Bobby was Hoover's boss, but Hoover was a one-man institution in Washington, D.C., with extensive political and big business connections and an admiring constituency out there among the anticommunist, pro-law-and-order electorate. It did not take long for the Kennedy brothers to discover exactly how and why Hoover had remained in office so long. The director's sources of information were ubiquitous and unparalleled, and he was not shy about using the particularly juicy nuggets of scandal and gossip that went directly into his private "Official and Confidential" files.

In December 1961, Hoover informed the attorney general about his father's dealings with Giancana and the mob and their role in his brother's election.

It's possible that this came as news to Bobby; Old Joe had been careful in many ways to insulate his sons from some of what it took to ensure the nascent dynasty's ability to perpetually extend its influence and power over the nation while making still more millions of dollars to add to the family coffers.

Soon after, an angry Bobby confronted his aged father at the family compound in Hyannis Port, Massachusetts. What was said on both sides can only be imagined, but within a few days of the showdown, Old Joe suffered a debilitating stroke from which he never fully recovered.

Hoover had only begun to play out his string. On February 27, 1962, he informed the attorney general that a surveillance of Johnny Rosselli's frequent companion, Judith Campbell Exner, had discovered that she had made a series of phone calls—over seventy—to one of JFK's restricted-access White House phone lines. There was more. She'd been conducting an affair with JFK since February 1960 and had made visits to the White House.

During the last six months, she'd been simultaneously conducting affairs with JFK and Sam Giancana, the latter especially getting a kick out of bedding the president's girlfriend. Exner later stated for the record that she and JFK had been lovers and that Giancana had used her as a courier to deliver several sealed envelopes to Kennedy—what those envelopes contained, she knew not.

The only thing more vexing to the attorney general than the knowledge that his brother the president was having an affair with the girlfriend of a mob boss that the AG was trying to put out of business, was the fact that Hoover knew it, too.

Going in for the kill, Hoover lunched privately with the president on March 22, 1962, acquainting him with the fact that he, Hoover, was well acquainted with all the dirty doings on the dark side of Camelot.

That was the day that JFK broke off the affair with Judy Exner. White House phone records show that that was the last day on which she spoke by phone to the president.

Hoover's machinations put the kibosh on any plans the Kennedys had to force him into early retirement. He would stay on as FBI director for as long as he liked. He was also cognizant of the CIA-Mafia Kill-Castro plots, as he also made clear to Bobby Kennedy. As if that weren't enough, he was also in possession of information about their involvement with screen sex goddess Marilyn Monroe. JFK had had a casual affair with her, but Bobby had had a more extensive relationship.

On top of everything else, Fidel Castro was up to his old tricks and some disturbing new ones. In 1962, he allowed Soviet technicians in Cuba to install missiles capable of hitting the United States, a development that JFK tried to ignore until presented with irrefutable proof by the CIA of the accuracy of the claims. The matter deepened into a crisis in October 1962 that threatened a possible nuclear exchange with the Soviet Union before the matter was defused.

The Kennedy brothers wanted Fidel dead now more than ever. Bobby Kennedy kept pressing CIA bigs to take action against Castro. The Kill-Castro plot was still alive, but now it had morphed. Off the case was Robert Maheu, replaced by legendary cold war intelligence great William "King" Harvey.

Harvey, who like Maheu had been a G-man before working for the agency, was once described by CIA head Allen Dulles as a "conspiratorial cop," adding, "The trouble is, I don't know if he's more conspirator or more cop."

Harvey and Rosselli hit it off, working well together. Giancana was officially out of the loop, dropped from the program. Rosselli was the go-between for Harvey and his CIA bosses and Florida mob boss Santos Trafficante, who Rosselli used for the assassination plot infrastructure.

Teams of Cuban exiles and assassins—action men and shooters—were smuggled by boat back to the island on various attempts to kill Fidel. All disappeared into Cuba and were never heard from again. Presumably, they were apprehended, tortured, imprisoned, and executed. Castro's intelligence apparatus, G-2, had agents planted throughout the anti-Castro movement in Florida and other U.S.

areas with a large Cuban exile community. G-2 had a reputation for effectiveness, but were they that good that they could nip every assassination plot in the bud, or did they have some inside information?

It all came to an end on November 22, 1963, in Dallas, Texas, when President Kennedy was assassinated, shot dead by a scoped rifle while riding in an open car in a motorcade. The official version is that he was killed by deranged loner and self-professed "Marxist-Leninist" Lee Harvey Oswald.

For over two decades, public opinion polls have steadily reflected the belief of a majority of the American people that John F. Kennedy was killed not by a lone gunman, but as a result of a conspiracy.

In 1968, after winning the California Democratic primary, Bobby Kennedy was positioned to stake his claim as his party's frontrunner and inevitable candidate in that year's presidential election. He was shot dead by assassin Sirhan B. Sirhan, another "lone nut" gunman. So goes the official version.

Great events cast long shadows over the years. The Watergate scandals forced President Richard M. Nixon to resign from his office on August 8, 1974, precipitating a short-lived spasm of national reflection and institutional correction. It spawned several congressional committees with the formidable task of trying to make some kind of sense out of the last decade of U.S. covert history.

The Senate Select Committee on Intelligence Activities was chaired by Senator Frank Church, leading it to be called the Church Committee. Among the red-hot items of recent secret history was the revelation of CIA-Mafia plots to kill Castro. Politicians expressed shock and outrage that an arm of U.S. clandestine services would have teamed with organized crime to murder a foreign leader in peacetime. Some of them might actually have sincerely believed it.

The committee scheduled two pillars of the Mafia's part in the plot to testify: Johnny Rosselli and Sam Giancana.

The years following the JFK assassination hadn't been so great for either of them. They'd had their ups and downs, mostly downs.

Rosselli had been busted in 1968 for his participation in an organized card-cheating scheme at the Beverly Hills chapter of the world-famed Friar's Club, the organization whose membership is comprised mainly of showbiz professionals. The cheaters battened on to the club's high-stakes card games, bilking such stars as singer Tony Martin and funnyman Phil Silvers out of tens of thousands of dollars. Rosselli served a year or two in jail for his involvement in the caper. After his release, he was still dogged by the government, which scrutinized his tax returns and sources of income and also threatened to deport him as an unregistered alien—Rosselli had never become a U.S citizen.

Giancana's fortunes had been no less ill starred. His initial embrace of and then later war with the Kennedys had poisoned his standing in the Outfit. In 1966, his masters showed him who was boss by taking away his power.

He'd never been the boss, only the acting boss, standing front and center and doing the heavy lifting while the likes of Accardo and Humphreys stood watching in the shadows of the wings. But theirs was the real power in the Commission.

Everybody was sick of seeing Sam Giancana in the headlines; he was catching too much heat and spreading it around on the rest of the mob.

He was removed from power in what cannot even be labeled a bloodless coup; it was more of an administrative removal. A banishment. Giancana relinquished his power and perks, leaving the country to take up residence in Mexico. He prospered during his exile in the gambling cruise boat business, making some serious money.

On July 17, 1974, he fell victim to the old switcheroo, as his government contacts turned hostile overnight and had him deported from Mexico back to the United States. The deportation was rigged in such a way that Giancana had to forfeit the millions of dollars he'd salted away in Mexican banks over the long years of exile, delivering him a major financial body blow.

He returned to Chicago, where the Outfit could keep a closer eye on him. He was now suffering serious health problems and was only a shadow of his once ferocious self, mostly piss and not much vinegar.

Such were the respective positions of Rosselli and Giancana when they were called to testify in Washington to the Church Committee on CIA-Mafia murder plots.

The Hit

Giancana's condition was already shaky before he was subpoenaed to testify before the committee. Ongoing tax troubles and legal woes had stressed him out to the point where he was heard expressing the undiplomatic sentiment that he'd do anything to stay out of jail.

On June 18, 1975, a week before he was due to testify in Washington, Giancana had dinner with one of his daughters and her husband, plus two trusted henchmen, tough guys Chuckie English and Butch Blasi. The guests all left at about 10:00 P.M. Giancana retired to his basement den, a fortified bunker equipped with a kitchen and all the amenities. A housekeeper was present in her room in the aboveground area of the house.

Sometime between ten and midnight, Giancana was joined by a visitor whose identity is unknown. Whoever it was, Giancana felt comfortable around him—trusted him. Around midnight, Giancana prepared a snack of sausage, escarole, and beans. While he was occupied preparing the food, his guest shot him once in the back of the head, killing him. The weapon was a .22 handgun, whose low caliber belies its high-velocity effectiveness.

Giancana lay on the floor, dead, while his killer fired another bullet in his mouth, then five more slugs under his chin, stitching a semicircle there. It was a message, of course. The bullet in the mouth was a warning to others to keep silent. The bullets in a semicircle in the throat are said to indicate that Giancana couldn't be trusted to obey the iron law of omerta.

The housekeeper told police that she'd thought Giancana was alone in the cellar and had been unaware that he'd received any visitor.

A week later, on June 24, Johnny Rosselli delivered his testimony to the committee. He was careful to minimize the role of Santos Trafficante in the Kill-Castro plot.

A month after that, on July 30, 1975, deposed Teamsters head Jimmy Hoffa disappeared. Hoffa, the object of Bobby Kennedy's Ahab-like obsession, had been paroled from prison in 1973 and was looking to reclaim his place as head of the union, a goal that did not sit well with mobsters who preferred the status quo to rocking the boat. There was also concern that Hoffa was cooperating with federal authorities.

Most authorities believe that Hoffa was lured into a car by someone he trusted, where he was garroted and his body disposed of. The contract is said to have been handled by mobsters Russell Buffalino and New Jersey labor racketeer Anthony "Tony Pro" Provenzano. Despite many false alarms throughout the years, Hoffa's remains have never been found.

Johnny Rosselli testified three times to congressional committees. The third and final time, a secret session on the assassination of President Kennedy, was held in April 1976.

Perhaps in an effort to disarm others' suspicions by showing he had nothing to hide and no fear of retaliation, Rosselli resided in Florida in Trafficante's turf, where the gang boss showed him every sign of respect and affection and even importuned him to come to work for him. Rosselli enjoyed a number of social occasions with Trafficante and his wife. Twelve days before he disappeared, he'd dined with Trafficante in Fort Lauderdale.

On July 28, 1976, Rosselli was drugged, kidnapped, and murdered.

On August 8, a fifty-five-gallon drum bobbed up in the Intracoastal Waterway off North Miami. In it were the remains of Johnny Rosselli, his legs sawn off and placed in the drum with him. Evidence showed that he'd been kidnapped and drugged, then asphyxiated and shot in the chest. Asphyxiation was the cause of death. Rigor mortis having set in, the dead man's legs were cut off so he could be fitted into the drum.

It was a brutal end for the star-spangled mafioso.

STRATEGY

High-ranking elements of the CIA and the Mafia had no desire to see any further exposure of the Kill-Castro plot. The alliance was only the tip of an iceberg that involved such matters as the fraud of the 1960 presidential election, which put Kennedy in office; JFK's sharing a mistress with Giancana and Rosselli; the Kennedy brothers' tangled involvement with Marilyn Monroe and her untimely death; and the full extent of the partnership between the nation's clandestine services and the Mafia.

Giancana was a potential weak link. He was aging and infirm, in bad health. A prison term would kill him. He might well decide to spill his guts to the feds to avoid going to jail. He'd lived by the laws of the Mafia and might well choose to keep his mouth shut and die in prison, but why take chances? It's not the Mafia way to leave such important matters to chance.

He was on the outs with Outfit boss Tony Accardo, another factor that negatively affected his prospects. The real threat to Giancana came not so much from the Outfit, though, but from one man who could be damaged by his testimony: Santos Trafficante.

The Florida mob boss had been present at the creation of the CIA-Mafia Kill-Castro alliance. The plot had been a private undertaking by Rosselli, Giancana, and Trafficante, one that they had initiated without prior clearance from the Commission and that they kept secret from their fellow mobsters.

The different plots had been carried out mostly by anti-Castro Cubans in the exile community in Florida, Trafficante's turf. Rosselli had relied on Trafficante's organization to carry out the chores needed to facilitate the succession of murder teams sent against Castro.

The question exists: How committed was Trafficante to the Kill-Castro effort? Rosselli was fully invested in the scheme and seriously dedicated to its accomplishment; Giancana less so, especially as he soured under Justice Department pressure.

It has been suggested that the reason that none of the assassination plots hatched against Castro reached fruition is not because of the excellence of Fidel's G-2 intelligence apparatus, but because he was tipped off in advance of each plot. A likely candidate for the role of tipster would be Trafficante, who could have bartered the information in exchange for Castro's cooperation in supplying him with a steady flow of narcotics. Apart from the lucrative profits that such an arrangement would generate to both partners, Castro could also have rationalized that increasing the amount of theiving dope addicts in America could only help further destabilize the capitalist colossus in the north.

Trafficante and the Outfit bosses both had their reasons to wish that Giancana was no more. Eliminating him presented no great challenge.

Giancana, aging and infirm, lacked mobility and was pinned down in the house that was his refuge and fortress. Keeping tabs on his comings and goings was child's play to the Chicago organization. The real threat would come if one of the law enforcement agencies such as the FBI was keeping him under close surveillance to keep him alive. The fact that the hit went down as easily and hassle free as it did is proof that no such monitoring efforts were being made by the government. The plotters had a clear field.

The identity of the killer is still unknown, but it can be assumed that Giancana knew and trusted him. This was a textbook classic mob hit, using as the killer a person whom the mark would never suspect of harboring such lethal designs.

A potential rough spot in the plan was the presence of Giancana's housekeeper on the premises. But it was far from being an insurmountable obstacle. Had she seen someone or something that she shouldn't, it would have been her funeral—literally. In his house, the inner sanctum where he felt safest, was where Giancana was most vulnerable. It was a closed site, with no witnesses but those inside it. It was the optimum locale for the hit. The housekeeper could have and would have been eliminated if necessary. Lucky for her that she chose that night to stay in her room.

Deduct 1 point for the housekeeper being onsite.

STRATEGY: 4

Tactics

In many ways, the execution followed the pattern used to put down unwanted mob bigs who have outlived their usefulness. It was not without a certain respect. Giancana was an inconvenience and potentially worse, but so far he had obeyed the iron rules of Mafia and followed the code of omerta.

In classic fashion, the condemned man, unknowing of his imminent fate, ate a hearty meal. Giancana's last night on earth was spent in the congenial company of family and friends, with no apprehension of the axe about to fall. The evening broke up and the others went home, leaving Giancana alone in the house with his housekeeper.

How the killer later gained admittance to Giancana's bunker basement is a mystery. The housekeeper told investigators that she had admitted no visitors and had heard no one entering. She might have slept through it or simply not heard Giancana letting the visitor in.

In classic fashion, Giancana was taken unawares, shot and killed before he'd had time to realize that something was happening. That's as merciful as a gangland execution gets.

The killer's choice of weapon is interesting and instructive. A .22 handgun packs a hell of a wallop, making it a valuable tool for professional killers. Its low caliber ensures that its report is not overly loud, even without a silencer. It is neat and lethal in the hands of a competent marksman.

The sound of the shots going off in the basement would have registered as a string of popping noises, ones that very likely would have been muffled to inaudibility by the thick-walled basement bunker.

The subsequent mutilation of Giancana's body by shooting into his mouth and under his chin was part of the package, sending a clear message: Keep silent, do not speak.

The killer also exited the house and made his getaway as silently and unseen as he had entered it.

TACTICS: 5

RESULTS

The execution of Sam Giancana bears certain similarities to that of Willie Moretti. Like Moretti, Giancana was liquidated not so much for what he had done, but what he might do. It was a matter of closing doors before the feds could enter them. A kind of more-in-sorrow-than-in-anger kill.

The hit went down smoothly. The press handled the story as a gangland kill, largely ignoring the political angles. Giancana's death could only have come as a relief to the Chicago mob and to Santos Trafficante. Dead men tell no tales.

RESULTS: 10

Murder Meter Box Score
   STRATEGY: 4
   TACTICS: 5
   RESULTS: 10

   TOTAL: 19

Outliving all who thirsted for his blood is Fidel Castro. Presidents, spy chiefs, and mob bosses who burned to see Castro dead have long since gone to the grave. His immunity to assassination has condemned the Cuban people to enduring over four-and-a-half decades of his crackpot brand of obsolescent communist tyranny. A tyranny that dwarfs that of mobsters such as Giancana and Trafficante even in their heyday, making them look like pikers.

9

Give the Man a Cigar:
Carmine Galante

Narcotics and the Mafia have long walked hand in hand. They're an item. Part of organized crime exists to supply the public with illegal and forbidden commodities it craves: prostitutes, gambling, and drugs. This may be called the syndicate's "service sector." (Of course, the other half of organized crime exists to squeeze money out of unwilling civilians such as union members, contractors, small business owners, and the public at large. This part may be labeled the "extraction" component.)

Drugs offer high profits and high risk. Charlie "Lucky" Luciano, Louis "Lepke" Buchalter, Meyer Lansky, Benjamin "Bugsy" Siegel, Albert Anastasia, and Vito Genovese, to name but a few top mobsters, were involved with narcotics trafficking throughout their careers.

Frank Costello famously expressed his belief that the mob should stay out of the dope business, but he was located in a stratospheric level where big business, politics, and organized crime intersected, allowing for the making of big money in less risky endeavors. However, most mobsters were not in that rarefied position where they could afford to forego the big money generated by narcotics.

And for all his public posturing against the drug trade, which may have been no more than disinformation offered in hopes of misleading law enforcement and public opinion, Costello was in combination with Luciano, Lansky, and Ansastasia, who were deep into the dope business. It's also significant that the antitrafficking Costello was forced into retirement by Genovese, who possessed no such scruples against the trade.

The downside of the narcotics racket was the long prison sentences that were handed out to traffickers. These penalties were maximized in 1956, when Congress passed the Boggs-Taylor Narcotics Control Act, providing for prison terms of forty years for trafficking.

This was serious business. Even the Mafia, with its internal discipline and ability to punish transgressors of its laws, and their families, was concerned that the threat of such heavy prison time wielded by the law would tempt arrested members to violate omerta and cut a deal to spare themselves the worst.

On October 10–14, 1957, less than half a year after the abortive attack on Frank Costello, an extraordinary meeting was held in Sicily between top-ranking American mafiosi and their Sicilian counterparts. Historically, the American and Sicilian branches of the Mafia had operated almost exclusively in their separate spheres, as two essentially independent operations. No unifying council existed to coordinate their organizations, though there were numerous examples of cooperation between various U.S. and Sicilian crime families.

The line between the two had begun to blur when Luciano was deported from the United States. Operating in Sicily and Italy, he labored to establish new narcotics pipelines to America. Initially, his focus was on diverting heroin and morphine from Italy's legitimate pharmaceutical stocks to the illicit trade; by the mid-1950s, though, the action had shifted to an alliance where the opium crop was grown in Turkey and shipped to refineries in Italy, Corsica, and Marseille, France, to be transformed into white-powder heroin. Turkish opium supplies were soon augmented by shipments from the former French colony of Vietnam.

Luciano worked with local mafiosi in his area, as well as with the Unione Corse, the Corsican "mafia." He was also served by a cadre of mobsters who, like him, had never become U.S. citizens and so were deported to their native Italian and Sicilian homelands. Emissaries from the Commission continually shuttled back and forth between New York and Naples, where Luciano generally resided, bringing him suitcases full of cash and conferring with him to receive his intructions for the acting bosses back home.

The meeting in October 1957 was held at Palermo's Hotel des Palmes, a world-famous luxury hotel that had seen its best days several generations earlier. Luciano was present, of course, as were some leading Sicilian mob chiefs. From the United States came a delegation spearheaded by mob boss Joe "Joe Bananas" Bonanno and his consigliere, Carmine Galante, seconded by some lesser figures such as three members of the Magadino family of Buffalo, New York, and Santo Sorge, a relative of one of the top men in the Sicilian Mafia.

Joe Bonanno had been one of the original five family heads appointed to the Commission in 1931; now, in 1957, only he and Joe Profaci remained of that original group. Bonanno came from Castellammare del Golfo, that Sicilian port city that had featured so prominently in the Castellammarese War between transplanted native son Joe the Boss Masseria and his opponent Don Salvatore Maranzano.

Of the original five family heads, Bonanno (aka Don Peppino) was the most old school, insisting that his Sicilian dialect be spoken in his New York crime family.

He would have preferred that only Sicilians be allowed into the Mafia, closing the membership rolls even to Italian-born mobsters. Unlike other Commission members, he generally shunned ventures involving nonmember associates.

Bonanno regarded himself as being in the tradition of the old-country Mafia dons, a man of honor, feared and respected, upright and proud—though that tradition existed largely in folklore and popular ballads divorced from the reality of the Sicilian Mafia's feudal ways and terrorist tactics.

His underboss, Carmine Galante, was born in New York in 1910, but both his parents had come from Castellammare. Galante was five feet, three inches of dynamite, an implacable stone killer and enforcer with a wicked disposition and an icy professionalism. He'd followed the traditional gangster career path from young hooligan to street gang member to hardened criminal and murderer before being recruited into the Bonanno gang. His criminal compeers tagged him with the nickname "Lilo," Italian for a little cigar. Galante himself was an enthusiastic cigar smoker.

Like Sam Giancana with Paul Ricca, Galante had been a chauffeur for his boss, Joe Bonanno, and like Giancana, Galante would ultimately rise to leadership of his family. Unlike Giancana with his explosive outbursts, though, Galante was a coolheaded killer; he was ice to Giancana's fire. Galante shared with Vito Genovese the ability to deal out murder wholesale without getting himself worked up over it.

In 1930, Galante was arrested for shooting a police officer in the leg during a truck hijacking. Sentenced to twelve and a half years in prison, he was paroled in 1939. Back on the streets, he sharpened his skills by carrying out a number of contract murders. Authorities believe that in his crime career he participated in or ordered some eighty or so murders. Believing, however, is not the same as proving in court.

Working with the government to kill a foreign foe was nothing new for Galante, who'd done just that almost two decades before the CIA-Mafia Kill-Castro plot. In his case, the year was 1943, the government was fascist Italy, and the target was Carlo Tresca, anarchist and exile, the writer and publisher of an Italian-language paper in New York who'd gotten under the skin of dictator Benito Mussolini. The hit was brokered through Vito Genovese, then in his incarnation of Il Duce's favorite mafioso. It is widely held that Galante was the actual triggerman in the hit.

Galante, at age forty, was made consigliere and put in charge of the Bonanno family's lucrative narcotics business. In the post–World War II era, Joe Bonanno was the first to establish a Mafia presence in Montreal. Galante went there in 1953 to set up a key transit point on a narcotics pipeline between Europe and America. It was a locale that he would use to great effect two decades later when importing a small army of Sicilian mafiosi into the United States.

In 1957, though, his stony and impenetrable presence was kept in the background as his boss, Joe Bonanno, took the spotlight at the American-Sicilian Mafia palaver at Palermo's Hotel des Palmes. The work of the conclave was done at meetings held at the site's Sala Wagner, a room where a century earlier composer Richard Wagner had created some of his greatest operas.

The conference revolved around the issue of narcotics. In light of the 1956 law mandating stiff penalties for traffickers, the American Mafia leadership was in a quandary. On the one hand, the profits from dope trafficking were too great to resist, with crime bosses and street soldiers alike generally unable to withstand the temptation. On the other hand, there was fear that maximum prison terms would pressure the arrested into breaking omerta and cooperating with the law to cut themselves a better deal. In 1957, over a third of the membership of the Bonanno family had been arrested for narcotics dealing. The ratio was matched or surpassed by the other five families, who at that time imported the lion's share of heroin coming into the United States.

The purpose of the meeting was to broker a deal allowing the Sicilian Mafia to take over the importation and distribution of narcotics in America. In essence, the American Mafia was doing what gamblers and bookmakers do, hedging their bet by laying off some of the action on their Sicilian counterparts. There was also a feeling that Sicilian mafiosi were made of sterner stuff than their American cousins, who presumably had fallen away from some of the iron traditions of omerta that still held sway in the old country.

The Sicilians would be licensed to bring in dope and would have permission to operate in the territories of U.S. crime families. American and Sicilian mobsters alike would profit from the deal, which would supply the Americans with a steady stream of the big-money revenue generated by narcotics, while laying off some of the crime-and-punishment risks on the Sicilians.

The deal was done, allowing some time for visiting American delegates like Joe Bonanno to be hosted and feted in their native land and see some of the sights.

Two weeks later, back in New York, the other shoe dropped in

the abortive assassination attempt of Frank Costello with the execution of his bulwark "Mr. Terror": Albert Anastasia. Behind it lay the
hand of Vito Genovese, making his bid for supreme power.
Anastasia had hit Commission member Vince Mangano to make
himself boss of their Brooklyn crime family. Now, Genovese had hit
Commission member Anastasia to become the boss of bosses.

The old order was destablized by fear and greed—fear of Genovese's
rapacious appetite for domination and the violence and murder it
had generated and might again; and greed for the colossal profits of
the dope trade. The Commission's balance of power had shifted,
leaving the last two original members, Bonanno and Joe Profaci, in
the minority and the three newer members, Genovese, Thomas
Lucchese, and Carlo Gambino, in the majority.

Similar stresses worked down to the family level. Genovese had
liquidated Anastasia in part by allying with Anastasia's underboss
Carlo Gambino, who in return took over the Brooklyn crime family.

Gambino had jumped over rival contender Anniello "Neil"
Dellacroce, an Anastasia loyalist and practitioner of his mentor's
brutal ways. There was some tension involved while waiting to see
which way Dellacroce would jump: whether he would acquiesce in
the transfer of power, or make war to take the throne for himself.
Dellacroce elected to take the number-two slot, solidifying Gambino's
mastery of the family. After Apalachin, New York, the American
Mafia made a conscious effort to be seen by law enforcement agencies and the public as having disassociated themselves from the narcotics trade. The word was put out that narcotics trafficking was
henceforth to be forbidden to members on pain of death.

This was disingenuous, to say the least. What it really meant was
that those members who were involved in narcotics trafficking
must, on pain of death, refrain from being seen or associated with
members who were not so involved, for fear of bringing the heat
down on them. The trafficking continued, but with a firewall of insulation that would allow deniability when a member was arrested
for the crime. That way the line could be advanced that the offend-
ers had been acting on their own, contrary to Mafia rules.

The truth was quite different. Until his death in 1962, Luciano was deeply involved in the heroin trade. His one-time underboss and current successor Vito Genovese was rapacious and relentless in his narcotics dealing. Genovese's arrest and conviction on trafficking charges in 1958 landed him a fifteen-year sentence.

Behind bars in the federal prison in Atlanta, Genovese still fancied himself the boss of bosses and handed out death sentences to underlings in the outside world whose behavior had offended him or who had otherwise lost his trust. It didn't take much to lose his trust, and those who had were soon dead.

In 1960, Joe Bonanno's henchman Carmine Galante was busted on narcotics charges. His first trial ended in a mistrial. Two years later, he was convicted and sent away on a long prison stretch.

Joe Bonanno's closest ally on the Commission was Joe Profaci, an alliance cemented by the marriage of Bonanno's eldest son, Salvatore "Bill", to Profaci's niece, Rosalie. Their wedding had been one of the signature mob galas of the postwar era, attended by a galaxy of Mafia notables.

But now Profaci, sick and aging, was weak and unsteady, even in quelling disorder within the ranks of his own family. In 1961, the Gallo brothers, dissatisfied with the share of the take coming their way for handling some of the family's strong-arm and murder chores, turned renegade. Leader Larry Gallo, sided by siblings Joseph "Crazy Joe" and Albert "Kid Blast" and some equally wild and uninhibited sidemen, struck hard against Profaci. They kidnapped family underboss Joe Magliocco, ransoming him for $100,000, and killed several Profaci lieutenants.

Such antics could only have further undermined the health of Profaci, who on June 11, 1962, died of cancer.

Joe Bonanno, now fifty-eight and readier than ever to rumble, backed Magliocco for the post of Gambino family head and Commission member. But Magliocco's bid was undercut by the rebellious Gallo brothers, prompting the power duo of Carlo Gambino and Thomas Lucchese to block his accession to the title.

The haughty Don Peppino Bonanno with his old-world airs, preening self-regard, and vaunting ambition, had bigger fish to fry.

Murder was on his mind in 1963: specifically, the assassination of Commission members Carlo Gambino and Thomas Lucchese and of Buffalo's longtime Mafia chief Stephen Magadino.

The deaths of Gambino and Lucchese would make Bonanno the big boss. Magadino, his cousin, had offended him by his resistance to Bonanno's incursions into his territory of Toronto, Canada. Presumably, the incarcerated Vito Genovese was considered to pose no threat to Bonanno's takeover bid.

It would have been a master stroke of murder if not for the intervention of Joe Columbo. Bonanno had given the kill orders to Magliocco, who gave the contract to Columbo, a midlevel Profaci capo with a smooth line in financial swindles and several murders under his belt. Instead of carrying out the orders, though, Columbo went to Carlo Gambino and told him the tale, putting Bonanno's murder ploy in check.

Magliocco was summoned before the Commission. His life could have been forfeit, but the Commission chose the next worse punishment: banishment from the Mafia. He was also assessed a fine of $43,000 as a kind of "court cost" for the Commission's time and trouble in examining his case. The unhappy Magliocco died not long after of natural causes—if not of a broken heart.

Joe Bonanno was also summoned before the Commission, a summons he chose to ignore. The machinery was already in motion to suppress him. From Chicago, Sam Giancana put in his two cents on Bonanno's recalcitrance: "Hit him!"

Bonanno was also being pressed hard by an antiracketeering grand jury probe headed by Robert Kennedy acolyte and Manhattan District Attorney Robert Morgenthau. On the night of October 20, 1964—the eve of his scheduled appearance before the grand jury—Bonanno vanished under mysterious circumstances that seemed to suggest that he'd been abducted (at the least, if not done away with). A closer look, however, exposed a number of holes and inconsistencies in the cover story, indicating that he'd faked the abduction as a way of making himself scarce and removing himself from the line of fire of his fellow mobsters and the subpoenas of federal crime probers.

His disappearance opened a period of sniping, hits, and intermittent low-level warfare between his crime family and those of the Commission—the so-called Bananas War.

Bonanno resurfaced two years later in May 1966, offering by way of explanation for his absence the story that he'd been kidnapped by rival gangsters who'd held him for several months, over which time he managed to bargain for his life and freedom; and that not until the time of his resurfacing had it been safe for him to show his face.

Federal prosecutors weren't buying and tried to have him jailed for ducking his grand jury date back in 1964. The battle raged for five years in court, with Bonanno ultimately beating the rap.

The suspicion was that Bonanno's return was prompted on a wild, failed murder attempt on his son and acting boss, Bill. Bonanno went before the Commission, offering to retire in exchange for a cessation of hostilities. The deal was taken, causing him to relocate to Arizona, where he dabbled in a few regional rackets.

Bonanno's abdication put his son Bill's leadership in eclipse, throwing the question of his successor into question. With logical candidate Carmine Galante in jail for the foreseeable future, mobster Phillip "Rusty" Rastelli was installed in the top spot.

In prison, Galante had confided to intimates his ambitions to restore the Bonanno family's power and prestige and take it to new levels and had made no secret of his intent to see himself not only as family head but ultimately as boss of bosses. His release in 1972 occasioned no small amount of tension between himself and the official family boss, Rusty Rastelli. In 1974, Rastelli was convicted on extortion and racketeering charges and given a six-year prison term, promoting Galante to the top slot as acting boss. Galante now began building an operation that would install him as the vital middleman between the Commission and the Sicilian Mafia heroin dealers who they'd licensed to operate in the United States.

The roots of the scheme went back to 1964. When events looked like Joe Bonnano was going to have to go to war with the rest of the Commission, he decided to import several dozen Sicilian gunmen to beef up his defenses.

On becoming Bonanno family head in 1974, Carmine Galante was to take this concept and put it on steroids, setting in motion an operation to import not dozens but scores and possibly hundreds of Sicilian mafiosi into the United States. This was done in conjunction with a massive expansion of the heroin trade, which the Sicilian newcomers would handle on American soil under a cooperative venture with the American Mafia. It was the same arrangement as that brokered in Sicily in 1957, but platformed into a whole higher level.

The Sicilians came through Canada into the United States, following the same pipeline route as the fresh tons of heroin they were now bringing into North America. In the United States, primarily on the Atlantic seaboard, they operated a high-volume heroin distribution network through a front consisting of chains of takeout pizza parlors—the infamous "Pizza Connection" dope ring that would be exposed in New York courts in the 1980s.

Galante recruited a sizeable contingent of them to fortify and expand the ranks of his street soldiers in New York. The Sicilians' names, faces, and lengthy police records were unknown to homegrown American law enforcement agencies, giving them a powerful initial advantage in setting up their networks.

The Sicilian contingent was referred to by the American Mafia members as "Zips," a word whose derivation is obscure but may come from a bit of Sicilian slang or wordplay meaning a rustic or other type of crude, raw fellow from the sticks. The Zips were regarded by their American counterparts, probably rightly, as being hard-core, old-school killers, fearsome and relentless.

Many of the new arrivals settled in Brooklyn, in the Knickerbocker Avenue area. One who'd come in advance of the 1970s wave was Salvatore Catalano, who'd arrived in 1966 and operated from the cover of a modest store that sold newspapers and magazines. In the 1970s, he emerged as a power in the area, buttressed by two more recent Sicilian immigrants, Baldassere "Baldo" Amato and Cesare Bonventre.

The latter two, who both hailed from Castellammare del Golfo, were a kind of watered-down version of that stellar Sicilian murder duo of the Capone era, Albert Anselmi and John Scalise.

The Bonanno capo on Knickerbocker Avenue was Peter Licati, who forbade the membership in his domain from drug dealing. Catalano and his two sidemen liquidated Licati, with Catalano taking over the dead capo's spot. This development was evidently far from unwelcome to Carmine Galante, since he began using Amato and Bonventre, while Catalano continued to hold and thrive in his newly won post.

Galante cherished the romantic fallacy that the Zips were true devotees of the Sicilian Mafia's man of honor tradition, more trustworthy and loyal, and less likely if arrested and facing heavy prison time to break omerta and be turned by the law to inform on their crime confederates. Which goes to show that a hardened mob chief is as much a mark as anyone for a beautiful dream.

Law enforcement agents and mob watchers now began to speak of the "Sicilian contingent" of the Bonanno family.

On May 15, 1976, Carlo Gambino, the canny white-haired, beak-nosed patriarch of his Brooklyn crime family, died of natural causes at age seventy-four. He left behind an organization that was the wealthiest and most powerful of the five families.

The line of succession was tricky. Gambino's family had developed along a two-track pattern, as exemplified by two lieutenants, Paul "Big Paul" Castellano and Neil Dellacroce. Castellano handled the family's more corporate operations, its financial schemes and rackets, including the penetration and ownership of legitimate businesses as fronts. He also had the additional credibility that came from being Gambino's brother-in-law and second cousin.

Dellacroce was a gutter-tough disciple of his mentor, Anastasia, bossing a crew of enforcers, strong arms, and killers who operated such traditional rackets as prostitution, drugs, gambling, loansharking, hijacking, and labor racketeering. Under Gambino, Neil bossed about half the family's rackets.

Gambino's dying wish was that Castellano become head of the family. At the time of Gambino's death, Dellacroce had been doing time, serving a sentence for tax evasion. Again, as in 1957 when Anastasia had been hit, he was now once more put in the position of being passed over for the top slot by a rival.

A refusal to accept the second slot could have resulted in a bloody intrafamily gang war. Tensions ran high at the all-important sit-down between newly anointed boss Castellano and Dellacroce.

Castellano said, "Anything you had with Carlo, you keep. Anything more you want, we talk."

This proved to be a basis for negotiation and Dellacroce was content for a time to accept the subordinate slot, and peace was maintained in the Gambino family.

Gambino's passing only encouraged Carmine Galante to put himself forward as the "first among equals" of the Commission. He had made a special status for himself by his role as overseer of the regular collecting of the American Mafia's cut of the Sicilians' U.S. heroin "take" and its distribution to the Commission members.

Fabulous sums of money were routinely channeled through him to the other five family heads. It was a position of wealth and power that might well have turned the head of another not quite so greedy as Lilo. But his insatiable money lust ensured that more and more of the take would find its way into his coffers.

His doling out of the heroin trade rake-off to his Commission associates became irregular and highly suspect in their eyes. His ordering the slaying of eight Gambino members in various hits during a long-running, low-intensity drug war had also put him at the top of the to do list of Gambino head Paul Castellano and underboss Neil Dellacroce.

The Hit

On July 12, 1979, at around midday, Carmine Galante was driven to the Joe and Mary Italian American Restaurant on Knickerbocker Avenue in Brooklyn. Owner Guiseppe Turano, a distant cousin of Galante's, was going on a trip to Sicily, and the planned get-together was a kind of going-away party. Galante, Turano, his wife, Mary, and his children, Constonza and John, ate at a table in the restaurant's outdoor patio. Also present was Angelo Presenzano, a Bonanno family member and Galante follower. Early on in the meal, the seventy-two-year-old Presenzano excused himself and left.

A short time later, a trio of newcomers arrived: drug dealer Leonardo Coppola, a Galante loyalist, accompanied by Baldo Amato and Cesare Bonventre, Lilo's trusted Zip bodyguards.

Host Turano expressed his surprise at Coppola's presence, since the two disliked each other. Galante expansively said that he would function as peacemaker. Coppola, Amato, and Bonventre were invited to Galante's table to join the celebration.

There was a lull after the main meal was eaten and before dessert was to be served. At that time, about 2:45 in the afternoon, three ski-masked intruders armed with handguns and shotguns entered the restaurant through the front of the building.

Turano's son, John, saw them and tried to run. He was brought down by a shot in the back, but survived.

The assassins stormed the outdoor patio, cutting loose with a fusillade that chopped Galante, Turano, and Coppola. Galante was in the process of lighting up a cigar when he was surprised by a shotgun blast at point-blank range. Turano and Coppola were also killed.

Galante's bodyguard Bonventre rose and fired two shots into his boss's body—a pointless exercise, since the shotgun blast had already killed Galante. The ski-masked trio fled the restaurant. Amato and Bonventre followed them out of the building. Once on the street, they all went their separate ways.

Police arriving at the scene found the body of Carmine Galante with a cigar still clamped between his jaws.

STRATEGY

Carmine Galante's problem was that he'd gotten too full of himself. His role as collector and bagman for the Commission's cut of the Sicilian heroin racket put him in an extraordinary position of power. When he began cutting back on disbursements to his fellow Commission members, he sealed his own doom. It was greed, pure and simple, that put the finger on him; greed plus the fear of what he might do in the future.

If he disrespected his fellows enough to steal from them, it would not be so great a step for him to try to kill them. For he must surely know that if and when his dishonesty was discovered, his death would be decreed.

He had committed a mortal sin and he had to be stopped before he descended further into the same fatal folly that had deluded Joe Bonanno into thinking he could make a clean sweep of his Commission opponents and keep all the marbles for himself.

As always, the principal is to strike where the mark feels the safest and is therefore the most vulnerable.

Galante seems to have had no suspicion that he was on the chopping block or he would have taken steps to protect himself. Clearly, he had no doubts about the loyalty of his bodyguards.

In the case of Leonardo Coppola, his instincts were correct. Coppola was loyal to him. That's why the murder plot had included Coppola's being lured to the restaurant so he could be assassinated along with his boss, to prevent his mounting any opposition or retaliatory strikes in the aftermath of the kill.

Amato and Bonventre had other loyalties. Their allegiance was not to Galante, but to the Mafia itself. They were easily suborned to turn against their boss. Their most important role in the hit was to deliver Coppola to the chopping block. That was their primary task. Their secondary role was to serve as backup for the ski-masked trio of shooters in the event of trouble or complications.

Bonventre made a big mistake when he put two slugs into Galante, a potentially fatal error that could have resulted in his arrest and the naming of the higher-ups who'd ordered the kill. It didn't, but it could have. That's a loose end, and loose ends are always dangerous.

Deduct 1 point for the use of Bonventre as a backup: bad personnel choice.

STRATEGY: 4

TACTICS

An interesting though unsolvable question is the role of Galante associate Angelo Presenzano. The elderly mobster was allegedly loyal to Galante. However, his sudden departure from the luncheon cannot help but raise the suspicion that he could have served as the spotter or fingerman in the kill, certifying that the mark (Galante) was on the scene at the appointed hour. He could have tipped off the three ski-masked killers that Galante was in place.

His part in the play, if any, must remain an open question. While hiding out after the hit, he died of a heart attack.

The Sicilian Zips, Amato and Bonventre, had a dual role. A major part of their function was to get Coppola on the scene without raising his suspicions. Their secondary task was that of backup. The plotters were taking no chances. Besides three masked killers with shotguns and handguns, Amato and Bonventre were present to provide an extra edge if for some reason the massive assault by the trio should go awry.

Not since Anastasia had a Commission member been killed so publicly and so bloodily. (Joe Columbo was the victim of an assassination attempt at an Italian American Unity Day rally, the triggerman being black man Jerome Johnson, believed to have been recruited by Crazy Joe Gallo. Johnson was killed on the spot by an unknown shooter. But the Columbo shooting was made to appear to be one of the "lone nut" pieces of political gunplay that had destabilized American politics in the 1960s and 1970s. Columbo did not die, though the shooting rendered him comatose and brain-dead.)

Galante and Coppola were marked for death. It's an open question as to whether Joe Turano was also slated for execution or simply was in the wrong place at the wrong time.

The Galante hit was a big kill, with three hitters armed with heavy firepower assaulting the mobster in broad daylight. An old saying goes, "If you strike at the king, strike hard!" The killers struck hard, all right, with maximum force, murderous and irresistible. The hit had certain aspects of a raw, ragged Wild West gundown.

The masked trio had made the kill. Galante was dead, as was

Coppola and Turano. Their getaway was clean. The hit turned sloppy when Zip bodyguard Bonventre pumped two slugs in Galante's body. By so doing, he implicated himself and his partner in the hit.

And it was all so unnecessary. After taking a shotgun blast to the torso at close range, Galante was a dead man. There's no surviving that kind of damage.

Did Bonventre lose his cool and panic? Or maybe his bloodlust was stirred by the gunplay and he couldn't let the occasion pass without getting in a few licks of his own. In either case, it was a mistake. Had he done nothing, he and Amato would have been in the clear. They could have fled then, with no imputation of involvement in the hit, because no hoodlum could be blamed for not sticking around after the murder to wait for the police to arrive.

A second blunder was then committed by the Zips when they failed to kill the remaining living witnesses, which included Turano's wife, Mary, daughter Constanza and wounded son John. Amato and Bonventre were lucky that the survivors had seen no evidence of their treachery or, if they had, were too imbued with the mystique of omerta and the fear of retaliation to speak of it.

Regardless, the Zip duo managed to avoid incrimination and arrest in the kill. That was luck, not skill. A professional doesn't count on luck to save the day. They made a bad mistake when Bonventre blasted his dead boss and compounded it by leaving the witnesses alive.

Deduct 1 point for Bonventre's rash action in showing his and Amato's hand.
Deduct 1 point for their leaving the witnesses alive.

TACTICS: 3

RESULTS

Who benefitted most from the death of Carmine Galante?

First, his fellow Commission members. The memory of Joe Bonanno's ambitious blueprint for murder and takeover was still fresh in the minds of the board members who sat in judgment on

Lilo. His sins were those they could understand. The sin of greed and overreaching. He was just too greedy to live.

Gambino family head Paul Castellano could not help but rejoice at the elimination of a murder-minded rival who'd already caused the deaths of eight members of his family in a drug dispute.

Years later, Gambino member Arthur "Bruno" Indelicato was convicted for his participation in Galante's murder. Indelicato's links to Neil Dellacroce indicate the possibility of Dellacroce's involvement in the hit. Dellacroce certainly had the qualifications and the manpower—and the will—to have masterminded Galante's execution.

Some big kills are simple at base. Dutch Schultz defied the Commission and died. Johnny Rosselli broke omerta and died. Carmine Galante got too greedy and pushy and died.

Galante's place was filled, incredibly, by Salvatore Catalano, the Knickerbocker Avenue capo who'd earned that particular post by knocking off Bonanno family member Peter Licati. Now Carmine Galante was dead and Catalano moved to occupy his spot.

It was a signal change: a Sicilian mafioso taking over one of the five families and a spot on the Commission. This, then, was the ultimate result of the "Sicilian defense" pioneered by Joe Bonanno fifteen years earlier and brought to its fullest development by Carmine Galante. But Galante had been too blind to see that he'd created a Frankenstein that would turn against him and usurp his place at the helm of the Bonanno family.

Catalano's reign was short lived, as within a year or so he voluntarily abdicated his position on the grounds that his difficulty with speaking and understanding the English language had proved an impassable bar to his maintaining proper leadership of his New York crime family.

The affair marks the highwater mark of the Sicilian Mafia's power and influence on the five families and through them, the Commission.

Baldo Amato would eventually be tried and convicted in the Pizza Connection heroin prosecutions of the 1980s. Cesare Bonventre fell victim to a gangland execution; his dismembered body parts found their final resting place in three fifty-five-gallon drums.

The showy splatter of the Galante hit was a high-profile news event whose prominence was not hurt by its having occurred in New York City, the media capital of the world. It was old school, a real cowboy kill. It was not the kind of publicity the American Mafia needed in the last decades of the twentieth century.

It furnished prosecutors with a weapon that they would wield to great effect in the investigations and trials of the 1980s; namely, concrete proof that the Mafia was not an illusory phantom compounded of Hollywood screenwriters' imaginations and the tall tales told by old crooks in their dotage, but was a vicious, murderous reality.

Mafia in America today works best as a secret thing, a twilight state of being buried as far below the media radar (not to mention that of the police) as possible. When the press gets on a hot story, the glare of publicity makes it impossible for the subject to lead a normal life.

Galante's bloody demise made for good pictures and good television and were endlessly showcased in headlines and transmitted around the world. Such publicity is poison for organized crime.

It's the kiss of death for a modern Mafia chief, as will be shown in the cautionary tale of John Gotti, which follows.

Deduct 3 points for a showy, splattery, headline-grabbing kill.

RESULTS: 7

Murder Meter Box Score
   STRATEGY: 4
   TACTICS: 3
   RESULTS: 7

TOTAL: 14

10

The Big Hit: Paul Castellano

Paul Castellano was a butcher's son and in his youth had followed the professional meatcutter's trade before moving on to Mafia greatness.

While head of the Gambinos, the most powerful crime family in the country, he owned a company that specialized in selling high-quality cuts of meat to top restaurants. When dining out, his custom was to examine the cuts of raw steaks, chops, and prime rib and passing on them before having them cooked for his meal. His interest in food was compounded by his ownership of a variety of meat and poultry outlets and several major supermarket chains in the Northeast. In short, Big Paul liked a good piece of meat.

He therefore had reason for anticipation on December 16, 1985, when he was scheduled to have dinner with three associates at Sparks Steak House in midtown Manhattan. The restaurant was one of the top steakhouses in the Metro area.

He didn't know that the menu's featured special of the day would be himself and that he was about to be served up well done.

He was born Constantino Paul Castellano on June 26, 1915, in Brooklyn, New York, to immigrant parents. His father was a butcher who also worked an Italian lottery on the side. Young Paul was an indifferent student who left school early to follow in his father's footsteps as both meatcutter and illegal lottery operator. Growing to a height of six feet, two inches, he came by the appellation of "Big Paul" honestly.

Crime called; he heard the call, becoming a burglar, gambler, and ultimately made Mafia member.

His career prospects were not hampered by the fact that he was not only the brother-in-law of Carlo Gambino, who married his sister, but also Gambino's second cousin. But his rise was no case of nepotism; he excelled both in traditional organized crime paths such as loansharking and labor racketeering, as well as in showing a facility for penetration and takeover of businesses and unions vital to the economy.

Stresses dating back to the Albert Anastasia hit threatened to open fault lines in what became the Gambino crime family. In brief, Gambino had teamed with Vito Genovese to liquidate Anastasia. In the aftermath, Gambino managed to reach a working arrangement with Anastasia loyalist and potential rival Aniello "Neil" Dellacroce, making him underboss. A disciple of Anastasia's aggressive attitudes and methods, Dellacroce was hard-line, old-school Mafia, a tough guy with no qualms about breaking bones and heads as needed.

He was content to accept the number-two spot.

Gambino sought to extend the family's reach beyond its traditional organized crime pursuits and deeper into such areas as construction, waste management, trucking, and the like.

In this, able assistance was provided by Paul Castellano. Big Paul was a big earner with an aptitude for money crimes. He owned poultry and meatpacking companies and wholesale food operations and controlled key unions whose work stoppages could paralyze whole segments of the city and regional economy at his command. He patterned himself on the big-business model, in dress and deportment. He became Gambino's favorite and most trusted capo.

The Gambinos became the city's—and thus the nation's—most powerful and influential crime family, with about 500 soldiers and a thousand or more associates.

Before dying in 1976, Gambino made clear that his choice for successor was Big Paul. Neil Dellacroce, then in prison for income tax evasion, had yet to be heard from. After being released, Dellacroce came to an accommodation with Castellano.

While maintaining outward unity, the family would be split into two factions. Dellacroce would retain control of ten of the family's twenty crews and would oversee its interest in such traditional blue-collar rackets as gambling, loansharking, and hijacking. Castellano would be in charge of white-collar money crimes and business scams. His many interests included two major supermarket chains, construction and carting companies, control of several major unions, and many other basic services integral to the city and regional economy.

John Joseph Gotti was born on October 27, 1940, in the Bronx, to parents who were both immigrants from Naples. His father worked construction, and John was one of thirteen children, two of whom died in their youth. When he was twelve, his family moved to the East New York section of Brooklyn. At about that time, young Gotti began to fend for himself in the streets.

His neighborhood belonged to mobster Carmine Fatico, an Anastasia capo. After Anastasia's death, Fatico became part of the Gambino organization, serving as a capo for Neil Dellacroce. Gotti began as a gopher for the Fatico crowd, running errands for them. He was one of those who always wanted to be a wiseguy. He was about five feet, nine inches, solid, well built, tough, and defiant. A boyhood chum and best friend was Angelo "Fat Ange" Ruggiero, with whom he would be closely linked for much of his crime career (and not always to best advantage).

Gotti joined the Fulton-Rockaway street gang, raising hell and making a name for himself as a young rough and ready hoodlum. At seventeen, he was busted on a burglary rap and received probation. He was on the way up, soon attracting favorable notice from Neil Dellacroce; this was the start of a vital relationship in Gotti's life and crimes.

Carmine Fatico moved his operation to South Ozone Park in Queens, making his headquarters in a building that held his sardonically titled Bergin Hunt and Fish Club, the place being named for Bergen Street in their old East New York neighborhood. (The misspelling of Bergen to Bergin was an oversight none of Gotti's crew bothered to correct.) The site was strategically placed close to JFK International Airport, a world hub for warehousing and distribution of many millions of dollars' worth of air cargo. The airport was prime plundering ground for the mob and its gangs of cargo thieves and hijackers.

In 1966, Gotti joined the Fatico Bergin crew as a hijacker. By this time, he had a wife and several children to support. His partners on a number of hijacking jobs were his younger brother, Gene, and longtime chum Angelo Ruggiero.

In 1968, the trio was busted for stealing a truckful of dresses, a felony. John was sentenced to three years in the tough federal pen at Lewisburg, Pennsylvania. Released in January 1972, he returned to his old haunts to learn that capo Carmine Fatico was suffering legal troubles that required him to stay away from the Bergin Hunt and Fish Club. With Fatico's endorsement and an okay from Neil Dellacroce, Gotti was made acting capo of the crew. In this capacity, he enjoyed regular meetings with Neil, who became a kind of sponsor and mentor in postgraduate racketeering and thuggery.

In 1973, Gotti was called on to do an important service for family boss Carlo Gambino. A popular crime of the era was kidnapping well-heeled mobsters and holding them for ransom. Kidnap gangs prowled the bars, clubs, after-hours joints, and gambling dens looking for likely victims.

One such victim was Emmanuel Gambino, the godfather's nephew. The victim's wife mustered a sum of $100,000, which was passed to the abductors. Young Gambino was not returned until several months later, when his body was found with a bullet in his head in a New Jersey dump site. Later, witnesses to another gang kidnapping, that of a Staten Island gambler, wrote down the license plate number of the car into which he'd been hustled away by his captors.

It was traced to two men: Edward Maloney and James McBratney, members of a kidnap gang to be sure, but apparently not the gang that had abducted and killed Emmanuel Gambino. Carlo Gambino didn't care to draw such fine distinctions and wanted them taken care of.

Maloney made himself scarce, but McBratney stayed put, beefing up security by carrying a machine gun around in his car. Unfortunately for him, that's where it was, in his car, on the night of May 22, 1973, while inside Snoope's Bar and Grill in Staten Island McBratney sat at the bar sipping a crème de menthe.

Three burly strangers entered, moving in on McBratney and surrounding him. One said that they were detectives and told him he was under arrest. A second pulled out a pair of handcuffs. There was a struggle. McBratney was a big guy but so were they, and there were three of them.

A spectator on the sidelines shouted something about seeing some identification. The intruder who'd been doing the talking established his bonafides by firing a shot into the ceiling. Some patrons fled the bar, others ducked for cover.

The two other men held McBratney in place while the gunman shot him three times, killing him. The trio fled.

McBratney had had nothing to do with Emmanuel Gambino's death. But he was a kidnapper, and his liquidation would serve as an object lesson to deter other crooks from treading in his path.

It had been an amateurish hit—which didn't make the victim any less dead. The trio took McBratney in a well-lit bar filled with witnesses, when they could just have easily waited for him to exit, where they could have put the blast on him in relative privacy. Or if the public execution was part of the lesson, they could have covered up their faces.

Instead, witnesses got a good enough look at them to later identify two of them and pick their photos out of a police mug shot book. The ones picked out were Angelo Ruggiero and Ralph Galione, another Gambino-associated thug, with the latter being fingered as the triggerman. An informer in the Bergin Club orbit identified John Gotti as the third man.

Gunman Galione presently vanished, never to be seen again. Gotti and Ruggiero were arrested. Legal counsel was supplied by Carlo Gambino in the form of superlawyer Roy Cohn, once chief advisor to Red-hunting Senator Joe McCarthy and now a power in the shadow zone of New York—and Washington, D.C.—where high society intersects with low life. Cohn had major league political connections. He argued that Gotti and Ruggiero had come to the aid of their pal Galione in a barroom brawl, not knowing that Galione had a gun and was going to use it. Galione, of course, was not present to contradict the thesis.

Cohn had his clients plead guilty to attempted manslaughter with a maximum four-year sentence. Gotti wound up doing two years in New York state's Green Haven prison, less time than he'd drawn on the earlier hijacking beef.

He was released on July 28, 1977, and was soon to achieve a life-long dream, that of becoming a "made" member of the Mafia, what the insiders called "getting straightened out," maybe because it put new recruits on a straighter and more direct path to riches and power. The ceremony inducting John Gotti into the Mafia was presided over by Big Paul Castellano himself.

Gotti was made capo over the Bergin crew, where he did what came naturally: running gambling and loansharking operations. His gambling habit was as bad as anybody's; he was a compulsive bettor who routinely dropped tens of thousands of dollars a weekend on sports bets and slow horses.

Tragedy struck in March 1980, when Gotti's twelve-year-old son, Frank, was killed in an accident while riding a motorbike. The driver of the death car, a Gotti neighbor and family man, disappeared several months later under circumstances that indicated foul play.

The Justice Department was preparing to unleash an unprece-dented attack on the Mafia, unprecedented in scope and effective-ness. It was armed with two weapons: the Racketeer Influenced and Corrupt Organizations (RICO) Act and a new generation of elec-tronic eavesdropping devices.

Passed in 1970, RICO was a federal law allowing for the prosecu-tion of persons engaging in a "pattern of racketeering." It viewed criminal acts not as singular occurrences but as part of a continuum, a pattern of racketeering. The law meant that persons charged need not have committed a specific crime, such as robbery or murder, but need only have shared in profits that those acts helped generate. It set penalties of as much as forty years in prison for violators.

The tools to do the job came from new electronic eavesdropping equipment and technology. Historically, wiretaps and bugs had proven to be one of law enforcement's most effective weapons against organized crime. The new technology had really come into its own. Phone conversations could be listened in to without the delicate and sometimes dangerous business of actually tapping into phone wires; now, cooperative phone companies let the authorities listen in directly to the conversations themselves. Bugging devices, wireless transmitters, and the like were smaller, more powerful, and equipped with longer-lasting power sources.

So armed, the Justice Department mapped its strike at the head of the national crime syndicate: the Commission. The attack was a multipronged one. One of its barbs was targeted at Angelo Ruggiero, a made member of the Bergin crew who regularly waited attendance on Big Paul Castellano. He was also an inveterate gabber and gossipmonger, whose talkative ways had already earned him the derisive tag "Quack Quack" from other mobsters.

After a meeting with Big Paul, Ruggiero liked to yak with other criminal associates about his conversations with the boss. Sizing him up as a prize target, the FBI planted in the fall of 1981 a bug in a room in Ruggiero's house where he conducted much of his mob business.

The tapes provided invaluable intelligence, including a conversation between Ruggiero and nonmember hoodlum Edward Lino, in which Ruggiero spoke of the Commission. This in itself was a violation of Mafia law, which decreed that the Commission could not be mentioned to outsiders. It also provided the feds with a foothold in the door for a RICO prosecution, since the existence of the Commission would be prime evidence of that all-important pattern of racketeering required for big convictions.

Another violation of Mafia law was the prohibition against criticizing a boss or, worse, a Commission member. Ruggiero held forth not once but often on what he saw as Castellano's failings as family head, speaking in frank terms and pungent language that Big Paul could not fail to take offense at, should he ever become cognizant of them. But that was a minor offense compared to this, that the Ruggiero tapes helped establish legal probable cause for the bugging and/or wiretapping of Castellano and underboss Neil Dellacroce.

Fat Ange was the pivot man into a lot of things. More things than he knew, when the electronic surveillance is taken into account.

His brother, Salvatore, was a big-time drug dealer. He was not a Mafia member, so the Commission's stricture about dealing drugs did not affect him. He and his wife died in a private plane crash in 1982. Fat Ange overcame his grief long enough to take over his deceased brother's narcotics business, an enterprise in which he was partnered with another made member, Gene Gotti, John's younger brother and the sibling to which he was closest.

Gene and Ange found big dope money irresistible. Of course, now they were in violation of the Commission's prohibition against members dealing in drugs, a lapse that carried a possible death penalty. (Not that this ever stopped anyone.)

Their boss and Gambino family head Big Paul Castellano was a strong proponent of that no-drugs edict.

The year 1983 was a time of woe for the New York Mafia. That year saw the publication of *A Man of Honor*, aging mob boss Joe Bonanno's self-serving autobiography about his life in the Mafia. Even though carefully whitewashed, his descriptions of the Commission furnished federal investigators with a hook to call him before a grand jury for questioning.

By admitting the existence of the Commission and his role in it, he opened the door to the RICO Act's "pattern of racketeering." Bonanno was subpoenaed to tell a grand jury what he knew of the subject; he took the Fifth, was immunized to compel his testimony, still refused to talk, and spent a year and some months in prison until the grand jury's term had expired.

In the spring of 1983, federal agents planted a bug in the White House, the mansion on Todt Hill in Staten Island where Big Paul Castellano held court. Castellano was a homebody and something of a recluse. His underlings had to visit him there to report and receive their instructions. The FBI tap proved hugely productive during the four months it was in operation.

In August, Angelo Ruggiero, Gene Gotti, and three accomplices were indicted on narcotics charges. Thanks in part to leads derived from the bugging of Ruggiero, Big Paul Castellano and Neil Dellacroce were indicted in a landmark case charging them with

Commission-related racketeering. Rounding out the year's bad breaks for the mob, Neil Dellacroce and John Gotti were indicted for loansharking and gambling operations.

In 1984, Castellano was hit with a separate charge for involvement in a major car theft ring that stole a high volume of luxury cars and resold them in Kuwait. Muscle was provided for homicide-happy hitman and cocaine abuser Roy DeMeo, one of the family's most fearsome enforcers.

Law enforcement was crowding the New York mob hard, as the seriousness of the RICO-based prosecutions began to sink in. Bosses and Commission members realized that they could soon be looking at some hard time.

Gene Gotti and Angelo Ruggiero were in hot water with Paul Castellano because of their alleged narcotics involvement. Castellano had been strongly in favor of executing Little Pete Tambone for violating the no-drugs edict several years earlier. Tambone had avoided death when a majority of the Commission voted to spare him, but no thanks to Big Paul.

Castellano would be within his rights to whack Gene and Ange if they were proven guilty of drug dealing. He could also have John Gotti whacked. As capo, Gotti was responsible for the actions of those in his crew.

Castellano wanted transcripts of the FBI's Ruggiero tapes. Legally, he was entitled to them to prepare for his own case. Beyond the law, he was entitled to them by virtue of being Ruggiero's boss. His word should have been law, but Ruggiero was fighting him, refusing to yield the transcripts without a court battle. Besides material relating to his drug dealings, the tapes were rife with his profane and insulting comments on Castellano and other mob higher-ups. Ruggiero was way out of line in refusing to obey a direct order from his boss. Neil Dellacroce argued his case, but Big Paul kept pushing for the transcripts.

The clock was ticking on Ruggiero, and on Castellano, too, if the truth be known, but time would run out more swiftly still for Dellacroce, who succumbed to the ravages of cancer on December 2, 1985.

A watershed moment had arrived. Dellacroce was the buffer between John Gotti and Big Paul. With that buffer gone, Castellano would be able to demote Gotti, break up the Bergin crew, or order the deaths of John Gotti, Gene Gotti, and Angelo Ruggiero.

Bad feelings and paranoia were intensified by Castellano's wrongheaded decision not to attend Dellacroce's wake. Big Paul explained that his appearance at the rites would generate bad press that might impact negatively on his upcoming trial. Dellacroce had been a respected figure, and Castellano's absence and poor excuse made him look weak, which caused him to lose some prestige.

The slip was a telling one, showing that the boss was out of touch with the sentiments of the Gambino rank-and-file soldiers.

With serious jail time looming as a possibility, Castellano planned to rule his family from behind bars, as Lucky Luciano and Vito Genovese had done. His house must be set in order. Tension had been brewing in the family between his faction and the Dellacroce faction. Neil was dead and the logical successor to lead his faction was John Gotti and his Bergin crew. That was a dangerous source of dissension. Castellano had never much liked Gotti, anyhow, and his plans for the future were unlikely to feature much of a future for John Gotti.

Big Paul liked to present himself as a businessman, but he wasn't afraid to crack a few eggs if he had to. His daughter, Connie, had married Frank Amato, whose position as son-in-law guaranteed him a seat on the mob gravy train. Amato had been a wife beater and an abuser, though, and the marriage had broken up in 1973. Soon after, Amato vanished from the ken of man, gone as irrevocably as if the earth had swallowed him up. More recently, Castellano had ordered the execution of homicidal hitman and cocaine cowboy Roy DeMeo. No, Big Paul was not a man to be trifled with.

Adding more fuel to the fire, Castellano's justice system connections enabled him in December 1985 to get hold of a copy of the damning Angelo Ruggero tape transcripts.

For John Gotti, the crisis had arrived.

The Hit

On Monday, December 16, 1985, a black Lincoln drove from the White House on Todt Hill in Staten Island to Manhattan. Paul Castellano was being chauffeured by Thomas Bilotti, his body-guard, driver, trusted aide, and protégé. Big Paul was set on putting Bilotti in as the family's acting street boss. Alone and unarmed, they were both riding in the front seat.

Castellano had a dinner engagement later that day; during the afternoon, he attended to some seasonal chores, with Christmas being about a week away. He stopped at his lawyer's office to do some business and pass around a few gifts to the staff. Later, he did some shopping.

He was scheduled to have dinner at 5:00 P.M. at Sparks Steak House restaurant—one of the city's top steakhouses with prices to match—on Forty-sixth Street, between Second and Third Avenue. His companions would be three of his capos: Thomas Gambino, Carlo's son and a midtown trucking magnate; James Failla, big in the private garbage carting industry; and Frank DeCicco, a tough and popular family capo.

Midtown Manhattan, where the restaurant was located, is always thick with traffic during the evening rush hour; the congestion was compounded by the hordes of holiday shoppers and tourists thronging the streets.

The Lincoln poked its way along the route, pulling up in front of the restaurant's front entrance. Bilotti pulled into a No Parking space. A Police Benevolent Association emblem in the front wind-shield served as a talisman against parking tickets.

It was 5:45 P.M. Castellano and Bilotti got out of the car. Three men who'd been waiting on the sidewalk near the building's front suddenly bore down on Big Paul and Bilotti. They wore Russian-style fur hats and white raincoats and wielded handguns, .32s and .38s.

They opened fire, unleashing a blistering fusillade on the two men. Castellano was hit with six slugs in the head and chest; Bilotti, with four. They went down, Bilotti sprawling faceup in the street with his arms extended, Castellano falling back toward his car, stretched across the sidewalk.

A wild scene of chaos erupted as passersby ran for cover. One of the shooters stood over Castellano and delivered the coup de grâce with a bullet in the head. The trio fled, making their way toward Second Avenue.

The killers were not alone. Other individuals had been stationed as backup on both sides of Forty-sixth Street between the avenues. All made their way to Second Avenue, where the getaway cars were parked; no police were at hand to bar their escape, no civilians were so brave or foolhardy as to try to interfere with them. All made a clean getaway.

Big Paul Castellano was dead, the first assassination of a Commission member in Manhattan since Anastasia's execution in 1957. Thomas Bilotti, his bodyguard and trusted protégé, was dead, too.

STRATEGY

At the time of the hit, John Gotti had to regard the murder of Paul Castellano as a matter of kill or be killed.

At the heart of the conflict was Castellano's no-drugs edict. But Gotti's crew was involved in drugs. Whatever John Gotti's role in the trade, there was no doubt about the complicity of his brother, Gene, and his longtime friend and associate Angelo Ruggiero.

The bug planted in 1981 in Ruggiero's house had yielded damning tapes that lay at the heart of the government's prosecution of him (and Gene Gotti) for trafficking. Paul Castellano demanded transcripts of the tapes, to which he had every right in his role as family head. But Fat Ange wasn't giving them up. He was stonewalling in a lame and unconvincing manner. Not only Ruggiero but also John Gotti had reasons for wanting those tapes buried. Apart from putting Gene on the chopping block, they would reveal how Ruggiero's unauthorized communications and gossiping had helped the government make its RICO case against Big Paul and other Commission members.

Gotti's blueprint for murder must have been in the planning stages for several months, but Neil's death was the final incident that gave the team the green light. Gotti planned a bold strike at the top. His plan was a violation of a prime directive of Commission law, the unauthorized assassination of a sitting member.

Still, it had been done before, by Albert Anastasia and later by Carlo Gambino himself, when he paired with Vito Genovese to knock off Albert A. It was easier to square things with the Commission after the fact than to square being dead courtesy of executioners sent by Big Paul.

Politics were involved, though: Gambino crime family politics and Commission politics. Luckily for John Gotti, there was a lot to work with; namely, the animosity and hostility with which many rank-and-file Gambino family members in Castellano's own faction held toward their chief, Big Paul.

Gotti moved to rope them in. Angelo Ruggiero was the go-between who made contact with murderously efficient enforcer Salvatore "Sammy Bull" Gravano. Gravano was alienated from Big Paul's distant leadership and looking for a change; he contacted his boss, capo Frank DeCicco, bringing him into the plot. Several other capos from the Castellano crowd also joined the plot.

These strategic alliances went a long way toward providing John Gotti with the cover he needed to make the hit. He could go to the Commission and show how Big Paul's capos themselves were actively supporting the purge.

The alliance yielded additional benefits by suborning an inside man close to Castellano. The inside man was Frank DeCicco. It was DeCicco who passed the word to Gotti about the December 16 dinner at Sparks. That piece of invaluable intelligence was the last thing needed to make the murder plan a reality.

The public venue presented problems. The assassination was planned for a midtown street during the rush hour, at a time when the area would be crowded with traffic, and the usual hordes of pedestrians would be increased by tourists and holiday shoppers. There was also a good chance that there would be police officers on routine patrol in the area.

Tough. Innocent bystanders and cops would have to take their chances. The shooters would try to hit only the target but in a tense situation like that, things happen. If a civilian was wounded or killed during the hit, it would generate a mountain of bad press and hostile law enforcement activity. If a cop should happen on to the scene and try to interfere, he would have to be neutralized. The hitters wouldn't be shooting to wound or disable. This wasn't an old-time Western movie with a lot of trick shooting. If a hitman opened fire on a cop, he would try to take him down. So there was a very real chance that police officers could be killed if they intruded on the big hit. That would trigger law enforcement heat that would make the killing of a godfather look like jaywalking by comparison.

That was the risk the plotters would just have to take, a risk they judged was worth taking. As the saying goes, they can only hang you once.

The plan to kill Paul Castellano was bold, possibly reckless. It was shored up by stragetic alliances and empowered by the presence of an inside man.

Deduct 1 point for the risk of wounding or killing a civilian or cop.

STRATEGY: 4

TACTICS

The plotters were fielding a sizeable team: eleven men, all proven killers mostly associated with the Bergin crew. Information about the hit was on a need-to-know basis, with the kill team knowing it had an unspecified big job to do and holding itself ready to move, but not learning of the actual target and circumstances of the hit until the day it was scheduled to go down. It was a wise precautionary measure, considering the number of individuals involved and the risks that would ensue if any had known enough to talk out of turn.

The core unit of four shooters was stationed so that two were covering the restaurant's front entrance and another two were across the street. All were outfitted with Russian-style fur hats and white raincoats. This would make it easy for them to recognize each other, something not to be despised in the middle of a hot shootout, where one ran the risk of being mistakenly shot by one's compadres. They were armed with .32s and .38s and equipped with walkie-talkies. Other team members were stationed as backup at opposite ends of the street, to bar any escape in either direction if the targets should try to flee.

Parked at a corner on the street was a Lincoln Town Car containing John Gotti and Sammy Bull Gravano. They served a dual role, as spotters and as backup. If the hit went sour or the cops showed up at a critical time, they were prepared to intervene to ensure the success of the hit and the assassins' getaway. The heavyweight spotters actually saw Castellano and Bilotti arrive by car and communicated the alert to the shooters by walkie-talkie.

The hit went down smoother than the plotters had a right to expect. Castellano, the godfather of the biggest and strongest crime family in the city, was going out in public protected by only a single bodyguard, Bilotti—who was not even carrying a gun! Castellano had a rule against bringing guns to meetings and sitdowns. He and Bilotti walked into the trap like sheep to the slaughter.

That the plotters had done their work well in terms of keeping secret their murderous intentions was obvious. Castellano wasn't expecting a thing. That in itself shows how out of touch he had gotten. As a top Mafia kingpin, why wouldn't he have expected danger, just on a general principle of wary survivalism?

At seventy, Big Paul was dangerously out of touch. The ease with which the hit was accomplished demonstrates its inevitability.

Not only was the target so unwittingly obliging but also were the police, none of whom were around when the hit went down. No innocent bystanders were killed or wounded by stray shots. For a big gundown on a crowded midtown street during the evening rush hour, the operation was as clean and precise as a surgical strike.

One of the shooters had the professionalism to deliver the coup de grâce to Big Paul whether he needed it or not—a nice touch demonstrating solid technique. Nothing would be left to chance, not even the unlikelihood that Castellano could have been badly wounded but not dead. The last bullet in the head ensured his death, all right.

The killers fled east to Second Avenue, where their cars awaited, and made their getaway. The car with Gotti and Gravano rolled past Sparks, allowing for a view of Big Paul sprawled on the sidewalk. Later, the two heard on the car radio that Castellano was indeed dead.

TACTICS: 5

RESULTS

The short-term results of the big hit were everything the plotters could have wanted; in the mid- and long term, though, the picture was decidedly different.

The immediate aftermath of Big Paul's demise saw John Gotti claim the leadership of the Gambino crime family. In one stroke, Gotti had gone from being a capo in the Dellacroce faction to becoming boss of the entire organization. To paraphrase a Broadway cliché, he'd gone to Sparks as a capo and come back as a star.

Rewards were quickly distributed and power seized. Frank DeCicco, the Castellano faction capo who'd fingered Big Paul to the assassins, was made underboss of the Gambinos by Gotti. DeCicco had gone along with the plot in large part because he feared and resented Castellano's positioning of bodyguard Tom Bilotti in a slot above DeCicco. Now, the only place Bilotti was going was to the morgue, along with Big Paul.

Gotti had calculated right about the Commission's response, too. Pressured by the government's RICO law prosecutions, the Commission members had no desire to create any more strife or turmoil in the organization. They willingly acceded to Gotti's accession to power.

A comeback of sorts made itself felt on April 13, 1986, when Frank DeCicco's car was blown up by a bomb. He was in it at the time and all over the scene when the smoke cleared. A bigger fish had escaped the net, since John Gotti was supposed to have been meeting with DeCicco when the button was pushed on him.

It was an unusual kill. American Mafia assassins weren't so big on car bombs in the modern era. That indicated that the blast might have been laid by Zips, Sicilian-born mobsters and Big Paul loyalists who were paying back DeCicco for his treachery. The question of who triggered the blast remains open, but no similar attempts were made against John Gotti.

Angelo Ruggiero, whose tape transcripts lay at the heart of the hit and were also a prime motivator in some of the government's RICO cases against the Commission, became a pariah, shunned by fellow mobsters who took their lead from family head John Gotti. Fat Ange died of natural causes, going to the grave while waiting in vain for a conciliatory message or word from Gotti, his one-time close friend and lifelong companion in crime.

Big Paul's death and Gotti's preeminence moved the latter from the middle to the top of the law enforcement's to do list. Their efforts to bring down Gotti were aided by the man himself, whose flaws and limitations became evident early in his reign.

Indeed, the Castellano kill may be regarded as the height of his power, before his legal troubles really began. Nothing in Gotti's subsequent career following his assumption of leadership of the Gambinos shows the hard-headed planning and savvy risk-taking of the Castellano kill. One may well wonder if some of the smarts and skill that went into accomplishing Big Paul's demise was the work not of Gotti, but of that low-profile, hard-hitting enforcer, Sammy Bull Gravano.

Neil Dellacroce's headquarters had been based in the Ravenite Social Club on Mulberry Street in Little Italy in downtown Manhattan. It was a friendly ethnic enclave whose residents were wary of strangers who could be law enforcement agents. Gotti decided to make his headquarters at the Ravenite.

More, he scheduled weekly meetings at the site where he would hold court before an audience of his capos and key associates. Attendance at such meetings was mandatory, and a family member who disliked making the long drive down from Connecticut to attend the get-togethers was whacked as a lesson to the others.

In light of the damage done by the bugs planted in Angelo Ruggiero's and Paul Castellano's residences, it was a mistake to operate out of the too-public Ravenite locale.

The regular meetings with underlings was an even bigger mistake, offering as it did an unparalleled opportunity for law enforcement surveillants to keep the place under observation, identifying members and clocking their comings and goings. It presented a rich mosaic of intelligence data that could be used to further a RICO prosecution based on the self-evident "pattern of racketeering."

Gotti dismissed the threat. His ego was such that it craved the constant reinforcement of being seen as the boss, to be attended by fawning followers who jostled, flattered, and maneuvered to gain his favor.

Of course, the authorities managed to bug the Ravenite, installing listening devices in a hall and an upstairs apartment where Gotti went with associates when he had some confidential business to discuss. His secrets wound up on tape to be used against him in future trials that were just around the corner.

Like Al Capone, Benjamin Siegel, and Sam Giancana, John Gotti loved the spotlight. Not for him the stealthy self-effacement of a Carlo Gambino or the tightly held anonymity of a Thomas Lucchese. Gotti loved being seen as the boss. The sartorial splendor of his custom-made suits and outfits led the tabloids to tag him "the Dapper Don." His later acquittals in several highly publicized trials earned him a new nickname as "the Teflon don," the smooth gangster to which no government charges could stick.

Dutch Schultz could have warned him of the fate of mobsters who become headline writers' dreams.

John Gotti was gangster as rock star. Capone couldn't get away with that for more than a decade in the early part of the twentieth century; at the century's end, in the pervasive media environment and hype, Gotti's public posture as high-profile gang chief only ensured that law enforcement at the city, state, and national level would prioritize him as number one on their own personal hit parade.

No surprise; they got him. Key witness in the government's case was none other than Sammy Bull Gravano. Gravano, who'd participated in at least sixteen homicides, pulled an Abe Reles and turned against Gotti, whose bullying ways and deep-dyed megalomania had deeply alienated the Bull. His testimony was pivotal in 1992 in convicting John Gotti to multiple life terms to be served in what is perhaps America's harshest prison: the maximum-security federal correctional facility at Marion, Illinois.

John Gotti spent much of his term confined to his cell in lockdown for twenty-three hours a day, with one hour allowed for exercise in a prison yard. Embittered as the years dragged by, he railed and raged against not only the government but also against his brothers, Gene and Peter, and son, John A. Gotti, for their flailing efforts in keeping the crime family a going concern.

On June 10, 2002, John Gotti died of cancer of the head and throat. Whatever else may be said of him, it must be noted that he played his string out all the way to the end, dying as he had lived—as a tough guy.

Another tough guy, Sammy Bull Gravano, served minimum prison time before being put into the federal Witness Protection Program and relocated with a new identity in Arizona, courtesy of a government grateful for his testimony in nailing John Gotti.

But the leopard does not change his spots, or the wiseguy his lawbreaking ways. Gravano was subsequently arrested for running one of the Southwest's biggest rings for the distribution of the club drug ecstasy, and is now serving a long prison term.

Deduct 5 points for Gotti's disastrous reign in the aftermath of the Castellano kill.

RESULTS: 5

Murder Meter Box Score
    STRATEGY: 4
    TACTICS: 5
    RESULTS: 5

TOTAL: 14

Final Score: Mafia's Greatest Hit?

Like judging ice dancing or a gymnastics contest, rating the Mafia's greatest hits has a high degree of subjectivity. That's because a gangland execution, like other performances, is not a science but an art. That extends to the judging, too. What one analyst may rank as necessity, another may hold to be nothing more than a sidebar or distraction.

In handicapping the hits throughout the book, I have tried to set out a rationale for each rating, but in the final analysis, it's one man's opinion. Readers are invited and encouraged to judge for themselves, to enjoy and further the great and growing sport of analyzing and appreciating gangland's biggest kills.

And rest assured, there will be more.

What follows is my choice for the Mafia's greatest hit, plus a few other categories of interest.

Mafia's Greatest Hit

The assassination of Don Salvatore Maranzano.

In many ways, Salvatore Maranzano was an inspired leader, but not the man to bring a unified American Mafia into the twentieth

century and beyond. A product of the Sicilian Mafia who fled
Benito Mussolini's persecutions in the 1920s, Maranzano whipped
rival Joe Masseria in New York's Castellammarese War of 1930–1931.
Masseria was willing to sue for peace, but Maranzano was having
none of it. His continuation of the war prompted Masseria's underboss, Charlie "Lucky" Luciano, to cut a private deal with Maranzano
in which he, Luciano, would eliminate Masseria in return for
Maranzano's recognizing him as the new head of the Masseria faction. No doubt even then, both Luciano and Maranzano were both
already plotting how to get rid of the other.

In the aftermath of Masseria's death, Maranzano proclaimed a
new, unified American Mafia, laying out a blueprint for its infrastructure and for the acknowledgment of New York's five families.
He also claimed for himself the title Boss of Bosses.

Luciano liked everything about the plan except Maranzano's role
at the top of the heap. It was not long before Luciano's and
Maranzano's soldiers clashed in a labor racketeering dispute that
found them on opposite sides. At that time, the murder clock started
ticking in earnest, with both crime bosses plotting the elimination
of the other. The race to see who would kill the other first went right
down to the wire, with Luciano's Louis "Lepke" Buchalter–Meyer
Lansky gunmen assassinating Maranzano earlier in the same day
that Maranzano planned to have Vincent Coll liquidate Lucky.

Maranzano's death put Luciano in the top spot. Maranzano's dif-
ficulties with speaking the English language, his lack of familiarity
with the American crime scene, and his autocratic Old World attitudes rendered him unfit to lead a truly American Mafia.

Luciano was steeped in the American milieu and was tempera-
mentally more suited for the role, as can be seen by his wise choice
to avoid seeking the title and power of Boss of Bosses, instead taking a kind of first-among-equals role at the Commission table. Even
behind bars, Luciano was the supreme man of respect to whom the
other Commission members looked for guidance, an eminence that
he continued to hold even after his 1946 deportation to Italy.

From 1936 through 1946, Luciano's stewardship helped establish
the American Mafia at the hub of the national crime syndicate. It

was also a period of relative peace between the prickly Commission members that allowed the Mafia to expand and consolidate its hold on vast sectors of the national economy.

For these reasons, I rate the Maranzano murder as the Mafia's greatest hit.

Mafia's Second Greatest Hit

The 1957 assassination of Albert Anastasia.

This kill laid the foundation, for good and ill, for the Mafia's subsequent history in the latter half of the twentieth century. Key to its importance is its boosting of Carlo Gambino to overlordship of Anastasia's Brooklyn-based crime family. Clandestine and crafty, with no love for the limelight, Gambino was able to persuade hardline enforcer Aniello Dellacroce into accepting the post of underboss, thereby unifying the family and avoiding a bloody and divisive struggle for power.

Under Gambino's leadership, his crime family became the most numerous, powerful, and influential of all the five families, which meant that it was the most powerful Mafia group in the United States. Gambino's two-track method of expanding the family's reach into legitimate businesses generated mega-profits with minimal agitation and negative press. His choice of successor, Big Paul Castellano, extended the family's longevity and power for another decade.

Mafia's Ballsiest Hit

The death of Dutch Schultz.

It was a real cowboy job, and virtually a one-man job at that, the man being Charles "the Bug" Workman, an A-list Murder, Inc. enforcer. Despite minimal backing on the job by Emanuel "Mendy" Weiss and driver "Piggy," it was Workman who stalked into the Newark, New Jersey, Palace Chop House and shot Schultz, his mathematical whiz Otto "Abbadabba" Berman, and two very tough bodyguards. Abandoned by his cohorts, Workman managed to make a clean getaway and would most likely never have been caught had he not been fingered for the kill by some of his Murder, Inc. colleagues who spilled their guts to Assistant District Attorney Burton Turkus. Man, he sure was a piece of work.

Mafia's Most Mysterious Hit

The Abe Reles kill.

Nobody who knew Kid Twist believed that he went voluntarily out the window of the Half-Moon Hotel. I posit the theory that inside man Allie "Tick-Tock" Tannenbaum played a critical role in the kill, and I show how he could have worked it with the help of a crooked cop or two, but still—it's only a theory (see chapter 5). Almost as puzzling as how the hit was worked was how the plotters managed to sell it as a Reles "misadventure" and make it stick, but they did.

Mafia's Most Elaborate Hit

The St. Valentine's Day Massacre.

Here's a plan that was as finely tuned as a Swiss watch, except for one vital slip: primary target George "Bugs" Moran slipped the noose thanks to the mistaken identification of a lookalike, allowing the North Side gang boss to escape the slaughter. That slip ultimately proved fatal to key plotter Jack McGurn, who was on the receiving end of Moran's revenge a few years later. In hindsight, Capone and McGurn would have been served by a less ambitious plan targeting Moran only—it would also have saved them from catching the heat (especially federal) that followed the massacre and that was instrumental in mobilizing the forces that brought down Al Capone. The St. Valentine's Day Massacre could also qualify as the Mafia's most wrong-headed hit, if there was such a category.

John Gotti's hit of Big Paul Castellano also had its elaborate elements, with plenty of things that could have gone wrong. But they didn't, and as a hit, it was pretty damned slick and successful.

For Further Reading

Those who wish to delve deeper into the subjects covered in this book are invited to investigate the following books. Many are out of print, but the Internet with all its many bookfinding and book-selling sources, should prove of service in locating most titles at a reasonable price.

Asbury, Herbert. *The Gangs of Chicago*. Thunders Mouth Press, 2003.

Bergreen, Laurence. *Capone: The Man and the Era*. Simon and Schuster, 1994.

Brennan, Bill. *The Frank Costello Story*. Monarch, 1962.

Cannon, Jack, and Tom Cannon. *Nobody Asked Me, But . . . The World of Jimmy Cannon*. Berkley, 1979.

Carpozi, George Jr. *Bugsy*. Pinnacle, 1973.

Curzon, Sam. *Legs Diamond*. Belmont Tower, 1962.

Demaris, Ovid. *Captive City*. Pocket Book, 1970.

Denton, Sally, and Roger Morris. *The Money and the Power: The Making of Las Vegas and Its Hold on America, 1947–2000*. Alfred A. Knopf, 2001.

Feder, Sid, and Joachim Joesten. *The Luciano Story*. Award, 1954.

Gage, Nicholas, ed. *Mafia, USA*. Dell, 1972.

Gentry, Curt. *J. Edgar Hoover: The Man and the Secrets*. Norton, 1991.

Hanna, David. *Frank Costello: Gangster with a Thousand Faces*. Belmont Tower, 1974.

Kobler, John. *Capone: The Life and World of Al Capone*. Da Capo Press, 1971.

Maas, Peter. *The Valachi Papers*. Perennial, 2003.

Messick, Hank. *Lansky*. Berkley Medallion, 1971.

Mustain, Gene, and Jerry Capeci. *Murder Machine*. Onyx, 1993.

————. *Mob Star: The Story of John Gotti*. 2nd ed. Alpha, 2003.

Nash, Jay Robert. *Bloodletters and Badmen*, vols 2 and 3. Warner, 1975.

O'Brien, Joseph F., and Andris Kurins. *Boss of Bosses: The Fall of the Godfather: The FBI and Paul Castellano*. Simon and Schuster, 1991.

Raab, Selwyn. *Five Families*. Thomas Dunne/St. Martin's Press, 2005.

Rappleye, Charles, and Ed Becker. *All American Mafioso: The Johnny Rosselli Story*. Barricade, 1991.

Reid, Ed. *The Grim Reapers*. Bantam, 1969.

Russo, Gus. *The Outfit: The Role of Chicago's Underworld in the Shaping of Modern America*. Bloomsbury, 2001.

Pietrusza, David. *Rothstein: The Life, Times, and Murder of the Criminal Genius Who Fixed the 1919 World Series*. Carroll and Graf, 2003.

Sann, Paul. *Kill the Dutchman! The Story of Dutch Schultz*. Da Capo Press, 1971.

Scheim, David E. *Contract on America: The Mafia Murder of President John F. Kennedy*. Zebra, 1989.

Scott, Peter Dale. *Deep Politics and the Death of JFK*. University of California Press, 1993.

Spillane, Mickey. *Killer Mine*. Signet, 1965.

Sterling, Claire. *Octopus: The Long Reach of the International Sicilian Mafia*. Touchstone, 1990.

Summers, Anthony, and Robbyn Swan. *Sinatra: The Life*. Alfred A. Knopf, 2005.

Sutton, Willie, with Edward Linn. *Where the Money Was: Memoirs of a Bank Robber*. Viking, 1976.

Teresa, Vincent, with Thomas C. Renner. *My Life in the Mafia*. Fawcett Crest, 1974.

Turkus, Burton B., and Sid Feder. *Murder Inc.: The Inside Story of the Mob*. Manor, 1972.

Wolf, Marvin J., and Katherine Mader. *Fallen Angels: Chronicles of L.A. Crime and Mystery*. Ballantine, 1988.

Zeiger, Henry A. *The Jersey Mob*. Signet, 1975.